Praise for *Architects of World History*

"This is a fascinating story of how nine distinguished historians, dissatisfied with the severe limits of nation-state history, found their way, often serendipitously, to one another and to larger networks of like-minded professionals. In the process they helped establish world history as a fertile field of research and teaching."

Ross Dunn, San Diego State University

"This is a stimulating collection, at once presenting leading voices in the field and some of the key topical approaches within world history. The goal of attracting and guiding students toward a greater sense of how world history is done is particularly attractive."

Peter Stearns, George Mason University

"This collection clearly frames the methodological and historiographical trajectories that give coherence to world history as a field. The contributions from a wide range of scholars humanize broad patterns of inquiry and provide a fresh, original approach. *Architects of World History* is essential reading for scholars and teachers at all levels who want to grasp the history and scope of this dynamic field."

Laura J. Mitchell, University of California

"Each of the authors is a genuine architect and visionary in the field of world history. Collectively they provide a rich introduction to current approaches to teaching and research, while at the same time unfolding their own personal and often remarkable intellectual journeys that brought them to the forefront of world history."

Craig Benjamin, President of the World History Association (2014/2015)

Architects of World History

Researching the Global Past

Edited by

Kenneth R. Curtis and
Jerry H. Bentley

WILEY Blackwell

This edition first published 2014

Registered Office
John Wiley & Sons, Ltd, The Atrium, Southern Gate, Chichester, West Sussex, PO19 8SQ, UK

Editorial Offices
350 Main Street, Malden, MA 02148-5020, USA
9600 Garsington Road, Oxford, OX4 2DQ, UK
The Atrium, Southern Gate, Chichester, West Sussex, PO19 8SQ, UK

For details of our global editorial offices, for customer services, and for information about how to apply for permission to reuse the copyright material in this book please see our website at www.wiley.com/wiley-blackwell.

Library of Congress Cataloging-in-Publication Data

Architects of world history : researching the global past / edited by Kenneth R. Curtis and Jerry H. Bentley.
pages cm
Includes bibliographical references and index.
ISBN 978-1-118-29485-7 (cloth) – ISBN 978-1-118-29484-0 (paperback) 1. World history–Historiography. 2. Historians–Biography. 3. Historiography–Methodology. I. Curtis, Kenneth Robert. II. Bentley, Jerry H., 1949–
D13.A69 2014
907.2′022–dc23

2013042708

A catalogue record for this book is available from the British Library.

Cover image: Steel globe below Trump Tower, New York City © Dan Nguyen
Cover design by Design Deluxe

Set in 10.5/13.5pt Palatino by SPi Publisher Services, Pondicherry, India
Printed in Malaysia by Ho Printing (M) Sdn Bhd

1 2014

Contents

Notes on Contributors

Jerry H. Bentley was Professor of History at the University of Hawai'i at Mānoa, was a founding member of the World History Association and was Editor of the *Journal of World History* for 22 years. In addition to his early books and articles on Renaissance humanism, he wrote extensively on theories of world history, periodization, and premodern cross-cultural encounters, edited numerous volumes, as well as coauthored the popular textbook *Traditions and Encounters*.

Lauren Benton is Professor of History and Affiliate Professor of Law, New York University. Her publications on comparative legal history include *A Search for Sovereignty* (2010) and *Law and Colonial Cultures* (2002). Benton received her Ph.D. in History and Anthropology from Johns Hopkins University and her A.B. from Harvard University.

David Christian is by training a historian of Russia and the Soviet Union. He has spent most of his career at Macquarie University, in Sydney, and San Diego State University. He began teaching courses on big history in 1989 at Macquarie University. He published *Maps* *of Time: An Introduction to Big History* in 2004. In 2010, with Bill Gates, he founded the "Big History Project," which is building a free online high course in big history due for release in late 2013. David Christian is the founding President of the International Big History Association.

Kenneth R. Curtis is Professor of History at California State University, Long Beach, where he teachers modern African and contemporary world history. His most recent publication, coauthored with Valerie Hansen, is the second edition of *Voyages in World History* (2013). His current project involves reassessing twentieth-century history through the lens of travelers' accounts.

Karen Louise Jolly, Professor of History at the University of Hawai'i at Mānoa, is a cultural historian of medieval Europe. She has written on *Popular Religion in Late Saxon England*, the concept of magic in the Middle Ages, and the history of Christianity in a world context (*Tradition and Diversity*). Her most recent book, *The Community of St. Cuthbert in the Late Tenth Century*, explores a Northumbrian religious community through the lens of a single manuscript artifact.

J.R. McNeill is University Professor and School of Foreign Service at Georgetown University. His books include *Something New Under the Sun: An Environmental History of the Twentieth-Century World*, winner of three book prizes and translated into nine languages; *The Human Web: A Bird's-Eye View of World History*, coauthored with William McNeill and translated into seven languages; and *Mosquito Empires: Ecology and War in the Greater Caribbean, 1620–1914*, which won the Beveridge Prize from the American Historical Association.

Kenneth Pomeranz is a Professor of History at the University of Chicago; he previously taught at the University of California, Irvine. His work focuses mostly on China, though he is also very interested in comparative and world history. Most of his research is in social, economic, and environmental history, though he has also worked on state formation, imperialism, religion, gender, and other topics. His publications include *The Great Divergence: China, Europe, and the Making of the Modern World Economy* (2000), which won the John K. Fairbank Prize from the AHA and shared the World History Association book prize. He was one of the founding editors of the *Journal of Global History*. His current projects include a history of Chinese political economy from the seventeenth century to the present and a book called *Why Is China So Big*? which tries to explain, from various perspectives, how and why contemporary China's huge land mass and population have wound up forming a single political unit. He served in 2013 as President of the American Historical Association.

Dominic Sachsenmaier is Professor of Modern Asian History at Jacobs University in Bremen/Germany. Prior to this, he held faculty positions at Duke University and UC Santa Barbara. His main research interests are Chinese and Western approaches to global/world history, seventeenth-century Sino–Western cultural relations, as well as global currents in modern Chinese history.

Kerry Ward is Associate Professor of world history at Rice University. She is the author of *Networks of Empire: Forced Migration in the Dutch East India Company* (Cambridge 2009) and several articles and chapters on South African, Southeast Asian and Indian Ocean history. She was Secretary of the World History Association from 2009–2013. During 2013–2014 she was the Human Trafficking and Modern Day Slavery Fellow at the Gilder Lehrman Center for the Study of Slavery, Resistance, and Abolition at Yale University.

Merry E. Wiesner-Hanks is a Distinguished Professor and Chair of the History Department at the University of Wisconsin–Milwaukee. She is the senior editor of the *Sixteenth Century Journal*, an editor of the *Journal of Global History*, and the author or editor of 20 books and many articles that have appeared in English, German, Italian, Spanish, Greek, Chinese, Turkish, and Korean. Her research has been supported by grants from the Fulbright and Guggenheim

Foundations, among others. She has also written a number of source books and textbooks for use in the college classroom, a book for young adults, and a book for general readers, *The Marvelous Hairy Girls: The Gonzales Sisters and Their Worlds* (Yale, 2009) – the story of a family of extremely hairy people who lived in Europe in the late sixteenth century. She currently serves as the editor in chief of the forthcoming nine-volume *Cambridge History of the World*.

1

Architects of World History

Kenneth R. Curtis

What is world history? Like many professors, I started thinking about that question less in theory than in practice. It was a dark, cold Wisconsin morning as I prepared for an 8:30 a.m. "modern world history" lecture. Still completing my Ph.D. dissertation on the political dynamics of coffee production and marketing in colonial Tanzania, how would I convince a roomful of young people that I was the person to whom they should turn to learn about the sixteenth century Ottoman Empire? Apart from reading a different textbook from my students, I *did* have some tools to help me. An experienced colleague had very kindly given me his lecture notes for the class (using the latest electronic storage technology of 1989: a set of "floppy disks") that contained excellent scholarly and primary source quotations. More importantly, as an East Africanist, I had a firm grasp on the foundational beliefs and practices of Islam, without which my students would not be able to understand Ottoman history. Finally, I had been reading a good deal of comparative history,

Architects of World History: Researching the Global Past, First Edition.
Edited by Kenneth R. Curtis and Jerry H. Bentley.

so I knew something about how to connect historical dots to reveal a larger picture. But then a note of panic: What was the correct Turkish pronunciation of "Süleyman?" Access to the internet was still years away; I had no way of checking. I simply resolved to do my best and learn from the experience.

I suspect many of my world history colleagues can see a bit of themselves in this story (e.g., Getz, 2012). In the Ph.D. programs of those days (and not too much has changed), we focused on research, on teasing out all the potential complexities of what, to others, might seem a straightforward story (such as Africans growing and selling coffee). We spent little time thinking about teaching, which requires a skill that is nearly the exact opposite: the ability to render the complex in a straightforward way for nonspecialists. The implicit assumption was that eventual employment at a major research institution would allow us to focus on our specializations and leave the broad brush strokes of introductory courses to others. (Never mind that the actually existing jobs were mostly at places where teaching was primary: liberal arts colleges, state universities with poor research funding, and community colleges.) We started teaching never having been taught how to teach.

When my own undergraduate alma mater – Lawrence University – offered me a short-term teaching contract, it was a godsend, not only helping to pay the bills while I finished writing my dissertation but also giving me experience to cite in the coming round of tenure-track job applications. At Lawrence, I was offered the option of sticking with African history; instead, I *volunteered* to teach a section of world history because I thought it would enhance my resume in a tight job market. Indeed, I doubt if I would have been considered at California State University Long Beach (CSULB) the next year had I not been able to convince them that I "could teach world history."

Once permanently employed, I might have looked to avoid further world history teaching obligations. But in the early 1990s, globally relevant history seemed too important to ignore. The Tiananmen Massacre, the fall of the Berlin Wall, Nelson Mandela's release from prison, the winding down of the Cold War, and the rhetoric and reality of "globalization" all accompanied my transition from Wisconsin to California. I then began a more conscientious investigation of world history, having come belatedly (like others in this volume) to recognize it as a discrete and dynamic subfield in the historical discipline. (For the institutional development of world history, see Pomeranz and Segal, 2012; for world history in the context of contemporary globalization, see Bright and Geyer, 2012).

As I began to investigate world history more deeply, I came to recognize two "habits of mind" that characterized scholars in the field (to cite the original Advanced Placement World History (APWH) course description): "seeing global patterns and processes over time and space while connecting local developments to global ones" and "comparing within and among societies, including comparing societies' reactions to global processes." Like many other world historians, I was drawn to forms of historical writing that helped tie together the past and present, finding intellectual satisfaction in identifying transnational or global patterns and in making apt comparisons.

For example, as I gained experience with the modern world history survey, I began to see the later history of the Ottoman Empire as part of a broader pattern: the struggles faced by leaders of old land-based societies and empires (also including Qing China, Tokugawa Japan, and the Russian Empire) to adjust to the new economic and military realities of the industrial era. In every case, conservative and reforming factions fought for influence, with world changing outcomes. I found it both challenging and inspiring to explore such connections and comparisons.

Having come to world history through praxis, there still remained the question in theory: and there are in fact distinct and sometimes divergent opinions on what constitutes "world history." Some of those divergences reflect national variations, as Dominic Sachsenmaier (2011) has demonstrated: German and Chinese historians, for example, bring different conceptual understandings to "world history" than their North American colleagues. Still, it has largely been US-based historians who have dominated definitional conversations.

As a starting point, Patrick Manning (2003) provided a broadly applicable definition for world history, identifying it with a focus on "the story of connections within the human community" that "portray the crossing of boundaries and the linking of systems in the human past." Jerry Bentley gave a bit more precision (2002) when he referred to

> historical scholarship that explicitly compares experiences across the boundary lines of societies, or that examines interactions between peoples of different societies, or that analyzes large-scale historical patterns and processes that transcend individual societies. This kind of world history deals with historical processes that have not respected national, political, geographical, or cultural boundary lines, but rather have influenced affairs on transregional, continental, hemispheric, and global scales (p. 393).

Bentley went on to list the historical processes most characteristic of world history as "climatic changes, biological diffusions, the spread of infectious and contagious diseases, mass migrations, transfers of technology, campaigns of imperial expansion, cross-cultural trade, the spread of ideas and ideals, and the expansion of religious faiths and cultural traditions." It would be hard to imagine any historian who would not find something relevant on such an expansive list, but the point is that these topics in particular seem to call out for transregional or global investigation.

The opportunity to pursue such conversations with like-minded historians came when I attended a meeting of the World History Association (WHA) in Philadelphia in 1992. Now I found that my passion for global and comparative history was shared by fellow history educators from all across the United States and from several international locations as well. I immediately recognized that the culture of the WHA was inclusive of history educators from various types of institutions, including, uniquely, a strong presence of secondary school teachers.

WHA members, moreover, shared a sense of mission. In the early 1990s, world history was struggling for recognition within the historical profession. Especially at more elite research universities, world history could still be thought of only as fodder for high school students or college freshmen, certainly not a subject for serious scholars (Weinstein, 2012). Even at the college survey level its role was still being challenged by traditionalist supporters of the well-established "western civilization" approach (Levine, 2000). On the political front, global thinking about the human past was decried by some US conservatives as "political correctness," mired in a leveling cultural relativism that denigrated the unique achievements of "the west" (see Nash, Crabtree, and Dunn, 2000). By sharp contrast, many of the high school and college teachers in the WHA were idealists who believed in linking global knowledge and global understanding with the potential for global peace and justice (Allardyce, 2000).

Such was the congenial atmosphere of the WHA, where neophytes in world history (like me) could easily mix with and learn from leading lights in the field (like Jerry Bentley). The founding editor of the *Journal of World History* and organizer of the 1993 WHA conference on his home turf in Hawaii, Dr. Bentley was not only a pioneer in the theory and practice of what some were coming to call "the new world history" – an innovator in teaching, scholarly publication, as well as textbook authorship – but also a mentor to a very long list of historians who benefited from his advice, including everyone involved with this book. When he succumbed to cancer in the summer of 2012, he left a great void. Still, we have been able to include Jerry's final essay, an opportunity for us to reflect upon his impact as one of the architects of the now globalizing field of world history.

"Architects" of World History

How does the metaphor of architecture relate to world history? Our title implies vision preceding construction. Let us think of building a brick edifice. One requirement is an adequate supply of solid bricks. If there is insufficient raw material, the building cannot be finished; if the bricks are of poor quality, the building will not stand.

In this analogy, bricks are equivalent to historical facts: no effective historical argument can be made unless the factual evidence is sufficient in quantity and quality. Yet piles of strong bricks do not assemble themselves into buildings. Similarly, mere data about the past does not constitute history.

In order to build a strong edifice, one also needs the skills of a mason, the technical expertise necessary to combine bricks into an enduring wall. Historians are also "masons" in this sense, trained to assemble historical evidence into walls of causality. As Bentley put it, "History is not a chest of miscellaneous details or a box of data from which historians simply pluck pieces of information and try to fashion them into some kind of story. Rather, history represents a creative effort by historians to gain insights into the dynamics of historical development" (p. 217). But a wall is still not a finished building, any more than an explanation of cause and effect constitutes a complete historical argument.

That is where the vision of the historian-as-architect comes in. Before choosing the bricks, before making a plan for assembling the materials, the architects have a vision of the final edifice. Of course, she must have a strong grounding in materials science and engineering to assure that the vision of her blueprint can be realized, but without her original vision nothing beautiful, strong, or enduring can be built.

Thus, historians combine all these skills. They are brick makers, searching out the raw materials of history, often working silently and diligently in archives and libraries in pursuit of evidence. Historians are also like masons, skilled in the assemblage of the raw material of evidence into the solid walls of intelligible narrative. And historians who really make an impact are also like architects, envisioning historical constructions in original ways and fashioning narratives that are acts of creative argumentation. In this book, you will encounter eight such historians. Chosen to highlight important nodes of world history research to which they have made signal contributions, they are all quick to point out the indispensability of collaboration: "I suspect that world history is not so much to be found in the houses any one of us has built," writes Kenneth Pomeranz, "as in the neighborhood created by their juxtaposition" (p. 103).

The conversation that led to *Architects of World History* began with Tessa Harvey, an editor at Wiley-Blackwell (a well-respected publisher of academic texts.) Tessa's first priority was organizing the *Wiley-Blackwell Companion to World History* (Northrop, 2012, including essays by Pomeranz, Sachsenmaier, and Ward), an ideal supplemental resource for readers seeking to pursue lines of inquiry laid out in this book. Northrop's volume joins *The Oxford Handbook of World History* edited by Jerry Bentley (2011) and Ross Dunn's *The New World History: A Teacher's Companion* (2000) as essential reference works. For a sustained single-author analysis of the world history enterprise, Patrick Manning's *Navigating World History: Historians Create a Global Past* (2003) remains unsurpassed.

One difference between the Northrop, Bentley, Dunn, and Manning titles and *Architects of World History* is the intended audience. Those books were written by historians for historians; here our main goal is to provide points of initial orientation in the field for undergraduate and graduate *students* of history (though we also hope the book will also be useful to other audiences, such as teachers given world history assignments without much prior training or background).

The fact is that the available resources in the field have to date been somewhat unbalanced, intended either for sophisticated academic audiences or for basic survey courses. At one end of the history continuum, research in the field has taken off, leading to the need for resources like the *Wiley Blackwell Companion* and the *Oxford Handbook of World History*. On the other, the survey course has now become a staple of the US university curriculum, leading to the availability of better-quality materials to support world history instruction. (I have contributed to that literature by coauthoring a textbook, *Voyages in World History*, 2013, and a document reader, *Discovering the Global Past: A Look at the Evidence*, 2011.) That strong presence in foundational history and emerging strength as a research field has, however, left world history with something like a "missing middle" where the upper-division undergraduate course and the beginning graduate experience are found. One principal purpose of *Architects of World History* is to help fill that gap by helping advanced undergraduate students and beginning graduate students to understand the architecture of the field and by providing them with some guideposts toward areas of research they may wish to pursue.

The idea for this book fermented for some years while I was distracted by administrative responsibilities. Then I did what any sensible person with a world history concept would do: I consulted with Jerry Bentley. Jerry recalled with nostalgia *The Historian's Workshop*, a book similar to this one in format that he had read and appreciated as an undergraduate (Curtis, 1970), and when we met in London, as attendees of a conference hosted by the European Network in Universal and Global History, he agreed to serve as coeditor of *Architects of World History*. The "intellectual trajectories" of our authors would be the book's leitmotif, with an emphasis on the varying paths they had taken toward world history research.

Paths to World History

My own path to world history was founded on outward expansion from my initial training as an Africanist and on involvement with teacher training. Those experiences led, in the spring of 2003, to an invitation to contribute to "Globalizing History at the University of Florida: A Workshop for the Teaching and Research of World History," sponsored by the National Endowment for the Humanities. My talk was entitled "Change from Below: World History and American Public Education." Though well received, I do not think my explanation of the upward flow of global history perspectives from US secondary schools to universities made much of an impact. This was a traditional, research-oriented history department where only one of the graduate students in attendance expressed a focus on teaching. The apparent lack of connection between academic history and broader currents of history education did not surprise me, even as it differed greatly from my own experience at the California State University Long Beach (CSULB).

When I joined the history faculty at CSULB in 1990, the department already had a venerable tradition of engagement with K-12 teaching. It was home to the Society for History Education and its respected journal *The History Teacher*, which publishes articles on history pedagogy by school teachers and academics alike (Weber, 2012). That sense of common purpose and lack of hierarchy appealed to my democratic educational instincts (providing an antidote to the frequent obfuscations of French post-structuralism then ascendant in the academy). From a pragmatic standpoint, I knew that many of my students were thinking of pursuing credentials qualifying them to teach history in middle schools or high schools. Many CSULB students are the first in their families to attend college; many are children of immigrants. Since my spouse was herself a seventh grade world history teacher and since CSULB cultivated close relations with Long Beach Unified School District (and with Long Beach City College, as part of the Long Beach Education partnership), my path was clear: toward energetic engagement with public history education (Houck, 2004).

Working with teachers on African history was an obvious starting point. As Kerry Ward affirms, Africanists are perennially distressed by entrenched ignorance of African history and geography. I found that few local teachers had any prior academic exposure to African studies, raising the specter that inaccurate stereotypes would be passed to yet another generation. Fortunately, the implementation of new state standards for history/social science in the later 1990s gave scope (and funding) for intervention: student learning about Africa, in the context of world history, was now *required*. The new California standards were a mixed blessing, however. No world historians were consulted in their development, and the standards bore no relation to the richly connective and comparative study of the human past found, by later contrast, in the APWH program. In California's version of modern world history for tenth grade students, for example, American and Western European exceptionalism were still woven into the structure of the curriculum.

California's history standards were part of a broader national trend in the 1990s, when more rigorous standards were proposed as a cure for persistent US educational underachievement. Under the auspices of the National Endowment for the Humanities, a large and prestigious group of history educators from both secondary and higher education backgrounds coordinated a national conversation about setting National History Standards in US and world history. The results were fantastic from an educational and pedagogical standpoint, but disastrous politically. After the proposed standards came under attack by conservatives as "politically correct" distortions of traditional history, the U.S. Senate voted 99–1 to denounce them (Symcox, 2002).

Away from the glare of national politics, however, a group of forward-thinking world historians were lobbying the College Board for inclusion of their subject in the prestigious and rapidly growing Advanced Placement (AP) program. (Through AP courses and examinations, high school students are able to learn at the college level and potentially to earn college placement and credit.) That lobbying was successful, and in 2002 the College Board unveiled its new AP World History curriculum, one that did indeed reflect the "architecture" of the "new world history" by emphasizing themes of connection, comparison, and global context. (Disclosure: I was involved in the course's design and implementation, and still have an oversight role as a member of the College Board's History Academic Advisory Committee.) The program is robust not only in terms of academic content but also in terms of numbers. Of the 1 million high school students who took an AP exam in 2013 (mostly in the United States, but an increasing number internationally) over 220,000 attempted the APWH test, with roughly half doing well enough to qualify for college credit. It has been through the AP program that the alliance of secondary and university history educators fostered by the WHA has had its broadest public impact.

These struggles to establish world history learning standards in the schools – with mixed results at the state level, grave disappointment at the national level, and significant achievement in AP – point to an important observation: that the space occupied by world history in American education was substantially the result not of a top-down process of "outreach" from the scholarly nobility to workaday classroom plebs, but from the "upreach" of classroom teachers (at all levels) looking for scholarly guidance in their attempt to globalize history education. The fact that David Christian has been so proactive and enthusiastic in adapting his "big history" project for broader use in the schools is a direct consequence – I hope he would agree – of world history's now well-established tradition of working fluidly across and between educational strata; another notable example is the online *World History For Us All* program, conceived by Ross Dunn at San Diego State University.

As with teaching, so with area studies: my institutional position at CSULB made a virtue of broadening my expertise beyond my original training. In fact, faculty members at universities without well-resourced area studies programs routinely find themselves teaching outside their original areas, especially those whose expertise lies in what was once called "third world" regions. For many, world history becomes a principal means of navigating the trajectory from what Philip Curtin (2005) called the "fringes" toward the "center" of the historical discipline. Though decades of area studies advocacy has led to significantly greater geographic diversity to the curriculum of most history departments in the United States, the residual effects of traditional Eurocentrism often remain, with histories of societies outside the United States and Europe still sometimes lumped together in a residual "other" or "nonwestern" category. World history, with its more balanced incorporation of global regions, offers an escape from that curricular impasse.

Though committed to Africa, I remember looking at the history department offerings before my arrival in Madison and imagining all the fascinating courses I might take in Brazilian, Turkish, or South Asian history. Instead, my studies were focused firmly on Africa: I had a continent's worth of knowledge to catch up with (beyond a lifetime of study!) and, needing to make a fast start on the Swahili language, it did not make sense to dally, nor would my professors allow me to do so. Meanwhile, the African Studies Program had the great advantage of interdisciplinarity, fostering interactions between faculty and students from such fields as sociology, political science, anthropology, as well as African languages and literatures. Though I still regret all the other great history classes I might have taken, it is still a standard of graduate training that one needs to be thoroughly grounded in a particular place, time, and language (in my case: East Africa, British colonial era, and Swahili) before even thinking of moving on to broader comparative research (Streets-Salter, 2012).

African studies and other area studies programs first took institutional form in the United States in the context of the Cold War. The National Defense Education Act of 1958 provided funding for language training in less commonly taught languages (including Russian and Chinese) and laid the foundations for interdisciplinary learning centers around the country each focused on a different global region. With waves of newly sovereign states knocking at the door of the United Nations and new embassies and consulates about to be opened, the United States needed its own cadre of regional experts. Over half a century later, the legacy and continued productivity of those area studies programs has been fundamental to world history, for without the academic work of three generations of area studies scholars the raw material for much global and comparative historical work simply would not exist, nor would appropriate language training be available. As a recipient of federal funding for the study of Swahili, and of Fulbright awards for research in Tanzania and international education work in Germany, I can well attest to the importance of public sector support for area studies research.

Still, area studies scholars can become trapped in regional bubbles. The fact that I had little consciousness of "world history" as an intellectual option while attending the University of Wisconsin was ironic, given that a decade earlier the history department at Madison had been especially identified for its strength in comparative history (Lockard, 2000). That was largely the work of Dr. Philip Curtin, a Caribbean specialist turned Africanist turned world historian who was on the faculty in Madison from 1956 to 1975 (before moving to Johns Hopkins and influencing many more intellectual trajectories, including those of Lauren Benton and J.R. McNeill). The gulf between comparative history and area studies had once again widened after Curtin's departure and before my arrival (though I did experience a reverberation of that program's strength in an excellent comparative seminar in the history of slavery led by Dr. Steven Stern, attended by an equal number of Africanists and Latin Americanists).

So like many others from area studies backgrounds it was teaching responsibilities rather than a research agenda that led me to take world history seriously. My pathway was far from unique in coming to world history from "the bottom up" – beginning with classroom teaching – and "from the fringes to the center" – from a background in what used to be called "third world" studies. My own story is one in which, as Merry Wiesner-Hanks puts it elsewhere in this volume, "contingency, chance, and luck play as large a role as reason, planning, and preparation" (p. 61).

Still, in spite of the role played by serendipity in pushing myself and others onto the world history track, there are those "habits of mind" we all seem to share, such as aspiring to the parachutist's view of the past. That analogy was advanced by Emmanuel Le Roy Ladurie, who contrasted historians that, from a high altitude, survey the broad plains of the past with the "truffle snufflers" that delve deeply into very specific (locally or nationally bounded) aspects of history. All the historians in this volume – whether their interest was initially sparked by curricular reform and innovation; intellectual curiosity sparking a scholarly research agenda; or even international travel experiences – have all risen above the plain to view the broader patterns of transregional or global history.

Location can also matter in determining paths to world history. From Honolulu, Jerry Bentley shared my experience of gazing out at the Pacific Ocean every day. As Karen Jolly explains, Bentley's intellectual adjustment to his new island home was very much part of the transition he made as a young professor from Renaissance history to world history. In my case, working at a university located at the US crossroads between Latin America and Asia (about 35% of CSULB students have family roots in the former; nearly 25% in the latter), the story of "our" shared history is necessarily "world history." The mobility of populations around the world is making and will continue to make global and transregional history more relevant to more of the world's people than ever before.

Foundational Texts

Those new to world history now have a number of guides to the field, including this one. Like other *Architects* contributors, however, my own beginning acquaintance with the field's foundational texts was haphazard. One day as when I wandered through the library's open stacks a title jumped out at me: Eric Wolf's *Europe and the People without History* (1982). Wolf was an anthropologist who specialized in Mesoamerican peoples and whose classic book on Aztec history *Sons of the Shaking Earth* (1959) I had read as an undergraduate. The victims of modern Western imperialism, Wolf explained, had been doubly marginalized: not only had they been stripped of political sovereignty and economic resources, they had in a sense been stripped of their own histories. As a novice Africanist, I saw how Wolf's global point reinforced that of Walter Rodney, whose *How Europe Underdeveloped Africa* (1974) had been required reading for students of modern Africa since its first publication in 1972. I vividly remember the original cover image of Rodney's book: a pair of giant white hands ripping the African continent in two. The thesis was clear, and as with Eric Wolf's book, the connection between history and contemporary issues of social justice unmistakable. Like most historians I have subsequently come to see these two works as limited by their didactic purposes and lack of analytical subtlety. But they remain on my bookshelf as signposts on my path toward African and world history.

Other authors in this volume have their own stories of being influenced by "just the right book at just the right time." Having all been educated between the 1970s and the 1990s, it is not surprising to find that there were certain benchmark texts, and certain benchmark concepts of historical analysis, that we share in common. While it is not within the scope of *Architects of World History* to provide a comprehensive bibliographic guide, it may be useful here to cite some of those foundational scholarly works that had such broad influence.

The terms "underdevelopment," "dependency theory," and "core-periphery relations" were starting points toward global historical analysis of the kind embedded in those books by Wolf and Rodney.

In an undergraduate course in "Political Modernization," our conservative instructor gave us a radical book to read: *Dependency and Development in Latin America* (Cardoso and Enzo, 1979). Rejecting the promises of "modernization" theorists that open markets were the surest path to broad prosperity, these economists argued that capitalism was in fact the source of Latin America's traditional *underdevelopment*: capitalism was the historical *cause* of Latin America's poverty, not its solution. (Ironically, Cardoso would later serve as president of Brazil and, in changed global circumstances, implement neoliberal market reforms.) The path from this book led to the highly charged economic analyses of Andre Gunder Frank and his classic formulation of the *Development of Underdevelopment* (1966). These works were part of a broader literature (e.g., Amin 1977, 2010) that cast the oppressed peoples of the "third world" in the role of global proletariat: it was they (rather than the industrial workers of the west, as Marx had predicted) whose revolutionary actions would transform the world.

The insights of underdevelopment theorists were primarily drawn from the disciplines of sociology and economics. Their influence on historical studies came via the work of Immanuel Wallerstein (cited as an influence in this book by Benton, Ward and Pomeranz). Trained as a sociologist rather than as a historian, Wallerstein was more interested in global structures than human activities in his landmark *The Modern World System: Capitalist Agriculture and the Origins of the European World Economy in the Sixteenth Century* (1974). In this and subsequent works, Wallerstein described the relations between the global economic "core" established in the West in the early modern period and its predatory relationship to Asian, African, and Latin American "peripheries" that provided it with markets and raw materials, as well as outlets for surplus capital and surplus population. Through these historical processes (complicated but not negated by "semi-peripheral" cases), the poverty of the world's majority had been created as part and parcel of "modernity" (Chase-Dunn and Hall, 2012).

As an historical sociologist, Wallerstein's emphasis was on structures rather than people, on "capitalism" rather than "capitalists."

His "parachute" view was useful for framing the historical context of the development of the modern global capitalist economy, less so for framing an actual research agenda grounded in historical sources. World systems analysis, one might say, was all architectural vision, with little in the way of bricks and mortar.

Many historians in the 1970s and 1980s found more applicable inspiration in the works of Fernand Braudel; in fact, the word "Braudelian" has long since entered out vocabulary to refer to works that take a long view of history (the *longue durée*) with a focus on the intersection between geography and history, between landscape and long-term dynamics of change and continuity. As leader of the French *Annales* school (so named for its flagship journal), Braudel had a signal impact on postwar historical writing: J.R. McNeill and Lauren Benton were in good company in the deep influence they experienced in reading his three-part *The Mediterranean in the Age of Philip II* (Braudel, 1972). His later work *Civilization and Capitalism* (1977) richly combined an eye toward long-term structural change in European and world economies with a close reading of texts and detailed examination of culture. For historians interested in human agency and human action in broad historical frameworks, Braudel has been inspirational.

From such influences I had developed a special interest in the historical development of modern capitalism and the rise of modern bureaucratic states, especially in relationship to agrarian societies. Among the works of comparative history I found stimulating in thinking through such processes (also cited by Kerry Ward) was Barrington Moore's *Social Origins of Dictatorship and Democracy* (1966). Moore focused on class relations between peasants, landed elites, and urban merchant classes in a broad array of European and Asian societies in his examination of the varying outcomes of democracy, fascism and communism. While Moore's work (like Wallerstein's) was still too much in the "historical sociology" mode to be a template for research, it was useful in reinforcing the elemental fact that rural populations have played a fundamental role in the shaping of modern history.

Another path forward was the emergence of the new social history in the 1960s and 1970s, with its focus on "bottom up" history and the stories of common men and women. Two works were of particular importance in my own experience. The first was E.P. Thompson's *The Making of the English Working Class* (1966). I was astonished when reading this dense and closely argued description of the transformation of English peasants into an industrial proletariat to find many parallels with my beginning studies of colonial African history; for example, the evolving rhetoric of class difference in eighteenth-century England was not that different from the language used to mark racial difference in twentieth-century East Africa. Of similar influence was Eugene Genovese's *Roll, Jordan, Roll: The World the Slaves Made* (1976) that took the lives, thoughts, and experiences of slaves in the antebellum United States every bit as seriously as Thompson had done for the English working class. Genovese used the concept of "cultural hegemony" first developed by the Italian Marxist Antonio Gramsci to sensitively describe both modes of resistance to and conformity with slave status, another topic with strong resonance for history seen from what came to be called the "subaltern" standpoint of the colonized.

That attempt to see history from the "bottom up" gave my dissertation research and the publications that stemmed directly from it (Curtis, 1992, 1994, 2003) a tight geographic focus on the finely grained history of the ways in which the global commodity markets and state interventions came to influence the social and political life of villagers in northwestern Tanzania. This was "truffle snuffling" history, using colonial records that had been poorly maintained; some nearly destroyed by time, neglect, and humidity. Still, that work connected to the "parachute" views laid out, for example, in James Scott's studies of peasant moral economies and their relationships to bureaucratic states (1977, 1987). Admittedly, had I known then what I know now I would have been more explicit in teasing out such global–local connections. The perfect title for such a study exists, although already taken by Donald Wright for his work on a small Gambian community: *The World and a Very Small Place in Africa*

(2010). In Wright's book, the structure of large global changes is related to finely grained specifics rooted in local language, culture, experiences, and perceptions, an approach that could be more widely emulated (Gerritsen, 2012).

Having finished my dissertation, joined the academic work force, and discovered the WHA and the *Journal of World History*, I then made up for lost time, catching up with the "classics" of world history, many of which are mentioned in multiple essays in this volume.

Actually, I already had a copy of William McNeill's *Rise of the West* on my bookshelf (1963; its used bookstore price of $1.25 speaking to its antiquity) and took the chance of his visit to Long Beach to give a thorough reading to his other works, such as *Plagues and Peoples* (1976). For many years, McNeill was a lone voice calling for a return to the larger frame of world history after a long period when historians had become more and more narrowly specialized. Although the title of the *Rise of the West* sounds triumphalist, in fact the book contextualizes Western European history by placing it firmly in the context of what McNeill called the Eurasian *oikumene* (interconnecting world). He then showed how the intellectual and technological developments of late medieval and early modern Europe had resulted from transregional transference. *Plagues and Peoples* was another highly influential work dealing with the clearly transregional subject of disease history, which again provided the necessary framework for proper examination of epidemics such as the Black Death, which was clearly an Afro-Eurasian and not merely European phenomenon.

Another speaker at CSULB with whose work I was already familiar with was Alfred Crosby, who visited in 1992 in the context of the quincentennial of Columbus' first journey to the Americas. A pioneer in the study of biological exchanges in world history, I vividly remember Crosby telling us, "I am not sure if it is more true to say that Cortes conquered the Aztecs with the help of smallpox, or that smallpox conquered the Aztecs with the help of Cortes!" Crosby was being provocative, of course, but his point was that human affairs have frequently been driven by environmental and disease factors. That was a fresh perspective in the 1970s that has since sparked many innovative studies, including J.R. McNeill's *Mosquito Empires* (2010). It was Alfred Crosby who first coined the term "Columbian Exchange" (1972) to describe the transference of diseases, domesticated animals, and food crops between Europe, Africa, and the Americas, in the process demonstrating the historians wishing to pursue such topics had to equip themselves with interdisciplinary research abilities. His later work *Ecological Imperialism* (1986) explained how the world's flora was remade (sometimes with conscious intent, often accidentally) by European imperialists, with massive environmental consequences for people on every continent (and explaining the Australian trees outside my California office).

Another name that appears persistently in the following essays is that of Philip Curtin. Like Jerry Bentley, Curtin's importance to the field stemmed as much from his mentorship of young scholars as from his own writing, though in his case there was actually a strong connection between the two. Curtin's approach was to gather a group of bright young scholars, fix a seminar topic, and then set them to work on specific aspects of it. Through this inductive and collaborative approach (the opposite of historical sociology's deductive emphasis) Curtin's work was deeply grounded in the bricks and mortar of historical detail. The result was such widely cited works as *Cross-Cultural Trade in World History* (1984) and *The Rise and Fall of the Plantation Complex: Essays in Atlantic History* (1998).

Marshall Hodgson is another name referenced in several *Architects* essays. A colleague of McNeill's at the University of Chicago, Hodgson's influence came through the posthumous publication of his *Venture of Islam: Conscience and History in a World Civilization* (1974). Hodgson retained the "civilizational" paradigm subsequently transcended by many world historians, but within that framework emphasized historical dynamism and innovation (Burke, 2000). His emphasis on the circulation of ideas within Islamicate societies (as he called them) and between those societies and neighboring civilizations defied earlier static stereotypes. Similarly, Leften Stavrianos countered "orientalist" conceptions of Ottoman state and society by stressing how its internal dynamics of change were connected to its evolving relationships with neighbors in North Africa, Central

Europe, and Iran (see also, Islamoğlu, 2012). Both Hodgson and Stavrianos anticipated the literary critique by Edward Said in his influential book *Orientalism* (1979), which critiqued static and exotic Western tropes of the "Oriental other." Said's work became a pillar of postcolonial studies, cultural studies, and subaltern studies, fields that overlap with world history but originate from quite different rhetorical and research starting points. (For the intersection and disconnection between these scholarly enterprises, see Bentley, 2005 and Sachsenmaier, 2011.)

Architects and the Scholarship of World History

However we define "world history," I tell my students, we certainly cannot think of it as "everything that ever happened, to anyone, anywhere in the world." That would be too audacious and ambitious an undertaking. Or would it? David Christian's *Maps of Time: An Introduction to Big History* (2011) does *indeed* take all of time and all of space as its domain. For the faint of heart, for whom stellar history might be a step too far, Christian's *This Fleeting World* (2007) is restricted to the mere 250,000-year history of *Homo sapiens*. Christian's audacious initiative has spawned the International Big History Association and a number of articles and books (Spier, 2012), though for most historians his expansive approach still lies outside the mainstream.

It is more usual for world historians to the limit their domains of inquiry by time, space, theme, or some combination of the three. As Adam McKeown (2012) has emphasized, world historians must be exceptionally aware of geographic and temporal *scales*, choosing the chronological and spatial parameters most appropriate to the questions they have framed: "Each scale," as he writes, "illuminates different processes." Thus, Philip Curtin, in his essays on the "plantation complex," needed to address origins in the Mediterranean and events in Africa, Europe, and the Americas over three centuries. Fernand Braudel described the shores of the Mediterranean as a coherent area of historical study over the *longue durée*, while William

McNeill's history of plagues and epidemics took Eurasia as its starting point (even as other historians have extended his insights to Africa, the Americas, and Polynesia). Some scholars like Donald Wright focus on a small region over a long period of time (2010), others will pick a small slice of time and look at the entire world, as with John Wills in *1688: A Global History* (2002).

We have cited Jerry Bentley's list of topics most characteristic of world history, but he did not explicitly mention the thematic area with which my own research connects most closely: the study of commodity chains in modern world history (Levi, 2012). Some economic and social historians have found that by focusing on the production, trade, and consumption of a single commodity they can tease out significant historical interconnections. A landmark of this approach, though written by an anthropologist rather than an historian, was Sidney Mintz's *Sweetness and Power: The Place of Sugar in Modern History* (1986). Apart from influencing Lauren Benton, Mintz's book also inspired me in the composition of a chapter for *Discovering the Global Past*, using primary sources to tell the story of "Sweet Nexus: Sugar and the Origins of the Modern World" (2011). Another volume to which I contributed used coffee as its starting point for analysis of the relations between producers, commercial intermediaries, and consumers in the modern economy: *The Global Coffee Economy in Africa, Asia, and Latin America, 1500–1989* (Clarence-Smith and Topik, 2003). Other world history studies have focused on rubber (Tully, 2011), salt (Kurlansky, 2003), and cotton (Riello, 2013). Similarly, environmental world historians have sometimes focused on a single disease, such as malaria (Webb, 2008; more generally Pernick, 2012).

In the eight essays that follow, you will be introduced to some of the more interesting thematic developments in the world history scholarship over the past decade, with authors who employ diverse temporal and spatial scales. Of course, not every important area of world history research is covered: for example, scholarship reconsidering the history of empires and imperialism (e.g., Sinha, 2012) is not the direct focus of any one essay. Even as the goal of keeping pace with research trends grows more daunting, however, the reader can make a good start by accessing the tables of contents and reviews published in *The Journal of World History*, *The Journal of Global History*, and *World History Connected* (a free online journal with a stronger emphasis on pedagogy). The new online *Journal of World-Historical Information* and the World-Historical Dataverse archived by Patrick Manning's World History Center at the University of Pittsburgh is also of interest. Of course, there is no substitute for the networking available through membership in the WHA or another of the regional associations of the Network of Global and World History Organizations, or for the daily world history conversations available through subscription to the H-World discussion network.

Architects of World History is intended to provide readers with a broad appreciation of the field of world history and some of its main nodes of research; perhaps as well an incentive to think through their own "intellectual trajectories" and the place of connective and comparative global history therein. Readers are then strongly encouraged to delve more deeply into the works of one of these scholars and the subfields they represent, perhaps adding their own geographic or chronological specializations to the mix. Which is to say: students of history who use this book as a parachute to gain a high-altitude vision of world history scholarship will eventually have to descend earthward and replant themselves in a specific field of study. Once you've thought through larger contexts, connections, and comparisons, however, we doubt that your perspective will ever again be quite the same.

As different as our authors' approaches to world history have been, J.R. McNeill and Merry Wiesner-Hanks share something in common. Each had a starting point in a field of historical inquiry that hardly even existed 40 years ago – environmental history for McNeill, gender history for Wiesner-Hank. Wiesner-Hanks explores the reasons it has taken several decades for cross-fertilization between gender history and world history to begin to bear fruit; from the standpoint of environmental history, on the other hand, convergence across these disciplinary distinctions has been less problematic. McNeill and Wiesner-Hanks thereby remind us that "world history" is not a segregated specialization, but one that has grown and matured in conjunction with other developments in the historical discipline.

Kenneth Pomeranz and Dominic Sachsenmaier share the common experience of having analyzed different aspects of what D.E. Mungello has called (2005) the "great encounter" between China and the west. Pomeranz sparked an intense and ongoing debate with *The Great Divergence: China, Europe, and the Making of the Modern World Economy* (2001), bringing fresh research to bear on the question of why England industrialized in the nineteenth century while Qing China lagged behind. From a social and intellectual standpoint, meanwhile, Sachsenmaier is contributing to a re-evaluation of the development of early modern Christianity in China, bringing language skills and fresh archival resources to an area of inquiry that in the past has been far too Eurocentric. In addition, Sachsenmaier's unique experience of having viewed the development history from three widely varying national standpoints (German, American, and Chinese) led to the publication (2011) of the first full-scale study of the globalization of world history (see also Zhang, 2012 and Neumann, 2012).

There is an even more direct connection between the scholarship of Lauren Benton and Kerry Ward, who explicitly recognizes Benton's *Law and Colonial Cultures* (2001) as an influence on her own monograph *Networks of Empire* (2009). These are two examples of world historians finding new sources and developing fresh interpretations of traditional topics: legal and imperial history. Comparative legal history is a well-established field, but in the past legal historians tended to focus on normative descriptions of comparative legal systems, what societies said people should do rather than what they actually did. What Benton showed, first for legal history and then for a more expansive consideration of "sovereignty," is that judicial practice cannot be read simply from statutes and that even conquered or subjected peoples have something to say about legal practice. Building on such insights, Ward produced a study that spanned the Indian Ocean and connected African and Asian histories in tracing the migrations of convicts at the intersection of imperial history, legal history, religious history, social history, and biography. If we say that one of the characteristics of world history as a field is the priority given to stories of "movement" (Ward, 2012), her research is a perfect embodiment.

By this point the book readers' perspectives may have been sufficiently stretched to prepare them for David Christian's reflections on the origins and development of "big history." No mere parachutist, Christian is a *cosmonaut* of history. If research in world history has often involved the bringing of fresh global insights to conventional historical fields (legal or imperial history) or the dovetailing of global history with other emergent topics (environmental or gender history), then Christian is an exception. His imaginative leap toward "big history" takes him and like-minded colleagues beyond the bounds of historians' usual fields of endeavor and into conversation with astrophysicists, geologists, and evolutionary biologists.

Finally, from the vast cosmos back to the relative intimacy of human culture and cultural interactions, we end with Jerry Bentley's final essay. The last time I talked with Jerry he was brimming with ideas about how to describe his intellectual trajectory toward global cultural history, but he sounded very weak. A month later, after his passing, I learned he had been working on his *Architects* essay in his last days, and that his widow, Carol Mon Lee, deemed it worthy of publication. I also discovered, in communication with our mutual friend Alan Karras, that a colleague at the University of Hawaii, Karen Jolly, had interviewed Jerry toward the end of his life and had prepared a thoughtful intellectual obituary. Thus, we publish here in full the fragment of Jerry's essay, completed by Jolly's third-person narrative on his mature work and thought. As a modest reminder of Jerry Bentley's enduring influence on the field of world history, we dedicate this book to his memory.

References

Allardyce, Gilbert. 2000. "Toward World History: American Historians and the Coming of the World History Course," in Ross Dunn, ed. *The New World History: A Teacher's Companion*. New York: Bedford/ St. Martin's.

Amin, Samir. 1977. *Imperialism and Unequal Development*. New York: Monthly Review Press.

Amin, Samir. 2010. *Global History: A View from the South*. Oxford: Pambazuka Press.

Bentley, Jerry. 2002. "The New World History," in Lloyd Kramer and Sara Maza, eds. *A Companion to Western Historical Thought*. Oxford: Wiley-Blackwell.

Bentley, Jerry. 2005. "Myths, Wagers, and Some Moral Implications of World History," *Journal of World History* 16: 51–82.

Bentley, Jerry. 2011. *The Oxford Handbook of World History*. Oxford: Oxford University Press.

Benton, Lauren. 2001. *Law and Colonial Cultures: Legal Regimes in World History*. Cambridge: Cambridge University Press.

Braudel, Fernand. 1972. *The Mediterranean and the Mediterranean World in the Era of Philip II*, 2 vols. New York: Harper & Row.

Braudel, Fernand. 1977. *Civilization and Capitalism*, Berkeley, CA: University of California Press.

Bright, Charles and Michael Geyer. 2012. "Benchmarks of Globalization: The Global Condition, 1850–2010," in Douglas Northrop, ed. *Wiley-Blackwell Companion to World History*. Oxford: Wiley-Blackwell.

Burke, Edmund. 2000. "Marshall G.S. Hodgson and the Hemispheric Interregional Approach to World History," in Ross Dunn, ed. *The New World History: A Teacher's Companion*. New York: Bedford/St. Martin's.

Cardoso, Fernando Henrique and Faletto Enzo. 1979. *Dependency and Development in Latin America*. Berkeley, CA: University of California Press.

Chase-Dunn, Christopher and D. Thomas. 2012. "Global Scale Analysis in Human History," in Douglas Northrop, ed. *Wiley-Blackwell Companion to World History*. Oxford: Wiley-Blackwell.

Christian, David. 2007. *This Fleeting World: A Short History of Humanity*. Great Barrington, MA: Berkshire Publishing.

Christian, David. 2011. *Maps of Time: An Introduction to Big History*. Berkeley, CA: University of California Press.

Clarence-Smith, William Gervase and Steven Topik. 2003. *The Global Coffee Economy in Africa, Asia, and Latin America, 1500–1989*. Cambridge: Cambridge University Press.

Crosby, Alfred. 1972. *The Columbian Exchange: Biological and Cultural Consequences of 1492*. Westport, CT: Greenwood Publishing.

Crosby, Alfred. 1986. *Ecological Imperialism: The Biological Expansion of Europe*. Cambridge: Cambridge University Press.

Curtin, Philip. 1984. *Cross-Cultural Trade in World History*. Cambridge: Cambridge University Press.

Curtin, Philip. 1998. *The Rise and Fall of the Plantation Complex: Essays in Atlantic History*, 2nd edition. Cambridge: Cambridge University Press.

Curtin, Philip. 2005. *On the Fringes of History: A Memoir*. Athens: Ohio University Press.

Curtis, Lewis Perry. 1970. *The Historians' Workshop: Original Essays by Sixteen Historians*. New York: Knopf.

Curtis, Kenneth R. 1992. "Cooperation and Co-optation: The Struggle for Market Control in the Bukoba District of Colonial Tanganyika," *The International Journal of African Historical Studies* 12/3: 505–538.

Curtis, Kenneth R. 1994. "Neo-traditionalism in Colonial Buhaya: A Public Debate," in Robert W. Harms, Joseph C. Miller, David S. Newbury and Michelle D. Wagner, eds. *Paths to the Past: African Historical Essays in Honor of Jan Vansina*. Atlanta, GA: African Studies Association Press.

Curtis, Kenneth R. 2003. "Coffee and Colonialism: Conflict or Consensus? Moral Economy and Bureaucratic Paternalism in Tanganyika, 1920–1960," in William Gervase Clarence-Smith and Steven Topik, eds. *The Global Coffee Economy in Africa, Asia, and Latin America, 1500–1989*, Cambridge: Cambridge University Press.

Curtis, Kenneth R. 2011. *Discovering the Global Past: A Look at the Evidence*, 4th edition, with Bruce Wheeler, Merry Wiesner-Hanks, and Frank Doeringer. Boston, MA: Wadsworth.

Curtis, Kenneth R. 2013. *Voyages in World History*. 2nd edition, with Valerie Hansen. Boston, MA: Wadsworth.

Dunn, Ross. 2000. *The New World History: A Teacher's Companion*. New York: Bedford/St. Martin's.

Frank, Andre Gunder. 1966. *The Development of Underdevelopment*. Boston, MA: New England Free Press.

Genovese, Eugene. 1976. *Roll, Jordan, Roll: The World the Slaves Made*. New York: Vintage.

Gerritsen, Anne. 2012. "Scales of a Local: The Place of Locality in a Globalizing World," in Douglas Northrop, ed. *Wiley-Blackwell Companion to World History*. Oxford: Wiley-Blackwell.

Getz, Trevor. 2012. "Teaching World History at the College Level," in Douglas Northrop, ed. *Wiley-Blackwell Companion to World History*. Oxford: Wiley-Blackwell.

Hodgson, Marshall. 1974. *Venture of Islam: Conscience and History in a World Civilization*. Chicago, IL: University of Chicago Press.

Houck, Jean. 2004. *Partnering to Lead Educational Renewal*. New York: Teachers College Press.

Islamoğlu, Huri. 2012. "Islamicate World Histories?," in Douglas Northrop, ed. *Wiley-Blackwell Companion to World History*. Oxford: Wiley-Blackwell.

Kurlansky, Mark. 2003. *Salt: A World History*. New York: Penguin.

Levi, Scott C. 2012. "Objects in Motion," in Douglas Northrop, ed. *Wiley-Blackwell Companion to World History*. Oxford: Wiley-Blackwell.

Levine, Lawrence W. 2000. "Looking Eastward: The Career of Western Civ," in Ross Dunn, ed. *The New World History: A Teacher's Companion*. New York: Bedford/St. Martin's.

Lockard, Craig A. 2000. "The Contributions of Philip Curtin and the "Wisconsin School" to the Study and Promotion of Comparative World History," in Ross Dunn, ed. *The New World History: A Teacher's Companion*. New York: Bedford/St. Martin's.

Manning, Patrick. 2003. *Navigating World History: Historians Create a Global Past*. New York: Palgrave Macmillan.

McKeown, Adam. 2012. "What Are the Units of World History?," in Douglas Northrop, ed. *Wiley-Blackwell Companion to World History*. Oxford: Wiley-Blackwell.

McNeill, William. 1963. *The Rise of the West: A History of the Human Community*. Chicago, IL: University of Chicago Press.

McNeill, William. 1976. *Plagues and Peoples*. Norwell, MA: Anchor Press.

McNeill, J.R. 2010. *Mosquito Empires: Ecology and War in the Greater Caribbean*. Cambridge: Cambridge University Press.

Mintz, Sidney. 1986. *Sweetness and Power: The Place of Sugar in Modern History*. New York: Penguin.

Moore, Barrington. 1966. *The Social Origins of Dictatorship and Democracy*. Boston, MA: Beacon Press.

Mungello, David E. 2005. *The Great Encounter of China and the West, 1500–1800*. Lanham, MD: Rowman & Littlefield.

Nash, Gary, Charlotte Crabtree, and Ross Dunn. 2000. *History on Trial: Culture Wars and the Teaching of the Past*. New York: Vintage.

Neumann, Katja. 2012. "(Re) Writing World Histories in Europe," in Douglas Northrop, ed. *Wiley-Blackwell Companion to World History*. Oxford: Wiley-Blackwell.

Northrop, Douglas. 2012. *Wiley-Blackwell Companion to World History*. Oxford: Wiley-Blackwell.

Pernick, Martin S. 2012. "Diseases in Motion," in Douglas Northrop, ed. *Wiley-Blackwell Companion to World History*. Oxford: Wiley-Blackwell.

Pomeranz, Kenneth. 2001. *The Great Divergence: China, Europe, and the Making of the Modern World Economy*. Princeton, NJ: Princeton University Press.

Pomeranz, Kenneth and Daniel A. Segal. 2012. "World History: Departures and Variations," in Douglas Northrop, ed. *Wiley-Blackwell Companion to World History*. Oxford: Wiley-Blackwell.

Riello, Giorgio. 2013. *Cotton: The Fabric that Made the Modern World*. Cambridge: Cambridge University Press.

Rodney, Walter. 1974. *How Europe Underdeveloped Africa*. Washington, DC: Howard University Press.

Sachsenmaier, Dominic. 2011. *Global Perspectives on Global History: Theories and Approaches in a Connected World*. Cambridge: Cambridge University Press.

Said, Edward. 1979. *Orientalism*. New York: Vintage.

Scott, James. 1977. *The Moral Economy of the Peasant: Rebellion and Subsistence in Southeast Asia*. New Haven, CT: Yale University Press.

Scott, James. 1987. *Weapons of the Weak: Everyday Forms of Peasant Resistance*. New Haven, CT: Yale University Press.

Sinha, Mrinalini. 2012. *"Projecting Power: Empires, Colonies, and World History,"* in Douglas Northrop, ed. Wiley-Blackwell Companion to World History. Oxford: Wiley-Blackwell.

Spier, Fred. 2012. "Big History," in Douglas Northrop, ed. *Wiley-Blackwell Companion to World History*. Oxford: Wiley-Blackwell.

Streets-Salter, Heather. 2012. "Becoming a World Historian: The State of Graduate Training in World History and Placement in the Academic World," in Douglas Northrop, ed. *Wiley-Blackwell Companion to World History*. Oxford: Wiley-Blackwell.

Symox, Linda. 2002. *Whose History?: The Struggle for National Standards in American Classrooms*. New York: Teachers College Press.

Thompson, E.P. 1966. *The Making of the English Working Class*. New York: Vintage.

Tully, John. 2011. *The Devil's Milk: A Social History of Rubber*. New York: Monthly Review Press.

Wallerstein, Immanuel. 1974. *The Modern World-System, Vol. I: Capitalist Agriculture and the Origins of the European World-Economy in the Sixteenth Century*. New York: Academic Press.

Ward, Kerry. 2009. *Networks of Empire: Forced Migration in the Dutch East India Company*. Cambridge: Cambridge University Press.

Ward, Kerry. 2012. "People in Motion," in Douglas Northrop, ed. *Wiley-Blackwell Companion to World History*. Oxford: Wiley-Blackwell.

Webb, James. 2008. *Humanity's Burden: A Global History of Malaria*. Cambridge: Cambridge University Press.

Weber, William. 2012. "The Evolution of *The History Teacher* and the Reform of History Education," *The History Teacher* 45/3: 329–357.

Weinstein, Barbara. 2012. "The World Is Your Archive? The Challenges of World History as a Field of Research," in Douglas Northrop, ed. *Wiley-Blackwell Companion to World History*. Oxford: Wiley-Blackwell.

Wills, John. 2002. *1688: A Global History*. New York: W.W. Norton.

Wolf, Eric. 1982. *Europe and the People Without History*. Berkeley, CA: University of California Press.

Wright, Donald. 2010 *The World and a Very Small Place in Africa: The History of Globalization in Niumi, the Gambia*, 3rd edition. Armonk, NY: M.E. Sharpe.

Zhang, Weiwei. 2012. "The World from China," in Douglas Northrop, ed. *Wiley-Blackwell Companion to World History*. Oxford: Wiley-Blackwell.

2

En Route to World Environmental History

J.R. McNeill

My path to world history must be among the easiest ever trod. I did not have to rebel against upbringing and socialization to embrace the gospel of world history. I was born into a missionary family.

One of my grandfathers, John T. McNeill (1885–1975), was born on a farm in Prince Edward Island in the Canadian Maritimes. He uprooted for Montreal, Vancouver, Toronto, Chicago, and New York, leaving behind the blind certainties of provincial Presbyterianism of a century ago. He preferred the uncertainties of university life and made an academic career, writing church histories as if all Christians were created equal. My other grandfather, a ne'er-do-well named Robert S. Darbishire (1886–1949), was born near Tampa, Florida to parents convinced of the superiority of all things English. He might have liked an academic career, but came no closer than teaching English to Greek schoolboys. He tried to educate himself about Islam and for a while studied Arabic and Turkish in the 1920s and 1930s, when such ambitions were surpassingly rare. He did not get far, but

Architects of World History: Researching the Global Past, First Edition.
Edited by Kenneth R. Curtis and Jerry H. Bentley.

his inclinations were ecumenical. Or so it seems from reading his letters; I never met him.

My father, William H. McNeill, born in Vancouver in 1917, became one of the most visible world historians of his time. As he recounts it (McNeill, 2005), he found the history education offered by his teachers at the University of Chicago and Cornell constraining, and was dazzled by the global vision on display in the work of Arnold J. Toynbee's *A Study of History*. He planned from an early age to write his own history of the world, hoping to improve upon Toynbee. While I was learning to read, my father was finishing *The Rise of the West* (1963), a milestone in the emergence of world history in the United States. The book was a modest popular success and still won admiration from scholars, in part for its emphasis on the interactions among societies. I expect I frequently heard about the virtues of world history at the dinner table growing up, although I am certain I paid little heed.

My grandmothers and my mother, so far as I know, were neither interested in world history nor ecumenical in outlook. They fulfilled the expectations for women in their times and devoted themselves to their families. Their devotion included nourishing any inclinations children might show toward reading and learning.

Environmental History

My own participation in world history has come mainly in the form of environmental history, to which I came accidentally. That story I will relate later, after some historiographical orientation.

The subfield of environmental history is now more than a generation old, pursued by scholars who deliberately write history as if nature existed. They (and I) believe that the natural environment serves not merely as a backdrop to human history, but evolves in its own right, both of its own accord and as a result of human actions. Environmental history, in short, is the history of the relations between human societies and the rest of nature on which they depend.

More than most varieties of history, environmental history is interdisciplinary. In addition to the customary published and archival texts beloved by historians, environmental historians routinely use the findings culled from bio-archives (such as pollen deposits that can tell us about former vegetation patterns) and geo-archives (such as soil profiles that can tell us about past land-use practices). Although the choice of sources emphasized normally differs, the subject matter of environmental history is often much the same as in historical geography or historical ecology.

Like everything in intellectual life, environmental history has tangled roots. Some of humankind's oldest texts, such as the Epic of Gilgamesh – the earliest versions of which are 4000 years old – deal with environmental change generated by human action (in this case, cutting cedar forests in the Levant). Many scholars of long ago, notably Ibn Khaldun (1332–1406) and the Baron de Montesquieu (1689–1755), found in the geographical variations in the natural world, and in climate especially, a key to human behavior. By today's standards, they rank as naïve environmental determinists. They did not see environments as changing, except perhaps on local scales. They tended to see nature as enduring, as divine creation, not easily altered by human effort. By the nineteenth century, however, scientists came to recognize that the Earth itself, and life on it, changed over time, affecting the opportunities open to humanity. A few even saw that humanity played a role in changing the biosphere (Agassiz and Gould, 1848; Marsh, 1864; Stoppani, 1871–1873).

Modern environmental history dates only to about 1970. Initially, it drew its energy from trends within society at large. Around the world, the 1960s and 1970s witnessed the coalescence of popular environmentalism as a cultural and political movement, spurred by recognition that people could indeed have profound impacts on the biosphere. In the United States, the new environmentalism helped inspire a few historians, initially almost all scholars of US history, to come together both intellectually and institutionally. They formed the American Society for Environmental History in 1976, the first of several such associations. Elsewhere, especially in Europe but eventually more broadly, historians also began to practice what increasingly came to be called environmental history (or *umweltgeschichte* or *storia ambientale* as the case may be).

In the 1970s and early 1980s, most of the influential work concerned US environmental history. A small handful of books acquired status as foundational texts. The first was Roderick Nash's *Wilderness and the American Mind* (1967), an intellectual history of nature-writing in the United States. Alfred Crosby's *Columbian Exchange* (1972) soon followed, one of the few books whose title became part of nearly every anglophone historian's vocabulary. Donald Worster's *Dust Bowl* (1978) took an iconic subject in US history and gave it a new twist, bringing new detail to historians' discussions of climate, soil, and grass, as well as to the human tragedies that played out on the southern plains in the 1930s. William Cronon's *Changes in the Land* (1984), which explored the transformations of southern New England's human ecology between 1600 and 1800, enjoyed great success. All these authors, and many more like them, wrote with modern environmentalist concerns looming over them, and typically lamented the changes they wrote about.

Younger recruits to the field often but not always shared this impulse to lamentation. A few of them took their approach beyond national borders, but none as yet sought to tackle environmental history on the world scale. By the early 1980s in the United States, environmental history was an up and coming subfield with professional meetings held once every 2 years and an academic journal. Aside from Crosby, however, no one consistently worked on large canvases. Outside the United States, through the early 1980s, the field remained thoroughly marginal, unless one counts the geographically aware rural histories of historians associated with the journal *Annales: E.S.C.* (which some do but I do not). In any case, environmental history and world history, both percolating provocatively in the 1970s, did not yet intersect.

Choosing History

None of this excitement penetrated my consciousness until after 1980. As an undergraduate at Swarthmore College (1971–1975), after a doomed flirtation with mathematics, I studied history, but neither world history nor environmental history. The offerings available to me were more conventional national histories, or in the case of Africa and Latin America, continental-scale history. Nonetheless, by accident rather than design, I learned something of the history of China, Russia, Africa, Europe, Latin America, and the foreign policy of the United States. I had plenty of opportunity for comparative world history on my own, although I do not remember ever taking the trouble to compare, say, the Russian and Chinese revolutions, each of which I studied in separate courses. I accepted as givens the national or regional frameworks of my professors, my classes, and the books I read for them.

When allowed to write a double-credit senior thesis at Swarthmore (about 160 double-spaced pages), I chose one of the most tedious subjects imaginable, railway finance in Britain circa 1830–1860. I spent the flower of my youth among the bulky gray microfilm readers of the University of Pennsylvania library, hand-copying data from lists of railway investors preserved in Britain's parliamentary papers. On one Friday evening I did not notice the library's closing bell and was locked in the microfilm reading room for the night. Although all my primary sources were from Britain, I did write sections of my thesis about India, Russia, Europe, and Canada, using published accounts. That probably represents my first uncertain lurch in the direction of world history. Although railroad-building would make a fine subject for environmental history, it never occurred to me to include such considerations. Nothing environmental figured anywhere in my undergraduate education. And I scarcely noticed the popular environmentalism of the early 1970s, although it was all around me.[1]

Upon graduation I went to Athens, like my grandfather before me. In the course of a year based there, I traveled to Turkey, Egypt, and for most of a summer, Tanzania. These travels, at age 21, were my first real exposure to a world very different from that into which I had been born. Despite having read a fair bit about peasants, subsistence crises, and famines in my Swarthmore education, the poverty and sickness in rural Egypt disturbed me. East Africa intrigued and puzzled me. On more than one occasion I was mystified in rural Tanzania by scenes of soldiers herding unarmed peasants in directions they clearly had no wish to go. I had no idea at the time (1976) what I was seeing, but it was the government's efforts to achieve self-sufficient, rationally planned farming villages, the so-called *ujamaa* program, which in parts of the country went over poorly.

A prospective job as an English teacher in Teheran fell through, so I returned to the United States in the fall of 1976 to begin graduate study in history at Duke University. My coursework there was conventional enough, focused mainly on Africa, Latin America, Canada, and modern Europe. I took two semesters of African history because my summer in Tanzania had sparked a curiosity in me. My other choices had little if any logic behind them. The geographic breadth of my studies was unusual among my fellow graduate students. I remember a sophomoric argument with one of my friends in which I accused him of knowing nothing of history outside of modern France, while he accused me of knowing nothing of anything in any depth. (We remained friends). Insofar as my studies had any coherence, their central theme was modern imperialism. I was, unawares and unintentionally, edging toward world history.

Floundering Toward World History

In the summer of 1980, I began to hurtle toward world history. While I was writing up my dissertation, a comparison of French and Spanish imperial regimes and economies in parts of the eighteenth-century Atlantic world, a historian of Britain and the British Empire, John Cell, asked me to team-teach what would be the first-ever world history class at Duke. The initiative was entirely Cell's. I had taken no courses with him and knew him only from the tennis court, where he competed with a ferocity I had rarely witnessed (he had been a varsity basketball player at Duke two decades before). But I was flattered to be asked, and we started in September. We used no textbook, only a series of primary sources that Cell had already assembled, and expected our class to weave these into a fabric the outlines of which we provided in alternating lectures. Cell's outlook was moderately Marxist, and his lectures emphasized social relations and class formation. Mine were often mainly about geography and agriculture, the least difficult subjects for me to prepare in a hurry.

After I completed my degree, in the summer of 1981, I was flamboyantly unsuccessful in the job market. Anne Scott, a historian of women in the American South and then chair of the Duke history department, asked me to teach modern world history on my own in spring of 1982, for which I was – and am – most grateful. I suspect no one else in the department wanted the assignment so it fell to an unemployed recent graduate. She assigned me to the cavernous office of Peter Wood, an early Americanist who was then on leave. Wood had a formidable collection of books lining the walls of his office, and I had time on my hands with only one class to teach. I discovered Emmanuel Le Roy Ladurie's *Peasants of Languedoc* (1974) and dozens of other books on rural history, some of which, like Le Roy Ladurie's study of the land, climate, and agriculture of southern France, had components of environmental history in them. One rainy afternoon I chanced upon Alfred Crosby's *Columbian Exchange*. I read it in one gulp and have never been quite the same since.

Floundering Toward Environmental History

Crosby served as my introduction to environmental history. At that point (1982) I was aware of some of the historiography that highlighted disease, partly because I had grown interested in the debates surrounding the size and fate of the pre-Columbian population of the Americas, and partly because my father had in 1977 published *Plagues and Peoples* (1977), which I had read in the summer of 1979. That book was the first general study of disease in history written by a historian. It is sometimes considered an example of environmental history, although (I can say with assurance) the author never thought of it as such.

Crosby's *Columbian Exchange* made what to my mind was an entirely convincing case for the importance of the transfers of crops, livestock, and pathogens between the Old and New Worlds in the wake of Columbus' voyages. I began to see new possibilities in my teaching, in which I was now free to experiment as I saw fit without the steadying influence of John Cell. With only one class to teach I had plenty of time to read, and with an income of $3000 per year, I could afford to do little else. So, under the spell of Crosby, I learned about crops, livestock, pathogens and related themes in every context I could. My students got a version of world history heavy on geography, agriculture, demography, and disease.

At the same time I was also engaged in trying to improve my dissertation in hopes of making it into a publishable book. Crosby's perspective nudged me in different directions with that project too, helping me to think of the North Atlantic cod fisheries and Cuban plantation agriculture in a slightly more ecological light (McNeill, 1985a). I learned to use the work of natural scientists, in this case mainly fisheries ecologists, to inform my speculations about the past.

None of this helped me in the academic job market, in which I was equally as unsuccessful in 1982–1983 and I had been the previous year. By this point, I had applied for upward of 100 tenure-track or short-term teaching jobs, in Latin American, early American, European, and other sorts of history, some as far afield as Singapore. Nobody wanted to hire me. I was surviving on odd jobs after the spring of 1982 and had begun to suspect I should seek something other than an academic career, but before I acted on that reasonable suspicion, John Richards intervened.

Richards (1938–2007) was a specialist in the history of Mughal India at Duke. He had taught me in an obligatory methodology seminar, which left me with no great impression of him and probably left him with plentiful doubts about me. By 1982, he had branched out as a historian from his Mughalist base and begun to work on early modern bullion flows around the world and, crucially for me, on deforestation in India. Late one Friday night I crossed paths with him in the stacks of the Duke library, remarking how inspiring it was to see a full professor there at such an hour. I noticed he had a book on Cuba under his arm, an island to which I had devoted half of my dissertation. We fell into conversation about Cuba and its forests, for Richards had begun to prepare to teach a global environmental history course. His course ultimately led to his magnum opus, *The Unending Frontier* (Richards, 2003), a global environmental history of the early modern centuries. Our conversation that evening revised my impression of him upward and perhaps eased his doubts about me.

Richards' work on deforestation had brought him into contact with natural scientists at Ecosystems Center, part of the Marine Biological Laboratory in Woods Hole, MA. A group there, led by ecologists George Woodwell and Richard Houghton, were then engaged in primitive modeling of the Earth's carbon cycle with a view to understanding the buildup of carbon dioxide in the atmosphere. Specifically, they wanted to know how much of elevated CO_2 levels could be attributed to the burning of fossil fuels and how much to burning of vegetation and other changes to land cover. To answer their questions, they needed historical data on vegetation changes in each of the nine regions into which they had divided the world. Richards was working with them on South and Southeast Asia.

Their next target was Latin America. At first, they contracted the research out to a high school teacher with a free summer, but the results apparently had left something to be desired. Richards suggested they try a trained historian who could read Spanish and Portuguese, and recommended me (although in fact I could scarcely read Portuguese). So, through Richards' influence, Ecosystems Center hired me to generate historical estimates, for 50-year intervals beginning in 1500, of the surface area of Latin America covered in forest, grass, annual crops, permanent crops, tree crops (and perhaps a few other things I have now forgotten). I did it by consulting UN FAO statistics, national statistical abstracts, and agricultural censuses when and where available, and especially for the early centuries, extrapolating liberally from the sketchy data on population and, in cases, crop exports. Most of the work was quantitative, so what little Portuguese I learned to work on Brazil proved good enough. Houghton and his colleagues would feed my data into their global carbon cycle model and calculate the contributions to atmospheric CO_2 made by vegetation changes in Latin America over the last five centuries. I was free to work when and where I chose and was paid what I called "science wages," rather more generous than my pay as a "visiting instructor" of world history at Duke.

The experience of working for Ecosystems Center pushed me further in the direction of environmental history in 1982–1983. The research I was doing fit with what I had read in Crosby and what I had learned about the catastrophic loss of population in the Americas in the sixteenth and seventeenth centuries. It taught me about the surge of deforestation in Amazonia and Central America in the latter half of the twentieth century. Richards organized a seminar or two on land-use history in South Asia, which allowed me to compare what I was learning about Latin America with what he and his associates were finding about South Asia. My science wages even allowed me to spend a month tramping around Nepal and northern India in the fall of 1982, which opened my eyes a little to a region I had never studied. Unlike my late teenage years at Swarthmore, when even obvious comparisons did not occur to me, now I found it interesting to think about the impact on forests of the population and economy of the Mughal Empire in India and the Spanish Empire in America. I started to think more carefully about the ecological consequences of population growth, of export agriculture, of livestock and other central concerns of environmental history.

In careerist terms, I was still floundering, unable to land what academics call "a real job." But I was making enough money to get by, indeed, given my skinflint habits, to save and travel. Aside from deep doubts about the viability of my chosen profession, I was happy. Thanks to John Richards and Ecosystems Center, I did not leave the profession of history at age 28 but decided to try the academic job market once again.

My luck changed in 1983. Goucher College in Towson, MD, hired me to teach European history. My duties, inherited from my predecessor, included national surveys of German and Russian history, an overview of modern Europe, and a survey of war and fascism in

Europe, 1914–1945. I taught these courses for 2 years. Goucher was a small women's college in those days, and its history department included only four full-time professors, all but me trained as Americanists. There was no room for world history in the curriculum, although I was given encouragement to develop a new course on Middle East history, which I would have taught had I remained at Goucher.

One of the good things about teaching at a college with only 60 faculty members in all was that I got to learn from the biologists and chemists well as from my fellow historians. We had only a single faculty research seminar across the entire college, so we had to present our scholarship in ways that avoided jargon and assumed no prior knowledge. I took part in seminars on aspects of population biology and labor economics, for example, and in turn strove to present my historical researches in ways that accounting professors and organic chemists alike would find interesting. This was good training as well as good fun and influenced the way I have tried to write books (not journal articles) ever since, hoping for an audience of general readers rather than only of fellow specialists.

While at Goucher, and living in the heart of Baltimore, I often attended a Johns Hopkins seminar on Atlantic history and culture run by Philip Curtin and the anthropologist Richard Price, an expert on Surinam. This was an intellectual experience of a different sort than the Goucher faculty seminar: a room full of distinguished specialists on Africa and Afro-America. I sat around the edges of the room and kept my mouth shut.

Nonetheless, I came to know Curtin a bit. He was perhaps the most prominent Africanist historian in the United States at that point, but had started out decades before as a historian of Jamaica. In his nearly 20 years on the faculty at Wisconsin, he had helped to set up a comparative world history program at the Ph.D. level, one in which John Richards had taken part before moving to Duke. Curtin was then finishing *Cross-Cultural Trade in World History* (1984) and getting into work on disease history that would result in *Death by Migration* (1989). I found his world-historical range dazzling and his ideas about the importance of malaria and yellow fever in

African and tropical American history especially exciting. In the course of my Ph.D. work on Cuba, I had come across many references to yellow fever and malaria and had given a paper on the subject in 1983. Conversations with Curtin helped me refine my thinking on the role of these two diseases, although 20 years would pass before I got around to further work in this vein.

Aside from discussions with Curtin, almost nothing in my time at Goucher (1983–1985) propelled me in the direction of either world history or environmental history. My teaching nudged me away from it. But my exposure to Richards had been a strong enough influence that I began to write up some of the work I had done for Ecosystems Center on Brazil for publication (McNeill, 1985b). And Curtin's example, no doubt combined on some level with my father's, confirmed my growing sense of the appeal of doing history on the world scale.

Teaching and Scholarship Intertwine

My circumstances, incentives, constraints, and opportunities changed in 1985 when, at age 30, I left Goucher for Georgetown University. In an astonishing failure of judgment, a dean at Georgetown had vetoed the possibility of appointing Alfred Crosby to a senior position (defined obscurely as "intersocietal history"), opening the door to a junior scholar such as myself.

At Georgetown I had three teaching responsibilities. The first was to teach intersocietal history to M.A. students in a highly regarded international affairs program, which I have done ever since. That class was required of all students, global in scope, and intended to acquaint ambitious people bound for careers in international business or politics with the range of ways in which societies have interacted in times past, and the ways in which international systems have functioned. I found ways to put some environmental history on the syllabus (e.g., Cronon, 1984; Crosby, 1986).

My second duty was to teach a one-semester survey course to freshmen on the history of Asia, Africa, and Latin America since

1500. I sometimes referred to it as the "antidote to Western Civ," which class students normally took in the fall before taking my course in the spring. Both courses were required of all undergraduates in the School of Foreign Service (a misnamed unit of Georgetown devoted to liberal arts education with an international flavor), and together amounted to something like world history. But the architecture of the two-semester sequence left many students with the impression that Western Civ was unique unto itself, worthy of more in-depth investigation than the history of any other part of the world. And, I expect, many of the deans and senior professors responsible for the curriculum believed precisely that.

My third duty was a two-semester undergraduate survey of African history. During my job interview I had been asked if I could teach African history and knew enough about job-seeking by this point to say "yes." I had taken one seminar in African history in my first year as a graduate student and had learned a few odds and ends sitting in on the Atlantic seminar at Hopkins. But teaching a two-semester survey with as slender a background as that was a strenuous assignment. In my first 2 years on the job, it had me up most days of the week before 5 a.m. trying to stay the proverbial hour ahead of my students.

This portfolio of teaching duties shaped my outlook as a historian in several ways. First of all, two of my courses were required and the third, African history, fulfilled a distribution requirement. This meant that almost all students in my classrooms were present only because they had to be. I struggled to make my classes seem important and relevant, to link the past to the present, and to opt for big themes over detail. Second, two of my three courses were either global or close to global in scale. I examined dozens of macro-scale history books each year when refining my syllabi, reading and teaching Stavrianos (1981), Wallerstein (1974), E.L. Jones (1981), Eric Wolf (1982), Abu-Lughod (1989), Hall (1990), and eventually Bentley (1993), Diamond (1995), Frank (1998), Pomeranz (2000), Bayly (2004) and many others in addition to the familiar tomes of Curtin and Crosby. And the third course, African history, allowed ample scope both for comparative perspectives and for consideration of Africa's relations with other parts of the world. Africanists (not that I was one) are very well represented in the ranks of world historians, and the nature of their subject is among the reasons why. I even considered trying to write a book about Africa in world history but decided to tackle something else first.

In the late 1980s, I took the step that confirmed my commitment to environmental history, and once again fortune smiled on me. Hitherto, all of my (meager) publications had derived from either my dissertation work on Cuba and Cape Breton or my Ecosystems Center work on Latin America (e.g., McNeill, 1985a, b). But in the summer before I moved to Georgetown I had taken part in an NEH seminar on southern European history run by Edward Malefakis of Columbia, a historian of twentieth-century Spain. Malefakis was of Greek extraction, spoke modern Greek and was trying to broaden his own historical scope outward from Spain.

Having some background in modern Greek, French, and Spanish I thought I might try to write an environmental history of the uplands of the Mediterranean world. I used Malefakis' seminar as an opportunity to prepare for this work, and wrote a sketch of the project. Like thousands of others, I had found Braudel's (1972) Mediterranean book inspirational, especially its first section on environmental constraints of southern European rural life. Braudel had by and large presented those constraints as timeless, which I thought was misleading especially for the mountainous regions I had seen 10 years before in my rambles in Greece. So I gradually conceived a circum-Mediterranean project on mountain areas that would explore the theme of environmental change and its meanings for peasants and herders. I began to study Italian and made plans to begin Turkish. I made no further progress in this direction in my first 2 years at Georgetown, what with teaching new subjects and facing large classes.

But one morning, probably in spring 1986, I was in my office early when a stranger poked his nose in to ask for one of my colleagues. The stranger, Frank Smith, was an editor at Cambridge University Press. He soon found that the colleague he sought was not yet in, so, as any editor would, he returned to my doorway and asked me about my work. It turned out that he had just launched a new book series in environmental history and so showed a keen interest in my ideas about Mediterranean uplands. He left with my NEH seminar paper. A few months later, after following the usual procedures, he offered a book contract. I suspect that contract helped me get a Fulbright for 1987–1988 in a now-defunct Western European Regional Research Program, which allowed me to spend 15 months in archives, libraries, villages, pastures, and forests of the Mediterranean. A few more summers invested in field and archival research, much sleep lost studying Turkish (with modest results), and eventually I had a book squarely in the field of environmental history, called *The Mountains of the Mediterranean World* (McNeill, 1992). It pays sometimes to be in one's office early.

While working on this book, I began to teach world environmental history for the first time. Georgetown wisely concluded it was worthwhile to invest in a real Africanist, so after 1990 I never taught the African history survey again, and gave up my plan of writing a book on Africa in world history. I was free, for the first time in my life, to design a course of my own choosing. Environmental history was my preference, and doing it on the global scale seemed the approach best calculated to attract students. My teaching was beginning to align with my main scholarly interests, whereas to this point my scholarly interests had evolved substantially in response to my teaching duties. It was at about this time that I began regularly to attend the meetings of the American Society for Environmental History and irregularly to go to the gatherings of the World History Association. At one of the WHA meetings, at Drexel University, perhaps in 1992, I first met Jerry Bentley.

Bentley (1949–2012) was an apostle for the world history creed whose enthusiasm was second to none. He led the charge to create the *Journal of World History* and encouraged everyone, including me, to submit pieces to the journal and to convince curriculum committees, department chairs, deans, and provosts if necessary that world history was a legitimate course to teach both as an undergraduate survey and as a graduate seminar. It was partly a result of Bentley's example and encouragement that I began to lobby for a true world history class, which I and others eventually taught at Georgetown. I also taught occasional Ph.D.-level classes (a new experience for me) in world history, at first with a syllabus modeled on the one Bentley had developed at the University of Hawaii – and was kind enough to share.

At Georgetown as elsewhere, world history met with some resistance. Some colleagues who taught a European history survey from the ancients to the Cold War sometimes maintained that their course represented the outer limits of what could be responsibly taught within a two-semester course. World history would be too much, too superficial, too incoherent. But my skeptical colleagues did not dig in their heels, and allowed me and others as well, to experiment with world history. For the last 20 years, my history department has offered both world history and Western Civ as courses that meet basic requirements. Over the years, more and more students have opted for world history. As elsewhere, finding willing instructors among the regular faculty has sometimes proved a challenge. Virtually no one is trained to teach world history, and professors with ambitions to publish or a heavy teaching load typically feel they don't have time to train themselves. World history is not necessarily too superficial and too incoherent, but it can be too much for instructors without ample time to prepare.

Going Global in Environmental History

My evolution in the direction of global environmental history, begun by my teaching in 1990, got a strong boost in 1993. Once again, a chance intervention played a large role. Paul Kennedy of Yale University was then recruiting authors for a 13-volume, thematically organized, history of the twentieth-century world to be published by W.W. Norton. Kennedy covered the conventional bases such as economic history, intellectual history and so forth, but he decided also to include an environmental history. This was the first occasion, I believe, when a multivolume series of this sort included an environmental history (unfortunately most of the books were never written). Somehow, perhaps after several others had declined the invitation, he asked me to write the environmental tome and I eagerly agreed, putting other ambitions aside for the next 7 years.

A global-scale book suited my circumstances at that point. Such books typically include no archival research but are based on secondary sources. As a new parent, I had good reasons to stay home and forswear trips to distant archives and landscapes of the sort I had enjoyed in researching *The Mountains of the Mediterranean*. After completing that research, for the next 19 years I did not venture inside an archive, except in 2003 when a friend invited me to occupy his house for a summer, enabling my family to transplant to a town within commuting distance of the Public Record Office (now the National Archives of the United Kingdom). Other than that happy summer, until 2007 I did my research no further afield than the Library of Congress, which luckily for me is only 4 miles from my campus. (One day, perhaps, when the holdings of most archives are available on line, original historical research and the demands of family life will be more easily compatible than they were in the olden days.)

While I was preparing for the book in Kennedy's series, global-scale environmental history was emerging in the 1990s. At first, the only global syntheses came not professional historians, but from geographers such as Ian Simmons (1989) and a former mandarin of the British Foreign Office, Clive Ponting (1992). A multidisciplinary magnum opus assembled by B.L. Turner *et al.* (1990), in which John Richards had a hand, helped spur historians to action.

Professional historians began by taking on manageable slices, with books on global fire history by Stephen Pyne (1995), or environmentalism by Ramachandra Guha (1999). Pyne's work, which grew out of his earlier studies of fire in American history, sought to discuss every aspect of the human relationship with fire, from cooking and the physiology of digestion to the cultural perceptions of wildfires. Guha's treatise on modern environmentalism showed the contrasts between the social movements that go by that name in, above all, India and the United States. Joachim Radkau (2000), whose background was in German intellectual history, was perhaps the first to bring the sensibilities of the historian to general global scale environmental history. His sprawling book was not a survey, but a series of soundings and reflections on everything from animal domestication to early modern timber shortages to contemporary tourism in the Himalaya.

My own effort, pursued in ignorance of Guha's and Radkau's, resulted in my first attempt at global-scale history, entitled *Something New under the Sun: An Environmental History of the Twentieth-Century World* (McNeill, 2000). That work did not, however, fit snugly with the usual themes of world history because it deals in depth only with the twentieth century and is relentlessly materialist in point of view. My book fit more easily with Radkau (2000), Hughes (2001), and Richards (2003) as part of a small surge of general works in global-scale environmental history. Richards' book, like mine, took on the globe for a restricted chunk of time, in his case the early modern centuries. He highlighted the ecological consequences of European overseas expansion. Hughes' work was intended more as a classroom book, in which vein others soon followed (e.g., Simmons, 2008; Penna, 2009).

All these works share some of the pitfalls of world history. No one can master all the relevant data and scholarship, as one can hope to do with sufficiently small subjects. The interdisciplinary requirements of environmental history compound the problem, as authors often need at least a nodding acquaintance with several disciplines ranging from anthropology to zoology. While the practical problems of such efforts will always remain, environmental history probably lends itself to global-scale work more readily than does, for example, labor history, women's history, or intellectual history. The chief reason for that is that so many of the issues and processes – deforestation, climate change, modern environmentalism – are inescapably global in nature. Local particularities exist, of course, as with all forms of history. But in environmental history they do not always dominate to the extent that they typically do in other arenas.

J.R. McNeill

A Curious Collaboration

As I completed the draft of *Something New under the Sun*, I happened to read Stephen Hawking's bestselling history of the Universe (Hawking, 1988). I erroneously concluded that if Hawking could write a history of 13.5 billion years of time in under 200 pages, then I ought to be able to write a history of humankind – maybe a quarter million years at the most – at similar length. I was still at a stage in family life where I needed a project I could do without straying outside the beltway. I began to outline my ideas, and soon decided, also erroneously, that the best and fastest way to get the job done would be to recruit my father as coauthor.

It may have been the best way, but it was not the fastest. For the next few years, we wrote chapters, exchanged drafts via the post office and occasionally in person, and argued over many points large and small. This procedure made the book, *The Human Web* (McNeill and McNeill, 2003) better, as almost every sentence had to be defended, but also made the process slower. Compromises abounded, as in all coauthored work, and there are passages in the book that I wish were different. No doubt my father feels the same way. I know he feels that a paragraph on the demise of cultural and biological Tasmanians, the last of whom, a woman named Trucanini, died in the 1876, is hard to justify in a book that does not even mention Otto von Bismarck. I thought, in contrast, that Trucanini represented an important world-historical process – the disappearance of small-scale cultures, languages, and peoples. Uneasy compromises notwithstanding, we're both pleased with the book in general. We did not manage to limit ourselves to 200pp and ended up with 324, perhaps too long to serve as an essay (my original intent) and too short to work as textbook (although a few brave instructors use it).

The Human Web is world history with an environmental tinge, but it is not environmental history. Instead, it is in the world history tradition that emphasizes interaction among cultures and tries to formalize that notion with the heuristic device of "webs" of interaction. In a very loose way, almost all humans at all times were involved in one network, a point on which my father insisted. But the book is really about more tightly connected webs of interaction, which grew with the transitions to sedentism, to farming, and to life with cities and states. The book follows the incremental increases in human interaction, more or less as Bentley (1993) did, but adds more geographic specificity, finding webs in some places but not others. It also includes the Americas, and recent centuries, which Bentley (1993) did not. It is more general and less economistic than the world systems work of Immanuel Wallerstein or Andre Gunder Frank.

After *The Human Web*, I retreated from genuine world history (and from coauthorship) for a while. I invested a few years developing my ideas about yellow fever and malaria in the imperial history of the Caribbean (McNeill, 2010). *Mosquito Empires* took me back to my conversations with Philip Curtin a quarter century before, and indeed all the way back to my graduate student days. That book is thoroughly environmental history, concerning, as it does, deforestation, mosquito habitat, population growth, and migration as they affected disease patterns and the results of settlement schemes, war, and revolutions in landscapes from Venezuela to Virginia.

It is also, at least in part, an archivally based history, reflecting a handful of brief sieges in archives mainly in Britain and Spain. Most historians, including myself, esteem archival work highly and feel somewhat sheepish if they abandon it for long. When my children grew old enough, I found it feasible to get back into archives briefly and felt more at ease with myself (as a historian, not as a father) in consequence. (Some historians, especially world historians, I hasten to add, are immune to archive-anxiety.)

I intended *Mosquito Empires* as an essay in Atlantic history, a genre in which I had dabbled before (McNeill, 1985b; Karras and McNeill, 1992). But it is speckled with world history perspectives too. I had taught Donald Wright's book (Wright, 2000) on, as he puts it, a very small place in Africa, and admired the way he integrated global trends into the story of a tiny community in Gambia. I tried to do analogous things, and from time to time brought up global patterns or made comparisons to other parts of the world. Wright's book, and I hope mine as well, show how world history thinking can enrich local and regional studies.

Conclusion

My route to world history began from a privileged start. From childhood I heard (even if I wasn't paying much attention) the gospel from a fervent believer and successful practitioner. I was never among those who regarded it as impossible, incoherent, or illegitimate. My route passed into the terrain of environmental history, which became and remains my primary identification as an historian. But the natural affinity between environmental history and world history made it easy, both in teaching and in scholarship, to inhabit both camps simultaneously.

At crucial stages along my route, helping hands guided me toward both world history and environmental history. John Cell invited me to team-teach world history and Anne Scott asked me to do it on my own when I was only a few months beyond my Ph.D. John Richards got me a job that kept me in the historical profession and gave me my first experience doing environmental history. Philip Curtin inspired me in general and encouraged me to delve into yellow fever and malaria history. Frank Smith poked his head into my office and soon after offered me a book contract. Paul Kennedy elected to include an environmental history in his global twentieth-century series and then asked me to write it. Throughout, of course, the example of my father's successes showed me what could be done if one (i) worked long hours, and (ii) conquered the anxiety that one could never know enough to write or teach world history.

As I see it, much luck is involved in shaping a life, whether a scholar's or anyone else's. In my case, that began with the family into which I was born, but did not stop there. It was (probably) good luck that I was not good enough in mathematics to pursue it far into my undergraduate years. It was by chance that John Cell decided Duke undergraduates needed world history while I happened to be there, and luck that he asked me, known to him chiefly through tennis, to join him in teaching it for the first time. It was (well-disguised) luck that I failed so miserably on the academic job market in the early 1980s, and was hanging around Duke when John Richards swerved toward environmental history. It was extraordinary good luck (for me) that a Georgetown dean passed on the chance to appoint Al Crosby. It was by luck that I was in my Georgetown office the morning Frank Smith came by (although I was there early almost every day). It was very good luck for me that Paul Kennedy did not choose someone else to write the environmental history for his series.

I never set out to work at the intersection of world history and environmental history. I merely responded to the opportunities others put in front of me. John Lennon, the musician, allegedly once said, "Life is what happens while you are busy making other plans." In my case I did not have much in the way of plans, but nonetheless my scholarly life is something that happened as much as something I set out to pursue. I do not recommend operating in life without much of a plan, but would advise being open to changing course if opportunities crop up.

The intersection of environmental history and world history is an exciting place to be. Opportunities abound. The great majority of environmental history work remains at the local, national, or regional level, despite the frequency with which ecological issues play themselves out on global scales. World historians, on the other hand, often recognize the environment as a worthy topic, especially recent textbook author teams. Some world historians put it at the center of their analyses (e.g., Pomeranz, 2000). But nonetheless, some of the strongest new interpretive works in world history almost entirely neglect it. Bayly (2004), for instance, in his insightful study of the nineteenth century – a time of considerable environmental flux – says next to nothing about it.

The confluence of world history and environmental history has some ways to go yet. Bayly's neglect of environmental themes suggested to me that there is room for a global study of the ecological implications of the Industrial Revolution, which I hope will be my next book. Others are working on such innovative topics as nitrogen, forests and forestry, the world's seventeenth-century crisis, climate politics, the modern ecology movement – and much else (Mercalli, 2010; Radkau, 2012; Gorman, 2013; Parker, 2013) Ingenuity seems to be running amok among global environmental historians. One would not want it any other way.

Note

1. Incidentally, I overlapped at Swarthmore with two students who would go on to distinguished careers and develop inclinations toward world history: Pamela Kyle Crossley of Dartmouth, a historian of China and Inner Asia who has written global-scale history; and Ronnie Po-chia Hsia of Penn State, a historian of early modern Europe and lately of European–Chinese interactions. They were both 2 years behind me and I scarcely knew either one.

References

Abu-Lughod, Janet. 1989. *Before European Hegemony*. New York: Oxford University Press.

Agassiz, Louis and Augustus A. Gould. 1848. *Principles of Zoology*. Boston, MA: Gould, Kendall and Lincoln.

Bayly, C.A. 2004. *The Birth of the Modern World, 1780–1914*. Oxford: Blackwell.

Bentley, Jerry. 1993. *Old World Encounters*. New York: Oxford University Press.

Braudel Fernand. 1972. *The Mediterranean and the Mediterranean World in the Era of Philip II*, 2 vols. New York: Harper & Row.

Cronon, William. 1984. *Changes in the Land: Indians, Colonists and the Ecology of New England*. New York: Hill & Wang.

Crosby, Alfred. 1972. *The Columbian Exchange: The Biological and Cultural Consequences of 1492*. Westport, CT: Greenwood Press.

Crosby, Alfred. 1986. *Ecological Imperialism: The Biological Expansion of Europe, 900–1900*. New York: Cambridge University Press.

Curtin, Philip. 1984. *Cross-Cultural Trade in World History*. New York: Cambridge University Press.

Curtin, Philip. 1989. *Death by Migration*. New York: Cambridge University Press.

Diamond, Jared. 1995. *Guns, Germs, and Steel: The Fates of Human Societies*. New York: Norton.
Frank, A.G. 1998. *Re-Orient: The Global Economy in the Asian Age*. Berkeley, CA: University of California Press.
Gorman, Hugh. 2013. *The Story of N: A Social History of the Nitrogen Cycle and the Challenge of Sustainability*. New Brunswick, NJ: Rutgers University Press.
Guha, Ramachandra. 1999. *Environmentalism: A Global History*. New York: Longman.
Hall, John. 1990. *Powers and Liberties: The Causes and Consequences of the Rise of the West*. Berkeley, CA: University of California Press.
Hawking, Stephen. 1988. *A Brief History of Time*. New York: Bantam Books.
Hughes, J. Donald. 2001. *An Environmental History of the World: Humankind's Changing Role in the Community of Life*. London: Routledge.
Jones, E.L. 1981. *The European Miracle*. New York: Cambridge University Press.
Karras, Alan and J.R. McNeill, eds. 1992. *Atlantic American Societies*. London: Routledge.
Le Roy Ladurie Emmanuel. 1974. *The Peasants of Languedoc*. Urbana, IL: University of Illinois Press.
McNeill, William H. 1963. *The Rise of the West*. Chicago, IL: University of Chicago Press.
McNeill, William H. 1977. *Plagues and Peoples*. New York: Doubleday.
McNeill, J.R. 1985a. *The Atlantic Empires of France and Spain: Louisbourg and Havana, 1700–1763*. Chapel Hill, NC: UNC Press.
McNeill, J.R. 1985b. "Agriculture, Forests, and Ecological History: Brazil, 1500–1983," *Environmental Review* 10/1986: 122–133.
McNeill, J.R. 1992. *The Mountains of the Mediterranean World: An Environmental History*. New York: Cambridge University Press.
McNeill, J.R. 2000. *Something New Under the Sun: An Environmental History of the Twentieth-Century World*. New York: Norton.
McNeill, William H. 2005. *The Pursuit of Truth: A Historian's Memoir*. Lexington, KY: University of Kentucky Press.
McNeill, J.R. 2010. *Mosquito Empires: Ecology and War in the Greater Caribbean, 1620–1914*. New York: Cambridge University Press.
McNeill, J.R. and William H. McNeill 2003. *The Human Web*. New York: Norton.
Marsh, George Perkins. 1864. *Man and Nature*. New York: Scribner.
Mercalli, Luca. 2010. Che tempo che fará. Milan: Rizzoli.
Nash, Roderick. 1967. *Wilderness and the American Mind*. New Haven, CT: Yale University Press.

Parker, Geoffrey. 2013. *Global Crisis: War, Climate Change, and Catastrophe in the Seventeenth Century*. New Haven, CT: Yale University Press.
Penna, Anthony. 2009. *The Human Footprint: A Global Environmental History*. Malden, MA: Blackwell.
Pomeranz, Kenneth. 2000. *The Great Divergence*. Princeton, NJ: Princeton University Press.
Ponting, Clive. 1992. *A Green History of the World*. Harmondsworth: Penguin.
Pyne, Stephen. 1995. *World Fire: The Culture of Fire on Earth*. Seattle, WA: University of Washington Press.
Radkau, Joachim. 2000. *Natur und Macht: Eine Weltgeschichte der Umwelt*. Munich: Beck.
Radkau, Joachim. 2012. *Wood: A History*. Malden, MA: Polity Press.
Richards, John. 2003. *The Unending Frontier: An Environmental History of the Early Modern World*. Berkeley, CA: University of California Press.
Simmons, Ian. 1989. *Changing the Face of the Earth*. Oxford: Blackwell.
Simmons, Ian. 2008. *Global Environmental History*. Chicago, IL: University of Chicago Press.
Stavrianos, Leften. 1981. *Global Rift: The Third World Comes of Age*. New York: Morrow.
Stoppani, Antonio. 1871–1873. *Corso di geologia*. Milan: Bernadoni & Brigola.
Turner, Billie Lee, William C. Clark, Robert W. Kates, John F. Richards, Jessica T. Mathews, and William B. Meyer, eds. 1990. *The Earth as Transformed by Human Action*. New York: Cambridge University Press.
Wallerstein, Immanuel. 1974. *The Modern World-System*. New York: Academic Press.
Wolf, Eric. 1982. *Europe and the People Without History*. Berkeley, CA: University of California Press.
Worster, Donald. 1978. *Dust Bowl*. New York: Oxford University Press.
Wright, Donald. *The World and a Very Small Place in Africa: The History of Globalization in Niumi, the Gambia*, 3rd edition. Armonk: M.E. Sharpe.

Further Reading

Aberth, John. 2012. *An Environmental History of the Middle Ages: The Crucible of Nature*. London: Routledge.
Beinart, William and Lotte Hughes. 2009. *Environment and Empire*. Oxford: Oxford University Press.

Bsumek, Erika, David Kinkela, and Mark Atwood Lawrence, eds. 2013. *Nation-States and the Global Environment: New Approaches to International Environmental History*. New York: Oxford University Press.

Burke, Edmund III and Kenneth Pomeranz, eds. 2009. *The Environment and World History*. Berkeley, CA: University of California Press.

Glacken, Clarence. 1967. *Traces on the Rhodian Shore: Nature and Culture in Western Thought from Ancient Times to the End of the Eighteenth Century*. Berkeley, CA: University of California Press.

Hughes, J. Donald. 2009. *An Environmental History of the World*. London: Routledge.

Le Roy Ladurie, Emmanuel. 2004–2009. *Histoire humaine et comparée du climat*, 3 vols. Paris: Fayard.

McNeill, J.R. 2003. "Observations on the Nature and Culture of Environmental History," *History and Theory* 42/4: 5–43.

McNeill, J.R. 2010. "The State of the Field of Environmental History," *Annual Review of Environment and Resources* 35: 345–374.

McNeill, J.R. and Erin S. Mauldin, eds. 2012. *A Companion to Global Environmental History*. Malden, MA: Blackwell.

Marks, Robert V. 2006. *The Origins of the Modern World: A Global and Ecological Narrative from the Fifteenth to the Twenty-First Century*. Lanham, MD: Rowman & Littlefield.

Radkau, Joachim. 2011. *Die Ära der Ökologie: Eine Weltgeschichte*. Munich: Beck.

Tucker, Richard P. 2000. *Insatiable Appetite*. Berkeley, CA: University of California Press.

Tucker, Richard P. and Edmund Russell, eds. 2004. *Natural Enemy, Natural Ally: Towards an Environmental History of War*. Corvallis, OR: Oregon State University Press.

Uekotter, Frank, ed. 2010. *The Turning Points of Environmental History*. Pittsburgh, PA: University of Pittsburgh Press.

3

Gender Intersections

Merry E. Wiesner-Hanks

Over the last 15 years, I have been engaged in teaching and research far different from what I anticipated when I finished graduate school nearly 35 years ago, with a dissertation on working women in sixteenth-century Nuremberg. At that point, I was well trained to teach courses in European history from the thirteenth century through the eighteenth and thought I could perhaps handle a course or two on Africa, as African history was my minor field in graduate school. I was first hired, however, to be one-quarter of the history department at Augustana, a small liberal arts college, and was responsible for teaching all of European history, what we then described as "Neanderthal to Nazis." Because I was female, and the first woman ever hired in the department, I was responsible for US women's history, too, although I had never taken a graduate course in US history.

In a panic about how to choose a textbook for my Western Civilization class – a course I had never had myself, and that covered

---

Architects of World History: Researching the Global Past, First Edition.
Edited by Kenneth R. Curtis and Jerry H. Bentley.

periods I had never studied – I talked with Pat Donnelly (officially J. Patrick Donnelly, S.J.), a friend who had been teaching at Marquette University for several decades. He passed along a great piece of advice: look at all the textbooks and pick the second best for your students, because you will need to take your lectures from somewhere, and you might as well take them from the best. That advice has come in handy many times since and been expanded beyond textbook choices.

When I moved to the University of Wisconsin-Milwaukee in 1985, becoming one-twenty-fourth instead of one-fourth of a department, I assumed that my days of dabbling were over, and that I would be able to teach what I really knew well. I was sadly mistaken. My experiences at Augustana were only the beginning, for at UWM I went from teaching courses in European history for which I had no formal training to teaching courses in many fields for which I was similarly unprepared. In the 1990s, I became the director of the Center for Women's Studies and taught a course in interdisciplinary feminist theory, having never taken a course that had either "feminism" or "theory" in the title in my life. In the History Department, my colleague David Buck and I decided in the late 1990s that we were dissatisfied teaching our courses in Western Civilization and Eastern Civilization because their East/West split did not represent the world that we and our students lived in. We put together a world history sequence, for which there were many splendid models taught elsewhere and several excellent textbooks. We brought in Jerry Bentley, the author of one of those excellent textbooks, as a consultant, and I learned from David how to pronounce Chinese names. I was to handle the first semester and began my very first lecture with a long explanation as to why UWM was now teaching world history. That lecture was September 4, 2001. Exactly 1 week later my explanation no longer seemed quite so necessary.

Through teaching feminist theory, I became familiar with the work of scholars in many fields who study women and gender. They increasingly emphasized the ways that categories of difference such as race, class, gender, religion, and sexual orientation intersect with one another, complicating any analysis. This chapter looks at one particular intersection, that of women's and gender history with world and global history, first in my own intellectual trajectory and then in the field of history as a whole.

My Own Journey

The geographic and disciplinary expansion that occurred in my teaching also happened in my research and publishing. My first book was on working women in south German cities in the sixteenth century, a widening of the geographic focus of my dissertation based on additional archival research in five more cities – Frankfurt, Memmingen, Munich, Strasbourg, and Stuttgart. The 500th anniversary of Luther's birth was in 1983, which resulted in a flurry of conferences. Some of the organizers of those conferences held in the United States thought that at least a nod ought to be made to the new-fangled field of women's history, so they asked me to give papers on "Luther and women." My protests that I wasn't a historian of religion, but an economic historian more comfortable with multivariate regressions than variant understandings of the Eucharist resulted in the comments along the lines of: well if you don't do this, there will be nothing on women. So I learned more about the Eucharist and other religious issues, drawing on the advice of Father Pat about textbooks: ask around, and read the best. There was wonderful scholarship available on many aspects of the Reformation through which I learned a great deal, and exactly one book and about 10 articles on women, so that on that particular topic I was able to read everything. (This has never been true since.) I spoke, and eventually wrote, about the impact of the Protestant Reformation on women, but also, because I was used to talking about what women actually *did*, I wrote about the impact of women on the Reformation.

Because I traced both positive and negative consequences of the Reformation, I expected that I would be criticized by Reformation historians, who often emphasize one or the other. They actually had few problems accepting my discussion of the range of consequences, but some did have problems accepting the notion that women in the sixteenth century actually had religious ideas and carried out actions based on their own ideas. As one put it: "You're not talking about women, you're talking about what women *think*!" My research into midwives and market-women had never provoked a reaction like this, so clearly some historians had more difficulty considering women as part of intellectual and religious history than they did as part of social and economic history.

In 1990, Cambridge University Press was beginning a new series of surveys designed for upper level students, with the imaginative title New Approaches to Modern European History. Robert Scribner, a member of the faculty at Cambridge and one of the editors of the series who I had met at a Luther conference, asked me if I would write a book on women and the family in early modern Europe, or something along those lines. I agreed, but instead of connecting women with the family, a link that seemed too limiting, I decided to connect women with gender, at that point a relatively new concept in history. This became my second book, *Women and Gender in Early Modern Europe* (Wiesner-Hanks, 1993).

In the 1980s, historians and scholars in other fields had begun to use "gender" to mean a culturally constructed and historically changing system of differences based to some degree on physical, morphological, and anatomical sexual differences, but also on many other things. Gender was thus quite novel when I wrote the proposal for this book. So novel, in fact, that the Cambridge University Press Board of Syndics, who approve all contracts, were somewhat dubious about whether they should support such a faddish project. That book became the first in the series that now has more than 50 titles, and has remained, I am pleased to say, its best seller. The book attempts to survey the life experience of half the European population from Portugal to Poland over 300 years, and of all of the European population – women and men – on certain issues. Writing it was an enterprise that required even more asking around about what and who to read than had my expansion into Reformation history. In the early 1990s, there was a fair amount published on women in the Western Europe, but very little on Eastern Europe and almost nothing on certain topics anywhere in

Europe, but people were very willing to let me read their unpublished work and graciously shared their expertise.

That book led directly to my research becoming global. After reading it, the historian of Southeast Asia Barbara Andaya invited me to what was the first conference in the world on gender in early modern Southeast Asia, held in 1995 at the University of Hawai'i. I was puzzled at the invitation, as I knew nothing about Southeast Asia, but Barbara explained that she wanted me there as a comparative voice, representing a part of the world with enough existing research that one could actually write a survey textbook. I was starting work on a book on Christianity and sexuality in the early modern period – for another series edited by Bob Scribner – and Barbara asked whether I was limiting the book to Europe, and if so, why. I had already decided that I should include the North American colonies and found that I didn't have a good answer for why I was stopping with what has since come to be called the "Atlantic world." Christian ideas and institutions shaped sexual attitudes and activities in much of the world in this era, with the most interesting challenges – and responses to those challenges – posed by colonial areas. So I made the book a global one and turned to an even wider circle of colleagues, friends, and acquaintances for advice on what was best and whose work I needed to read (Wiesner-Hanks, 2000).

At the same time, Jean Woy, the history editor at Houghton-Mifflin, suggested that because of the growth in world history courses, a world history version of an innovative Western Civ reader for which I was a coauthor would be a good idea. I agreed, not having yet learned that successful books for the college classroom bring a life sentence of doing new editions (Wiesner-Hanks *et al.*, 1997). This meant, although of course I did not know it then, that when I later began teaching world history myself I had a book that fit with the way I liked to teach: lots of primary sources and an emphasis on historical thinking skills.

As the writing on those books wound down, Constantin Fasolt at the University of Chicago asked me if I would be interested in doing a book on gender for a series with Wiley-Blackwell, again designed for students. I could not turn this down, and that book became one on gender in all of world history, titled simply *Gender in History* (Wiesner-Hanks, 2001). Not simply Neanderthal to Nazis, because world history demands an even broader time frame than a mere 10,000 years, what we might term Big Bang to Obama. So I read the work of primatologists and political scientists as well as that of historians, relying on still more people for advice about what was best. After writing that book I felt I could finally teach interdisciplinary feminist theory with some legitimacy, although of course by then I had already been teaching it for more than a decade.

My journey from German historian to global one is personal and idiosyncratic, but it is also in some ways typical of larger patterns. In this, it is like most stories we tell in world history, a local one, but with larger connections and a global context. It is a story in which contingency, chance, and luck play as large a role as reason, planning, and preparation. I have told the story here as one involving individuals, and have included their names, in part to acknowledge them, and in part because women's history has taught us that recording names is important. Too many women are in the historical record simply as "… and wife" or "… and his daughter," with only the man's name given.

Like all histories, this story involves change, but it also involves continuity, which in my case has been special attention to women and gender. Much that I teach and publish does not focus specifically on gender, but that is a lens through which I see all historical developments.

The Development of Women's and Gender History

The central role of gender in history (and in life) might seem self-evident in 2014, but it was not when I chose to be a history major more than four decades ago. At that point, the word "gender" was primarily used as a classification of nouns and pronouns in certain languages, yet another complexity that made learning those languages difficult. The women's movement changed that, as it changed so much else. Advocates of women's rights in the present, myself included, looked at what we had been taught about the past – as well as what we had been taught about literature, psychology, religion, biology, and most other disciplines – and realized we were only hearing half the story. Most of the studies we read or heard described the male experience – "man the artist," "man the hunter", "man and his environment" – though they often portrayed it as universal.

We began to investigate the lives of women in the past, first fitting them into the categories with which we were already comfortable – nations, historical periods, social classes, religious allegiance – and then realizing that this approach, sarcastically labeled "add women and stir," was unsatisfying. Focusing on women often disrupted the familiar categories, forcing us to rethink the way that history was organized and structured (Lerner, 1979). The European Renaissance and Enlightenment lost some of their luster once women were included, as did the democracy of ancient Athens or Jacksonian America. Even newer historical approaches, such as the emphasis on class analysis using social science techniques termed the New Social History that had developed during the 1960s, were found to be wanting in their consideration of differences between women's and men's experiences.

Research in women's history was accompanied by teaching. By the late 1970s, hundreds of colleges and universities in the United States and Canada offered courses in women's history, and many had separate programs in women's history or women's studies. Universities in Britain, Israel, and Australia were somewhat slower to include lectures and seminars on women, and universities in Western and Eastern Europe slower still. In Japan and elsewhere, much of the research on women was initially carried out by people outside the universities involved with local history societies or active in women's groups, so was not regarded as scholarly. The history done in any country is shaped by regional and world politics, and issues other than gender have often seemed more pressing to historians in Latin America, Eastern Europe, and other parts of the world where political and economic struggles have been intense. Universities and researchers in developing countries also have far fewer resources, which has hampered all historical research and limited opportunities for any new direction. Thus, an inordinate amount of the early work in women's history was done by English-speaking historians on English-speaking areas, especially the United States, although there was significant work done in many other parts of the world as well (Offen, Pierson, and Rendell, 1990).

As women's history was expanding as a research and teaching field, it was also changing. The disruption of well-known categories such as class ultimately included the topic that had long been considered the proper focus of all history – man. Viewing the male experience as universal had not only hidden women's history, but it had also prevented analyzing men's experiences as those of men. The very words we used to describe individuals – "artist" and "woman artist," for example, or "scientist" and "woman scientist" – kept us from thinking about how the experiences of Michelangelo or Picasso or Isaac Newton were shaped by the fact that they were male, while it forced us to think about how being female affected Georgia O'Keefe or Marie Curie. Historians familiar with studying women increasingly began to discuss the ways in which systems of sexual differentiation affected both women and men, and by the early 1980s to use the word "gender" to describe these systems. At that point, we differentiated primarily between "sex," by which we meant physical, morphological, and anatomical differences (what are often called "biological differences") and "gender," by which we meant a culturally constructed, historically changing, and often unstable system of differences. "Gender" was thus a cultural superstructure built on biological sex.

Most of the studies with "gender" in the title still focused on women – and women's history continued as its own field – but a few looked equally at both sexes or concentrated on the male experience, calling their work "men's history" or the "new men's studies." Several university presses started book series with "gender" in their titles, and scholars in many fields increasingly switched from "sex" to "gender" as the acceptable terminology: "sex roles" became "gender roles," "sex distinctions" became "gender distinctions," and so on.

Historians who developed this new perspective increasingly asserted that gender went far beyond the sexual. *Every* political, intellectual, religious, economic, social, and even military change had an impact of the actions and roles of men and women, and, conversely, a culture's gender structures influenced everything else. People's notions of gender shaped not only the way they thought about men and women, but about their society in general. As the historian Joan Scott put it in an extremely influential article that appeared in the *American Historical Review*: "Gender is a constitutive element of social relationships based on perceived differences between the sexes, and gender is a primary way of signifying relationships of power" (Scott, 1986, p. 1056). Thus, hierarchies in other realms of life were often expressed in terms of gender, with dominant individuals or groups described in masculine terms and dependent ones in feminine. These ideas in turn affected the way people acted, though explicit and symbolic ideas of gender could also conflict with the way men and women chose or were forced to operate in the world.

Complicating Categories

Just at the point, however, that historians and their students were gradually beginning to see the distinction between sex and gender (and an increasing number accepting the importance of gender as a category of analysis) that distinction became contested. Not only were there great debates about where the line should be drawn – were women "biologically" more peaceful and men "biologically" more skillful at math, or were such tendencies the result solely of their upbringing? – but some scholars wondered whether social gender and biological sex are so interrelated that any distinction between the two is meaningless (Butler, 1990). Most people's internal and external genitalia allow them to be categorized as "male" or "female," but for some these are ambiguous, a condition now called "intersexed." The same is true with chromosomes and hormones. Despite these variations, throughout history most intersexed people have been simply assigned to the sex they most closely resembled, sometimes with surgery or hormone treatment to reinforce this assignment. Thus, in these cases, cultural notions about gender – that everyone *should* be a man or a woman – determined the person's sex, rather than the other way around.

The distinction between sex and gender has also been challenged by transsexual and transgender individuals, that is, individuals whose sexual and reproductive organs and even chromosomal and hormonal patterns mark them as male or female, but mentally regard themselves as the other, a condition known medically as "gender dysphoria" or "gender identity disorder." In the 1950s, sex-reassigment operations became available for gender-dysphoric people who could afford them, and they became transsexuals. Sex-reassignment surgery could make the body fit more closely with the mind, but it also led to challenging questions: At what point in this process does a "man" become a "woman," or vice versa? With the loss or acquisition of a penis? Breasts? From the beginning? What does the answer to this imply about notions of gender difference? In the 1980s, such questions began to be made even more complex by individuals who understood themselves to be "transgendered," that is, not as moving from male to female or vice versa, but as *neither* male nor female or *both* male and female. (The prefix trans- in English carries this double meaning of "across" and "beyond.") As with intersexed and transexual people, transgender individuals provoked both philosophical and practical questions: What is the source of gender difference? Should such individuals be allowed in spaces designated "women only" or "men only"? Should they have to choose between them, or should there be more than two choices? (Fausto-Sterling, 2000)

In some of the world's cultures, there *are* more than two genders, and greater knowledge about these third genders has created still more doubts about the relationship between "biological" sex and "cultural" gender. Here the research of world historians and anthropologists has been especially important (Herdt, 1994). In a number of areas throughout the world, including Alaska, the Amazon region, North America, Australia, Siberia, Central and South Asia, Oceania, and the Sudan, individuals who were originally viewed as male or female assume (or assumed, for in many areas such practices have ended) the gender identity of the other sex or combine the tasks, behavior, and clothing of men and women (Ramet, 1996). Some of these individuals are intersexed and occasionally they are eunuchs (castrated males), but more commonly they are morphologically male or female. The best known of these are found among several Native American peoples, and the Europeans who first encountered them regarded them as homosexuals and called them "berdaches," from an Arabic word for male prostitute. Now most scholars choose to use the term "two-spirit people," and note that they are distinguished from other men more by their work or religious roles than by their sexual activities; they are usually thought of as a third gender rather than effeminate or homosexual males (Roscoe, 1998).

At the same time that historians of women and gender were puzzling over the relationship between sex and gender, many also became interested in questions about sexuality, as did other historians who had not previously focused on gender issues. Just as the women's movement created an enormous interest in women's history, so the gay liberation movement that also began in the 1970s led historians and activists to study same-sex relations in many periods. They initially focused primarily on men, but then also on women. Some historians put emphasis on continuities and similarities in the experiences of individuals and groups across time, and others emphasized differences (Greenburg, 1988). Many historians saw the late nineteenth century as a central turning point because that was when physicians, psychiatrists and scholars in other fields first defined those who were attracted to those of the same sex as "homosexuals," and first defined the notion of "sexual identity" or "sexual orientation." Before this point, many historians asserted, there were sexual acts, but not sexual identity. Other historians disputed this idea of one dramatic break, however, finding people who lived long before the nineteenth century who understood themselves to have what was later termed a sexual orientation. Still others argued that the idea of two sexual categories – homosexual and heterosexual – was simply a cultural construction from a particular time and place and did not represent the way many societies conceptualized sexual attraction. Like gender, sexuality was not a neat dichotomy, they asserted, but a complicated system, both distinct from and yet closely interwoven with gender (Murray, 2002).

Gender is thus a far more complex concept than when it was first devised, and it has been made even more complex by the insight that it does not operate alone in shaping people's experiences. The earliest women's history tended to focus, not surprisingly, on women who left the most record in historical sources, usually members of the elite. Generalizations were made about the role and experiences of women in one or another time or place – "the status of women in ancient Greece was ..." or "the role of women in colonial India was ..." – without differentiating much among women. Historians studying women who were not members of the elite challenged such generalizations, just as they challenged those studying nonelites to recognize differences created by gender. As the title of an influential 1993 collection of essays put it: *All the Women Are White, All the Blacks Are Men, But Some Of Us Are Brave* (Hull, Scott, and Smith, 1993). In this work, and in many others, scholars asserted that the experiences of women of color must be recognized as distinctive and that no one axis of difference (men/women, black/white, rich/poor, gay/straight) should be viewed as sufficient.

Historians of women and gender thus paid increasing attention to the many categories of difference that people envision or create – race, class, gender, ethnicity, religion, sexual orientation, nationality, marital status, age, able-bodiedness, and so on. More importantly, they emphasized that *all* categories of difference intersect with one another in complex ways that change over time. This insight led, in the 1990s, to theoretical perspectives that recognized multiple lines of difference. Postcolonial feminist theorists, for example, examine those who have been subordinated by race, ethnicity, or culture *and* by gender as part of the process of colonialism and imperialism, noting the ways in which these hierarchies both reinforce and weaken one another (McClintock, Mufti, and Shoalt, 1997). Somewhat to the contrary, other theorists argued that because categories were socially constructed and often oppressive, simply studying how they intersected was not enough. Scholars in gay and lesbian studies increasingly called for "queering" – that is, problematizing and complicating the categories used to describe and analyze things – and this line of thought was called "queer theory" (Jagose, 1996). They celebrated efforts at blurring or bending categories, and often spoke of gender and sexual categories in terms of performance rather than identity. The emphasis on both intersection and questioning was captured in the themes of the triennial Berkshire Women's History Conference, the largest women's history conference in the world; in 1996, the theme was "complicating categories," and in 1999 "breaking boundaries."

Gender History and Global History

This crossing and breaking of boundaries sometimes included national and regional ones, as women's and gender historians worried about the narrowness, the national parochialism, and the Eurocentrism of curricula. My own move from teaching Western Civilization to teaching World History was one that was happening in many places, both in general courses and in courses that focused on women and gender. Courses were developed that focused on international feminisms, African and South American women, and gender and development. At the 1996 Berkshire Women's History Conference, a session on teaching world and comparative history almost overflowed its room when the crowd it had drawn grew to more than a hundred, and many people in the audience commented that they had either decided or had been assigned to teach world history. Some even noted that this teaching assignment had been given them not only because they were young and untenured – and thus had less power to choose what they would teach – but specifically because they were female, and so (in the mind of their department chairs) somehow more sympathetic to the concerns of various "others."

Calls to internationalize or globalize the curriculum in the 1990s came from within for many historians of women and gender, but also from without, as universities, departments, schools, or school districts decided that they wished to broaden their course offerings beyond Europe and North America. In the United States, these changes arose from state mandates, as states tried – and continue to try – to figure out how best to prepare students for the global economy. Outside the United States, similar decisions were made by national departments of education.

Gender history and world history came together in the classroom before they came together as research fields. Until about 15 years ago, there was relatively little connection between the two in terms of research, for which I see three primary reasons. First, both developed as, in part, revisionist interpretations arguing that a standard story needed to be made broader and much more complex. Women's and gender historians called for history that included women and recognized that men had gender, and world and global historians called for history that did not center on the West. Both have thus been viewed by those hostile or uninterested as "having an agenda." Both concentrated on their own lines of revision, so did not pay much attention to what was going on in the other.

A second reason for the lack of connection is that the primary revisionary paths in women's/gender history and world/global history have been in opposite directions. World history has emphasized links, the crossing of boundaries, and convergence. In contrast, after an initial flurry of "sisterhood is global," gender history over the last several decades has spent much more time on *divergence*, making categories of difference ever more complex. Gender historians have emphasized that every key aspect of gender relations – the relationship between the family and the state, the relationship between gender and sexuality, and so on – is historically, culturally, and class specific. Today historians of masculinity speak of their subject only in plurals, as "multiple masculinities" appear to have emerged everywhere, just as have multiple sexualities in the works by historians of sexuality (Dudnik, Hagemann, and Tosh, 2004).

A third reason is the powerful materialist tradition in world and global history, which stands in sharp contrast to the largely cultural focus of gender history as this has developed over the last several decades. Most world history has focused on political and economic processes carried out by governments and commercial elites. Women's history also initially had a strong materialist wing, with many studies of labor systems and political movements, but since the 1980s, more attention has been paid to representation, meaning, and discourse.

Within the last several decades, however, women's and gender history and world and global history have begun to intersect. Some historians trained in women's and gender history have begun to become more global and transnational in their interests and approaches, the path that I took. Some global and world historians have begun to become more interested in issues of gender and sexuality. And younger historians have been trained in both fields right from the start, not dissuaded from developing research topics that seemed impossible or unwise several decades ago.

Gender/Global Intersections

Exciting scholarship that draws on *both* world history and the history of gender has thus begun to appear in a number of research areas. To use the term developed in gender history, they have begun to intersect. I would like to highlight just three of these: movements for women's and gay rights, colonialism and imperialism, and migration.

First are studies that focus on movements for women's rights and, more recently, for gay, lesbian, and transgender rights. The history of the movement for women's rights that began in the nineteenth century and continued into the twentieth, the "first wave" of the feminist movement, initially focused on the United States and Great Britain, but more recent scholarship has made clear that this movement was global, not simply something emanating from the Anglo-American world (Rupp, 1997). The "woman question," which, along with suffrage, debated the merits of women's greater access to education, property rights, more equitable marriage and divorce laws, temperance, and protection for women workers, was an international issue, though with different emphases in different parts of the world. Women's rights were linked to other social and political issues and to calls to broader democratic representation for all, not simply for women. Efforts to achieve women's rights and the actions of actual women have often been forgotten, or intentionally ignored in the nationalist historiographies of anticolonial struggles, however. Studies are beginning to revise this picture and examine the interplay between women's rights movements and state-building, sometimes setting this in a comparative or global context (Joannou and Purvis, 1998).

Women's suffrage was not always a force for more general notions of rights, however, but was also linked to racialized constructions of nation and empire. In many places, advocates of women's rights used ideas about racial and class superiority to bolster their arguments, noting how much more worthy and responsible honorable white middle-class women were than working-class, immigrant, or nonwhite men. Women understood to be "honorable" were married and generally mothers, of course, so such lines of reasoning were also heterosexist, although sexuality was never mentioned openly, in contrast to blatant and hostile race and class comparisons. Such arguments are one of the reasons that white women were granted the vote relatively early in Australia, New Zealand and South Africa, and that one of the first states in the United States to allow woman suffrage was conservative Utah, where Mormon women argued their votes would outnumber those of non-Mormon men. Whiteness also became part of notions of who was truly a man, as Marilyn Lake and Henry Reynolds have recently stressed in their study of "white men's countries" (Lake and Reynolds, 2008).

The second-wave feminist movement that began in the 1960s and 1970s was similarly international, and comparative studies are evaluating similarities and differences between feminisms in West and East, North and South. Some of these works are global, while others are regional, but still examine what happens when ideas, institutions, and individuals cross borders. Studies of transnational feminist networks of activists and organizations note class, racial, ethnic, and imperial tensions, but also their common agendas and similar programs (Moghadam, 2005).

A second area in which there is increasing fruitful intersection between gender history and world history is research on colonialism and imperialism. Both men and women were agents in imperial projects, and colonial powers shaped cultural constructions of masculinity and femininity. Many recent works demonstrate that imperial power is explicitly and implicitly linked with sexuality, and that images of colonial peoples were gendered and sexualized (Levine, 2007). Research on gender and sexuality in the context of imperialism has emphasized links between colonized areas and the colonizing country – what is often called the "metropole" – arguing that the process of colonization shaped gender ideologies and practices everywhere, and not simply in the colonies themselves (Wilson, 2003). European men's and women's perceptions of their national identity were shaped by colonial expansion, and their political ideas were transformed by colonial experiences.

Encounters between colonizers and colonized involved the gendered bodies of men and women, which served as metaphors for the nation and as sites where colonial power was exercised. Intermarriage and other types of sexual relationships among individuals from different groups occurred especially in colonies or border regions that can be seen as "gender frontiers" and were interwoven with developing notions of racial difference and national identity. In French colonial North America, for example, policy toward intermarriage changed depending on changing ideas about how best to increase both the colonies' and France's strength. Most immigrants were unemployed young men from urban environments, and for a brief period in the 1660s the French crown directly recruited young women to go to New France to be their wives, mostly poor women from charity hospitals. The crown paid for their passage, and about 800 did immigrate, but their numbers were never great enough to have a significant effect on the population. French finance minister Jean-Baptiste Colbert decided not to expand the program, however, because he worried it would depopulate France. Instead, he recommended that French men marry Native American women who had converted to Christianity and "make them French" in terms of clothing, language, work patterns, and lifestyle. The French hoped that such marriages would help the fur trade and strengthen ties between French and Native American communities and families. In a few cases, this policy had the effect that the government hoped it would, but in many more cases the opposite happened and the men adopted customs the French regarded as "savage." Official opinion changed and intermarriage was officially prohibited, although it continued to be a common practice, especially in frontier areas. Similar examples of shifting policy toward intermarriage and great variation in levels of enforcement can be found throughout the colonial world (Belmessous, 2013).

Colonialism and imperialism involved the migration of large numbers of people from one part of the world to another, and migration itself is a third area in which there is a growing number of studies that bring together gender history and world history. Approximately half of all long-distance migrants today are female, with women's migration patterns sometimes similar to those of men but sometimes quite different (Sharpe, 2001). Recent studies examine the transnational character of many migrants' lives, in which women and men physically move back and forth and culturally and socially create and maintain links across borders. Gendered and sexualized migration influenced (and continue to influence) the economies, societies, and polities through and across which people moved. Distance and movement shaped intimacy, and intimacy, or the prospect of intimacy, or the desire for intimacy, influenced the formation of imperial power.

Nations today determine who is and is not a citizen, and also control who will be allowed to emigrate and immigrate legally. Laws regarding migration are rarely gender neutral, and many countries refuse to allow in those judged to be homosexual, to say nothing of those who identify or appear to be transsexual (Canaday, 2009). Despite such restrictions, however, those whose sexual and/or gender identity and presentation were in some way non-normative have migrated extensively (Patton and Sánchez-Eppler, 2000). As with other aspects of life, such as religion, migrants challenged, adapted, appropriated, and reworked gender and sexual structures and concepts. Individuals blended and built on elements from many cultures to create hybridized or fluid sexual and gender identities.

On these three topics – womens' movements, colonialism, and migration – there has been a vast amount of research over the last 15 years that brings together gender history and world history, and much more is on the way. This is also true for a number of other topics as well, including the spread of religious ideas, third genders, marriage patterns, slavery, and comparative nationalism. The increasing amount of intersection between these two fields can be seen not only in books and articles, but also in conference themes. The organizers of the 2010 World History Association annual conference chose "gender" as one of their two themes, and the organizers of the 2011 Berkshire Women's History conference, in their words, "restructured the conference to take advantage of new upsurges of intellectual energy in global history, transnational and transregional history." There is thus much to look forward to, although also far too much to read.

This discussion of scholarly trends may make it appear as if focusing on women or using gender as a category of analysis has been uniformly accepted among world historians, and as if adopting a global perspective is now standard among gender and women's historians. This is far from the actual situation. Although investigating gender may seem self-evident to students and younger scholars, there are also many historians who continue to view this as a passing fad, despite the fact that such judgments become more difficult to maintain as the decades pass. (This is not only true of world historians, but also of those who study one region or one country.) Very few of the articles in the *Journal of World History* and the

Journal of Global History focus on women or gender, and there were no panels on gender at the most recent European Congresses of World and Global History, held in Dresden in 2008 and in London in 2011. Women in some countries still report that investigating the history of women can get them pegged as less than serious and be detrimental to their future careers as historians, and a 2012 issue of *L'HOMME: European Journal of Feminist History*, posed the question: Is global replacing gender? From the other side, studies of women, gender, and sexuality continue to be very unevenly distributed geographically, with research on the United States still vastly outweighing that on anywhere else. Some of this research considers issues that have been important in world history, such as migration, American neo-imperialism, and diasporas, but it is still about the United States.

I do not wish to end on a pessimistic note, however, so I will return to where I started, with my own story. Becoming a global historian has not simply meant expanding my research and teaching to encompass the world, but also changed the way that I think about Europe. For the third edition of *Women and Gender in Early Modern Europe*, published in 2008, I added a new chapter on gender in the colonial world, reflecting my own and many others' sense that European history must be connected to that of the rest of the world. In the early modern era, the lives of European women were shaped by developments beyond Europe more than they had been earlier, and European notions and patterns of gender were spread throughout much of the world. This was a time of dramatically increasing global interaction, with new contacts between peoples brought about primarily – though not only – by European voyages. Colonies saw varying degrees of immigration; some had large European populations and some only a few merchants, soldiers, and missionaries. Even if the number of European immigrants was small, however, European family forms, legal systems, religious beliefs and practices, political institutions, and economic systems confronted and blended with existing ideas and structures in colonial areas, creating new hybrid forms. As in the earlier example about French North America, European men (and sometimes women) also married and had other forms of sexual relations with indigenous people and with immigrants from other areas, creating populations, as well as ideas and institutions, that were mixed, or to use the Spanish word, *mestizo*.

Every aspect of the process of colonization was gendered. Letters, reports, and other documents by explorers, missionaries, and government officials describe territories they were seeing for the first time in highly sexualized metaphors, as "virgin lands." European explorers and colonizers described their conquests in sexualized terms, portraying themselves as virile, powerful, and masculine. Indigenous peoples were often feminized, described or portrayed visually as weak and passive in contrast to the dynamic masculine conquerors, or they were hypersexualized, regarded as animalistic and voracious. (Or sometimes both.)

Sometimes explorers linked women in Europe and indigenous people directly. For example, Jean de Léry, a French Protestant explorer in South America, used a description of a witches' sabbath from a book of European demonology to describe rituals of the Tupinambá people of Brazil. Pierre de Lancre, a French magistrate appointed in 1609 by King Henry IV to investigate the activities of witches in the Basque region of southern France, noted that the reason there were so many more witches in his day than earlier was the coming of European missionaries to the New World. Many of Satan's demons had left Europe centuries earlier when it had become Christian, he commented, but now they had returned. The demons traveled, in Lancre's opinion, with Basque fishing ships, remaining with the "impudent and undisciplined" Basque women when their husbands left again in search of cod. These women's only marketable agricultural commodity was apples, which de Lancre disapprovingly noted that they loved to eat instead of remembering that apples had been the fruit with which the snake tempted Eve in the Garden of Eden. Thus not only did European ideas about gender shape attitudes toward indigenous peoples, but those about indigenous people shaped ideas about European women.

The vast majority of European conquerors, merchants, and settlers who traveled great distances in the early modern period were men, which not only led to mixed social and cultural forms in colonial areas, but also shaped marriage patterns and other aspects of life in Europe. Because Christianity did not allow polygyny, male migration may have contributed to the entry of more women into convents in Catholic areas. In Protestant areas, male migration reinforced an existing pattern of late marriage and large numbers of women who remained single.

The early modern period saw a dramatic rise in the production, transport, and sale of consumer goods. Some of these, such as sugar and coffee, required vast amounts of heavy labor and are most profitably worked on a large scale, leading to the development of plantation economies in tropical areas with largely male slave work-forces. These slaves wore clothing made from cloth that was often produced in European households, speeding up the adoption of new techniques of production in some parts of Europe. This sometimes broke down traditional gender divisions of labor, so that men, women, and children all spun thread, instead of simply women doing this task. I had traced these changes in my dissertation and first book on German working women, but at that time I had not really thought about all the places that the cloth they were making might have gone. Some certainly ended up clothing slaves in the Caribbean, just as the guns that they were making – south Germany was a center of production for high-quality muskets and pistols – ended up in Africa being traded for those slaves. Women in Europe who were far from an ocean and never left their village or town were increasingly enmeshed in the global economy in the early modern period, and I could no longer tell their story as one that stopped at the Atlantic.

That was also true for the ways that I teach, speak, and write about all of European history. I no longer teach the Renaissance or the Reformation in the same way that I did when I thought of them as European events – or even more narrowly, as simply Italian or German events. When I designed a survey textbook on early modern Europe, it began with a chapter on "Europe in the world" in 1450, and included two more chapters that looked at relationships between

Europe and the rest of the world in terms of travel, trade, exploration, colonization, and other types of contacts.

Sailing into unfamiliar territories in teaching and research thus not only allows you to see new things, but it also allows you to bring new things home. This has been at times a frightening journey – who can pretend to know the history of the whole world? – but I can't imagine being stuck on the shore.

References

Belmessous, Saliha. 2013. *Assimilation and Empire: Uniformity in French and British Colonies, 1541–1954*. Oxford: Oxford University Press.

Butler, Judith. 1990. *Gender Trouble: Feminism and the Subversion of Identity*, new edition 2006. New York: Routledge.

Canaday, Margot. 2009. *The Straight State: Sexuality and Citizenship in Twentieth-Century America*. Princeton, NJ: Princeton University Press.

Dudnik, Stefan, Karen Hagemann, and Josh Tosh, eds. 2004. *Masculinities in Politics and War: Gendering Modern History*. Manchester: Manchester University Press.

Fausto-Sterling, Anne. 2000. *Sexing the Body: Gender Politics and the Construction of Sexuality*. New York: Basic Books.

Greenburg, David. 1988. *The Construction of Homosexuality*. Chicago, IL: University of Chicago Press.

Herdt, Gilbert, ed. 1994. *Third Sex, Third Gender: Beyond Sexual Dimorphism in Culture and History*. New York: Zone Books.

Hull, Gloria T., Patricia Scott, and Barbara Smith. 1993. *All the Women Are White, All the Blacks Are Men, But Some of Us Are Brave: Black Women's Studies*. New York: The Feminist Press at CUNY.

Jagose, Annamarie. 1996. *Queer Theory: An Introduction*. Washington Square, NY: New York University Press.

Joannou, Maroula and June Purvis, eds. 1998. *The Women's Suffrage Movement: New Feminist Perspectives*. Manchester: Manchester University Press.

Lake, Marilyn and Henry Reynolds. 2008. *Drawing the Global Colour Line: White Men's Countries and the International Challenge of Racial Equality*. Cambridge: Cambridge University Press.

Lerner, Gerda. 1979. *The Majority Finds its Past: Placing Women in History*, new edition 2005. New York: Oxford University Press. Chapel Hill, NC: University of North Carolina Press.

Levine, Phillipa, ed. 2007. *Gender and Empire*. Oxford: Oxford University Press.

McClintock, Anne, Aamir Mufti, and Ella Shoalt, eds. 1997. *Dangerous Liaisons: Gender, Nation and Post-Colonial Perspectives*, Minneapolis, MN: University of Minnesota Press.

Moghadam, Valentine M. 2005. *Globalizing Women: Transnational Feminist Networks*. Baltimore, MD: Johns Hopkins University Press.

Murray, Stephen O. 2002. *Homosexualities*. Chicago, IL: University of Chicago Press.

Offen, Karen, Ruth Roach Pierson, and Jane Rendell, eds. 1990. *Writing Women's History: International Perspectives*. Bloomington, IN: Indiana University Press.

Patton, Cindy and Benigno Sánchez-Eppler, eds. 2000. *Queer Diasporas*. Durham, NC: Duke University Press.

Ramet, Sabrina Petra, ed. 1996. *Gender Reversals and Gender Cultures: Anthropological and Historical Perspectives*. London: Routledge.

Roscoe, Will. 1998. *Changing Ones: Third and Fourth Genders in Native North America*. London: Macmillan Press.

Rupp, Leila. 1997. *Worlds of Women: The Making of an International Women's Movement*. Princeton, NJ: Princeton University Press.

Scott, Joan. 1986. "Gender: A Useful Category of Historical Analysis," *American Historical Review* 91/5: 1053–1075.

Sharpe, Pamela, ed. 2001. *Women, Gender, and Labour Migrations: Historical and Global Perspectives*. New York: Routledge.

Wiesner-Hanks, Merry E. 1993. *Women and Gender in Early Modern Europe*, 2nd edition 2000, 3rd edition 2008. Cambridge: Cambridge University Press.

Wiesner-Hanks, Merry E. 2000. *Christianity and Sexuality in the Early Modern World: Regulating Desire, Reforming Practice*. London: Routledge and Kegan Paul. 2nd edition 2010.

Wiesner-Hanks, Merry E. 2001. *Gender in History*, 2nd edition 2011. London: Blackwell.

Wiesner-Hanks, Merry E., William Bruce Wheeler, Franklin M. Doehringer, and Kenneth R. Curtis. 1997. *Discovering the Global Past: A Look at the Evidence*, Vols. I and II. Boston, MA: Houghton-Mifflin. 4th edition 2011.

Wilson, Kathleen. 2003. *The Island Race: Englishness, Empire and Gender in the Eighteenth Century*. New York: Routledge.

Further Reading

Ballantyne, Tony and Antoinette Burton, eds. 2005. *Bodies in Contact: Rethinking Colonial Encounters in World History*. Durham, NC: Duke University Press.

Ballantyne, Tony and Antoinette Burton, eds. 2009. *Moving Subjects: Gender, Mobility, and Intimacy in an Age of Global Empire*. Urbana, IL: University of Illinois Press.

Canning, Kathleen. 2006. *Gender History in Practice: Historical Perspectives on Bodies, Class, and Citizenship*. Ithaca, NY: Cornell University Press.

Fletcher, Ian Christopher, Laura E. Nym Mayhall, and Philippa Levine, eds. 2000. *Women's Suffrage in the British Empire: Citizenship, Nation, and Race*. New York: Routledge.

Hagemann, Karen and María Teresa Fernández-Aceves. 2007. "Gendering Trans/National Historiographies: Similarities and Differences in Comparison," *Journal of Women's History* 19/1: 151–213.

Hodes, Martha, ed. 1999. *Sex, Love, Race: Crossing Boundaries in North American History*. New York: New York University Press.

Meade, Teresa A. and Merry Wiesner-Hanks, eds. 2004. *Blackwell Companion to Gender History*. London: Blackwell.

Molyneux, Maxine. 2001. *Women's Movements in International Perspective: Latin America and Beyond*. New York: Palgrave.

Scott, Joan W., Joanne Meyerowitz, Heidi Tinsman, Maria Bucur, Dyan Elliot, and Wang Zheng, "*AHR* Forum: Revisiting 'Gender: A Useful Category of Historical Analysis'," 2008. *American Historical Review* 113/5: 1344–1430.

Smith Bonnie G., ed. 2000. *Global Feminisms Since 1945: A Survey of Issues and Controversies*. New York: Routledge.

Smith, Bonnie G., ed. 2004. *Women's History in Global Perspective*, 3 vols. Urbana, IL: University of Illinois Press.

Woollacott, Angela. 2006. *Gender and Empire*. New York: Palgrave Macmillan.

4

No Great Divergence? Reaching World History Through East Asian Studies

Kenneth Pomeranz

My path to world history led through East Asian area studies, given a particular spin by having nearly gone into European history; I continue to do some work that is more global in scope and some that speaks more to area specialists. This divided focus has its costs, sometimes making me feel I am cutting corners in both areas; but I think it has ultimately helped me write a kind of world history that area specialists can recognize as mattering to them. And while establishing world history as a research field – creating discussions about transregional topics that meet the same standards of rigor that we apply in other historical fields – has been a major development in its own right, we still have a long way to go in making these discussions matter to the discipline as a whole, as historians of gender and the environment (to name just two relatively recent insurgencies) have done.

In retrospect, I realize that I *began* doing world history well before I would have accepted or even recognized the label. But since world history is at least as much a matter of approach and consciously

Architects of World History: Researching the Global Past, First Edition.
Edited by Kenneth R. Curtis and Jerry H. Bentley.

chosen interpretation as of the material one covers, I wasn't *really* doing world history until I knew that I was doing so; gaining that awareness required encountering other people excited by the possibilities for creating such a field and discussing it with them. Since research is the part of an academic's life in which they have the greatest individual control, it was here that I could be most like an "architect," proceeding according to a plan I devised alone; but for the same reason, my research plans could keep evolving, and I was relatively free not to worry about what name to give them. Thus, teaching and service – areas in which it was essential to explain to others what I wanted to do, and solicit their cooperation, before I could do it – probably played more important roles in making me think of myself, and my research, as being in a field called "world history." Consequently, though most of this essay concerns my research career, the last third focuses on teaching and institution-building as central to my own development, to any lessons that story may have for others, and to certain tasks that I think are vital for our field today.

Discovering History, Academia, and China

My early life did not particularly point toward academia, or history. My parents had both fled Hitler's Germany as teenagers, and thus did not finish high school; but they both liked reading, and it was assumed that my sister and I would go to college. Like many of my male peers – I was born a year after Sputnik – I was encouraged to focus on the sciences, and initially did. But somewhere in junior high and high school, I found my interests shifting toward social sciences and humanities – a couple of excellent teachers helped (Pomeranz, 2013 describes one of them), but I suspect that the political ferment of the late 1960s and early 1970s mattered more.

My junior year of high school was probably decisive. Still thinking about the natural sciences, I took two Saturday physics classes in a program for "gifted" high school students at Columbia; they were certainly interesting but didn't make me feel as if I had found my calling. The same year, I took the PSATs and checked the box that allowed something called "Telluride Association" to contact me if my scores met the cutoff for their programs. I had never heard of Telluride, except as a town in Colorado; a chance to spend a summer in the Rockies sounded good.

That box changed my life. After a lengthy screening process, 32 of us wound up at Cornell University, taking one of two seminars with college faculty (in my case, one in American political theory), provided with some other structured activities, and encouraged to feed off each other – which we did, with a rare level of intensity. (I think I slept about 5 h per night.) The experience opened up many new vistas for me, of which a few are relevant here.

First, I learned – if I had had any remaining doubts – that the social sciences and humanities could be as challenging as the sciences, and that some of my peers thought so, too. Secondly, I got a sense that I was pretty good at this sort of thing, even within this selective subgroup. Third (and not unrelated to the first two), my college aspirations changed, and perhaps my career ambitions, too. Previously, I had figured that despite high grades and SATs, financial considerations meant that I would probably attend a State University of New York campus. (My father was a linotype printer, a field in which jobs were vanishing. His union ultimately made a deal that protected his cohort, but that happened later.) Now I had a new set of friends who assumed (rightly, as it turned out) that we were all going to elite colleges. The program was also my first exposure (aside from attending those Columbia physics lectures) to professional academics, and to some peers from academic families; the world they inhabited seemed appealing. When Telluride offered me – along with some of my friends from the summer – a slot in their program for Cornell students (which included a partial scholarship) I grabbed it and spent my college years in a small, academically intense community within a large research university.

I took a lot of history at Cornell, but didn't necessarily plan on becoming a historian, until quite late in the game. Certainly I had no idea of being a "world historian," or even any sense that such creatures existed. My courses were all in national history, except for two in what we would now call early modern Europe. To the extent that I hoped to construct a larger picture, I assumed it would come from assembling the relatively detailed pictures of particular times and places from upper division classes into some kind of mosaic. I never took a lower division "civ" survey, but that was because other courses looked more challenging, not because I had any critique, even an inchoate one, of the problems in reifying "civilizations": that is, treating units of study invented for our own intellectual convenience as if they were real, unified, clearly bounded entities. I do remember hearing parts of such a critique from John Najemy, a Renaissance historian. But his point, if I remember it right, was about the ideological dangers of an overly celebratory "Plato to NATO" narrative, rather than an epistemological argument about the dangers of treating *any* "civilization" as if it was a monad moving through history on its own. A fellow undergraduate, Dan Segal – still a major intellectual influence, as well as one of my closest friends – also made arguments about the dangers of reifying national or civilizational traditions, but I understood this mostly as a caution against a crude "West and the rest" dualism, and perhaps a plea for micro-level "thick description." (Dan was an Anthro major.) If the idea that one might instead or in addition take a unit larger than a single "civilization" – the whole world, or something like Marshall Hodgson's Afro-Eurasian ecumene – as an object of study, criticizing civilizational models from "above," I missed it.

To the extent that I acquired any seed of a more global approach, it probably came from studying what was then called history of foreign relations. Here I had a truly inspiring teacher in Walter LaFeber, from whom I learned an enormous amount. But for whatever reason, this also did not get me to think in terms of world history. Studying US foreign relations made me think about possibly going into government – an idea that did not survive the United States' rightward shift circa 1980 – but when I thought of a career as a historian, I was more excited by the idea of doing some kind of history focused on "ordinary people." And while international history was beginning to become less focused on state to state relations, and more on other kinds of cross-border interactions, it was doing so unbeknownst to me. (And even in this broader international history, the nonstate actors were more likely to be intellectuals, foundation officers, business people, or missionaries than small farmers or wage laborers.) Studying social and political movements, or perhaps economic development – some aspect of how ordinary people, in Charles Tilly's words(1985), "lived the big changes" – seemed more exciting to me; and given both the histories and languages with which I had some acquaintance, the logical time/place field had to be in modern Europe. By fall of my senior year, I was applying to graduate schools with the thought of doing either French or German history, of either the nineteenth or twentieth century. (I also thought about applying to law school, which seemed much more practical, but my true preferences were amply revealed when I couldn't motivate myself to register for the LSAT.)

Then something – and someone – happened. The someone was Sherman Cochran, who let me into his graduate/senior seminar in Chinese history even though I had no background, taught what may well be the best single course I've ever taken (though there are a lot of contenders) and then offered good advice as I pondered a question I had not anticipated asking: "If you like studying this stuff so much, and there are actually jobs doing it …" Once I explained that I was becoming increasingly intrigued by the idea of studying China, but already had applications in the mail saying I wanted to do modern European history, he thought a bit, and then offered me a list of books. The idea was that if I actually read these books in my spare time and over the summer, this would prove that my interest wasn't just a passing whim; it would also bring me about up to where I would have been had I done an East Asia concentration within an undergrad history major, except for – ahem – having no language skills. I could then knock on the door of the resident historian of China and see what that person suggested.

Graduate School: Lots of Dots, Not Yet Connected

I followed this advice, chose Yale for graduate school, and knocked on the door of Jonathan Spence. He explained that he taught 1-year-long graduate course that required no Chinese; if I did well enough in it, there might be money to support me over the summer while I started catching up on language skills. I worked hard and benefitted from Jonathan's tolerance for the errors created by my patchy knowledge and fondness for premature syntheses. In the spring, I was a teaching assistant in his huge lecture course and felt increasingly committed to this field (though, wanting to keep my options open, and needing to do at least one research paper using primary sources, I also kept working on twentieth-century Germany). In the summer I started Chinese, and determined that while my tones were never going to win any prizes, I could become good enough at Chinese to survive. After another year and half – at which point I was more or less reading modern Chinese, and no longer throwing classical Chinese texts across the room in frustration – I formally changed my major field to "China circa 1600–1949."

A lot went into this decision, some of it only dimly understood. In part, I was simply intrigued by how different China was – and how different it wasn't. Unlike some parts of the world, it had long had a recognizable state and bureaucracy, large towns and cities, private property, widespread literacy, and other phenomena familiar from Western history, but its history was nonetheless strikingly different from others I had studied. And explaining what then seemed the most salient piece of that difference – a peasant revolution that had built a twentieth-century state and a collectivist society – implied numerous questions that seemed tailor-made for anyone interested in history from the bottom-up. More generally, the relatively thin scholarly literature (especially in English) was at least as much an attraction as a drawback: there was plenty to do and no need to choose a narrow topic in order to avoid repeating the work of others.

The Ming-Qing archives in Beijing had been opened to Americans in 1979, so by the 1980s one could do Chinese history in "normal," professionally recognizable, ways; but the field also offered a sense of adventure. The still very uncertain shape of post-Mao society offered the promise of watching history unfold in the present – and perhaps even of seeing something that might be a model for other places; this was also very attractive, and I had some ideas (although fuzzy ones) about how studying and teaching China's past might connect to witnessing (or even participating in) its present transformations.

At another level, as the child of refugees from mid-century Germany, I think I also, subconsciously, wanted more separation between personal history and any history I would study professionally. That their own experiences had helped make my parents far less critical of the United States than growing up in the years bridging Nixon and Reagan had made me added another incentive to study some very different part of the world. And yet I didn't want to give up my interests in European (or for that matter American) history. I told myself that with native English, some French and German, and some graduate-level history courses under my belt, I could someday go back and "do something comparative"; but if I didn't learn Chinese and Japanese in my 20s, I was unlikely to learn them later. In retrospect, elements of a career in world history were coalescing, but at the time, "history" and "world" did not seem to go together much. Research that crossed national, even continental lines, seemed more in the bailiwick of political scientists, mostly using methods that did not appeal to me. (Conversations with my wife, a political science graduate student who left for law school, confirmed that the field was, on the whole, moving even further away from approaches that I found compelling.) Historians, it seemed, probed deeply into narrower geographic areas.

The dissertation topic I developed was certainly in that mold. It looked at a region of North China surrounding the Grand Canal – for centuries, the main transportation link between Beijing and China's economic heartland in the Yangzi Valley – during the period when the Canal decayed and railroads were built, by-passing "my" region. I chose the topic not to answer any single question but because it seemed to intersect many issues in modern Chinese history: What was happening to rural living standards in the decades before World War II? How were class relations and rural social structure changing? How did political power – as exercised from the village on up – and popular ideas influence economic behavior? Did imperialism/foreign contact matter much, one way or the other, to people in the countryside? Did any of this help explain the Chinese revolution?

And since the center of the region I studied was the intersection of the Grand Canal and the Yellow River, these questions were soon joined by questions about the region's environmental history – at a time when Chinese environmental history barely existed.

As I soon discovered, even a region chosen because it was *not* on the coast had had a variety of foreign visitors, whose writings I found very useful. But my research questions were still mostly contained within a Chinese historiographical frame. The theoretical influences came mostly from outside Sinology: the most important ones from the Annales school, on the one hand, and Charles Tilly's work on states, markets, and popular protest (1972, 1975, 1979, 1985, 1990; Tilly, Tilly, and Tilly, 1985), on the other hand. G. William Skinner – who wrote a series of enormously influential articles on the spatial organization of Chinese society, beginning from central place theory and analyses of local marketing networks (1964–1965, 1971, 1977a, b) – and Immanuel Wallerstein were also in there somewhere, as I struggled to understand how developments in "core" and "peripheral" areas had influenced each other.

Like many dissertation writers, I spent a lot of time noticing trees, while being unsure about the shape of the forest. Accurately or not, I remember exactly one "Aha!" moment from the process. Convinced that, in good Braudelian fashion, I needed to put the ecological setting first, I produced a 185-page "first chapter" describing the changes to the region's waterways. Even I knew that this was too long, but there was a lot to say. The mouth of the Yellow River had shifted by almost 300 miles just before my period began, while civil war and foreign incursions were forcing the Qing to rethink their political and economic priorities; years of politicking about what water conservancy should look like in the new order had followed. So when Prof. Spence noted that what I had given him didn't have to be the opening chapter, a light bulb went on. My story was, in large part, about how the landscape was the result of human choices, not just the setting for them; and the logics informing those choices had changed drastically as both the human and physical contexts shifted in the late nineteenth and early twentieth centuries. The "China-centered Chinese history" my cohort sought to write was turning out to be inseparable from "Chinese history in global context," though I wouldn't have phrased it that way yet.

Semi-Conscious (At Best) Steps Toward World History

The dissertation, fortunately, yielded a job, a well-received book (Pomeranz, 1993) and tenure at University of California Irvine. Irvine hired me to help build a China program – and perhaps also a "Pacific Rim" program. World history was not on the table. But my Chinese history colleague R. Bin Wong had, like me, a background in European history and comparative interests. And he had more experience than I did being the one Sinologist in rooms of historians and other social scientists studying the West; consequently, he had thought a lot about how to show such interlocutors that China need not be seen as a deviation from "normal" historical development. Years of conversations, exchanging drafts, and so on with Bin would not only make me a better historian of China, but help me rethink how China's history could matter to a particular history department, history more generally, and to adjacent academic fields.

Irvine's history department has always been undersized for a major research university; when I first arrived, it was very small. While this became a chronic problem, especially for graduate training, it also had some advantages: it encouraged people, especially in non-US fields, to connect with people working on other regions. One important connection for me was with Steven Topik, a Latin Americanist with whom I shared an interest in nineteenth- and twentieth-century economic history. Among other things, this led to my first, coauthored, book in world history: *The World that Trade Created* (1999).

That, too, began by accident. A Ph.D. student, Will Swaim, left UCI and started editing a monthly magazine called *World Trade*. He gave the last page of each issue to a historical feature called *Looking Back*, which he initially wrote himself; as he became too busy for this, he offered it to Steve, whom he had met at Irvine. In 1990, Steve suggested that he and I split the column, taking alternate months. Doing some writing for nonacademics seemed appealing, as did a little extra money; and initially, I could write columns without much new reading, using material I already knew. Before long, however, I needed to branch out geographically, which meant additional reading that was unlikely to feed my regular research or teaching. But that made the column a good excuse to read about other parts of the world. Discovering some of the literature on the Indian Ocean (Chaudhuri, 1985, 1990; Subrahmanyam, 1990, 1993) was particularly eye-opening; so was the new view of the growth of British power in Asia being developed by C.A. Bayly (1989). After 6 years, Steve and I had roughly 70 short articles (mostly 1200–1500 words) on several loosely related themes, which he suggested might form the core of a book. After a few demurrals, we found a publisher and then set to work. Eventually we grouped the articles into seven thematic chapters; writing introductory essays to tie each chapter together, highlight more general issues that emerged from the articles, and point to additional examples. While we originally aimed at general readers, we found our biggest audience in college and Advanced Placement classrooms: world history instructors liked having a choice of geographically varied, short articles on related themes.

But at least through the mid-1990s, I thought of myself very much as a historian of China who happened to have some other interests. So the second monograph I planned was at least as Sinological as the first: a study of how worship of the goddess of Mt. Tai – an important, understudied, North China deity – evolved over roughly 500 years. While researching my first book, I had noted interesting controversies over the goddess; but they did not fit that project. Now I retrieved those notes, made more, and began sketching how the goddess' story might illuminate Chinese history more broadly. I also did some reading on vaguely parallel phenomena elsewhere – hoping such cases would sharpen my questions about China, but not planning to write about other places. The goddess turned out to be connected to the bodhisattva Guanyin, who had Indian origins, spread from China to Japan, Korea, and beyond, and has been compared by some scholars to the Virgin Mary. So here, too, a "local" history had world history possibilities – but I wasn't looking for them.

In 1991, I succeeded in two grant competitions; the path to a second book seemed clear. Moreover, this topic seemed researchable in North American libraries, with just a short trip to China. This was very important since my wife also had a career, we had a 2 year old, and we wanted another child.

Things are rarely that simple. American libraries yielded some great finds, but not quite enough. Meanwhile, I learned that more material might be available in China than I'd realized: mostly at local levels, requiring elaborate preparations. Meanwhile, our "second child" became twins, while our older one (and, eventually, the twins, too) turned out to have developmental differences. So I needed a long trip to China and couldn't take one any time soon.

An Accidental World Historian

While this path forward became obstructed, another opened. A publisher asked for comments on their world history textbook; I criticized it at great (47 page) length. The text had begun as a western civ book; subsequently other authors added chapters on other regions, in patchwork fashion. Among other things, this created an odd "west and the rest" effect: because the Europe chapters took account of the preceding 25 years of social history literature, while the other sections (being shorter and having less literature to draw on) mostly covered elite politics, the book gave the impression that in Europe, lots of people had agency, while elsewhere only rulers did. It thus reinforced (presumably unintentionally) various bad ideas about a stagnant "Orient"; fixing that would require that the book take more account of new social and cultural histories being written about Asia, Africa, and Latin America. This made me think more about how to put what were often local histories in a global frame, and why simply juxtaposing national literatures was inadequate.

The authors were, unsurprisingly, not interested in my recommendations, which essentially required a new book. The publisher then asked me if I wanted to write my own textbook, which I did not; we turned instead to ideas for a possible world history book series. Trying to think of feasible scholarly projects spanning multiple world areas was challenging and fun. But I was still so far from thinking of myself as a world historian that I was very surprised when the publisher asked "Which one do you want to do?"

But once posed, the idea was immediately appealing – especially given the problems with my existing second book project. The topic that seemed most appropriate for me was one that that would look at the origins of a more or less integrated world economy from three perspectives, alternating among the North Atlantic, East Asia, and South Asia. I would be working on familiar themes, albeit on a much larger geographic scale: economic development, states and markets, resource issues and environmental change, imperialism, and how "local" social structures shaped responses to external shocks.

This idea became *The Great Divergence* (2000) – though after many further changes. As I worked on a background chapter, which would describe the state of various economies on the eve of British industrialization (and the growth of a new British empire in Asia), I became less and less convinced of the conventional claim that Europe, or even Northwest Europe, was already far more prosperous than anyplace else in say, 1770. My skepticism grew partly out of the European literature on standards of living, which showed no clear gains for most people, even in Britain, until well into the nineteenth century (e.g., Mokyr, 1988); partly from work on grain prices and real wages, which suggested that in much of Europe, unskilled real wages bought less food in 1800 than in 1400 (Abel, 1980; Phelps-Brown and Hopkins, 1981). It also came from reading through the long debates on "proto-industrialization," which showed how hard it was to make clear connections between the growth of rural handicrafts in the sixteenth to eighteenth century and the factory-based industrialization of the nineteenth (e.g., Kriedte, Medick and Schlumbohm, 1981; Levine, 1977). Indeed, much of the latter literature painted a picture that seemed not very different from the picture of Lower Yangzi handicraft production that Mark Elvin (1973) had famously called a "high level equilibrium trap." Increasingly, I began to think that the mainstream literatures on sixteenth- to eighteenth-century China and Europe were exaggerating the inevitability of economic stagnation and breakthrough, respectively, because we knew what had in fact happened later on, ignoring large and important areas of similarity. This was reinforced as I thought more about the geography of both places and problems with using modern nations as units for historical comparisons. After all, China more resembled Europe as a whole – in size, ecological diversity, and range of living standards circa 1750 – than it did any single European country; and Britain and the Netherlands were arguably less typical of Europe as a whole than the prosperous Yangzi Delta (with perhaps 15% of the empire's population in 1750) was of China. Yet in one chapter of the *Cambridge Economic History of Europe* where I kept track, roughly three-fourth of all references to "Europe" (without any geographic modifier) were based on data from the continent's wealthy Northwestern corner; when some Chinese Marxist historians had likewise relied heavily on Yangzi Delta evidence to show that late imperial China was incipiently "capitalist," the problem had been widely noted.

Before long, I had 100-plus pages arguing that at least parts of East Asia maintained rough economic parity until almost 1800, and that explanations of the nineteenth-century "great divergence" therefore had to rest on relatively recent and contingent developments. Looking for those developments, I was drawn to thinking about environmental and energy constraints – fundamental to what Braudel had called the "biological old regime" – and how they were relaxed for Britain (and later Europe more generally). Two great changes stood out: a huge increase in the use of fossil fuels, and soaring land-intensive imports from overseas, especially the Americas. The former story was an old one, but had recently been revisited, and its discontinuities emphasized, by E.A. Wrigley (1988). The latter story led back to voluminous debates about the significance of the Columbian exchange (Crosby, 2003(1972), 1986), colonial surplus extraction (Williams, 1944; O'Brien, 1982), and other issues. Along with Crosby, whose work I already taught, I was strongly influenced by 1990s scholarship that re-assessed the role of Latin American precious metals – and China's role as the ultimate destination for much of this treasure (Flynn, 1995; Flynn and

Giraldez, 1996; Von Glahn, 1996). That literature helped to challenge stereotypes in which early modern Europeans were active acquisitive consumers, while Chinese were, for better or worse, simply passive recipients of bullion (Wallerstein, 1974; Kindlberger, 1990); it also helped me rethink European colonization in the Americas as something that had been shaped – perhaps even sustained – by global relationships, not just bilateral ones. If I was right about the significance of Europe's overseas "ghost acres" (Jones, 1981) to industrialization, then arguing that the colonization that had made such ecological windfalls possible was best understood as a product of *world* history became even more significant.

A manuscript with such a revisionist argument could only be convincing if it were more densely footnoted and academic than the book my original publisher had wanted. It thus wound up, ironically, in Princeton's series on "The Economic History of the Western World." The argument was – and remains – controversial, but the book at least succeeded in mattering to both more traditional historiographies and an emerging world history field; it won a regionally specific East Asia book prize (from the American Historical Association), while sharing a prize from the World History Association.

More debates have followed and have moved in several directions. I have written about some of them elsewhere (e.g., Pomeranz, 2010, 2011a, 2012) and can mention just a few things here.

One area in which my work has thus far held up well is in its assessment of agriculture (Brenner and Isett, 2002; Huang, 2002; Pomeranz, 2002). As late as 1820, labor productivity in the Yangzi Delta was over 90% of that in England (while land productivity was far higher). This placed it roughly even with the Netherlands, and well above any place else in Europe – including some places where industrialization took off during the nineteenth century (Allen, 2009a, b; Li and Van Zanden, 2012). This highlights a crucial discontinuity between whatever factors explain the relative performance of preindustrial economies and those that explain industrialization. And by confirming that China was not "backward" in the largest sector of all preindustrial economies, it casts doubt on many broad-gauged explanations that assert long-standing, decisive differences in "economic freedom," "attitudes toward risk," and other characteristics attributed to whole civilizations.

Beyond this, however, disagreement reigns. Though some of the discussion has remained focused on the issues I emphasized, a lot has also moved toward discussions of science, technology, "human capital" (Mokyr, 2002, 2010; Van Zanden and Luiten, 2009), and geographic networks of early modern "collective learning" (Christian, 2004, pp. 392–394); toward reasons why European industry might have been biased toward urban-based and capital-intensive operations (Rosenthal and Wong, 2011); and toward technologies of warfare in particular (Hoffmann 2012). While some of these works have accepted the idea of a relatively late "divergence" (see also Goody, 2004), there is no consensus on this either; a boom in comparative studies of the ancient world has led some scholars to formulate new arguments for the early emergence of Western exceptionalism (Scheidel, 2007). More recently, Ian Morris has argued that while "the West" did not gain its current lead over "the East" until the 1770s, both that event and today's apparent re-convergence can only be understood with a framework that goes back 10,000 years (Morris, 2010; for a response, see Pomeranz, 2011b). Meanwhile, some scholars in other disciplines have taken the broad outlines of *The Great Divergence* as a point of departure for placing the twentieth-century resurgence of economic growth in East Asia in historical perspective, seeing this as a return to normalcy after a relatively brief Western interregnum (Sugihara, 2003; Arrighi, 2009). However, these arguments fare in the longer run, the debates have catalyzed considerable new research, and discussions that have made people relate their areas of specialization to others in new ways; shaking up old assumptions about what places each of us need to know about has itself been a significant step forward.

For my own personal trajectory, it was important that involvement in these debates made me more and more a part of conference and other circuits explicitly dedicated to world history. More generally, it is important note that most of these discussions were initially centered in the United States, where world history has grown faster than in the rest of the global academy. But *The Great Divergence* also brought me into contact with a lively set of discussions in Europe about global economic history, particularly at the London School of Economics, where Patrick O'Brien was building a new graduate program. Shortly thereafter, Patrick referenced the "divergence debate" in procuring funding for the Global Economic History Network, which ran several years' worth of valuable international conferences. (Its institutional offspring continue to do so.) A bit later, he helped persuade LSE and Cambridge University Press to support the founding of *The Journal of Global History*, this gave the field its second major journal and one that has dedicated considerable efforts to drawing in readers and writers outside North America. (I was the only one of the founding troika of editors based in the United States.)

Teaching World History

Meanwhile, I had also begun teaching world history – first at the undergraduate and then at the graduate level. A group of eight of us responded to a request from Irvine's Dean of Undergraduate Studies (Mike Burton, an anthropologist) that we create such a course and met periodically over a summer to generate syllabi. While we were markedly unrepresentative – lacking anyone working on Africa, Asia other than China, Latin America, Eastern Europe, or Oceania – this at least forced us to move beyond "representing" our own time/place field and to think thematically. And having tenure-track faculty committed to the course helped protect it from being taken less seriously than other surveys.

In fact, world history was probably the most difficult of the introductory sequences the department offered, precisely because it was organized thematically and often jumped across time/place boundaries. Moreover, it had embedded in it from the start theoretical arguments about what history was good for and how moving self-consciously among different spatial and temporal scales taught knowledge and skills that were hard to learn otherwise. Moreover, because not all our colleagues (or even all the teaching assistants assigned to us) were sure that this kind of course should exist, we paid an unusual amount of attention to explaining its uses. No doubt many students, who were often simply fulfilling a distribution requirement, overlooked this. But one pedagogical advantage of world history is that it exposes the choices we make in defining historical topics, which are more easily papered over in classes on topics that seem more self-evidently "real" (such as nations) and are bounded in intuitively obvious ways. World history makes it harder to simply stand up and start telling a story, without saying something to explain what is and is not being covered, and why individual classes look so different (e.g., a lecture on nineteen-century urbanization that jumps from Paris to Chicago to Buenos Aires to Shanghai, followed by a lecture on the Russian Revolution that stays firmly in one place). It is tempting to rush past these questions in class, so as to save time for another substantive "case," but that risks throwing away a particularly good opportunity to introduce history *as a discipline* – with distinctive goals, methods, assumptions, points of consensus, and currently active debates, – rather than just an accumulated store of "background" on today's world. For me, this helps tip the scales between encouraging students to do world history and adding additional courses in area studies regions

One advantage of teaching a more self-conscious kind of world history survey was the room it opened up for dialogue with graduate student TAs: the weekly staff meetings came to be less about adequately supervising the TAs in a set of self-evident tasks than about having our own discussion of the materials and how to use them. Since the TAs also seemed to find this intellectually engaging – and it was becoming increasingly clear that having a "world history" credential would help them find jobs – it made sense to start thinking about creating graduate courses and a graduate field in world history. At the time (circa 1996/1997), there were few models for this and big questions about what graduate world history should do: Should there be dissertations in world history? If not, were we simply preparing students to teach? Or was there another possibility: a research field that would produce few dissertations, given the problems with prolonging graduate school, but that did have a canon of respected works and evolving research-based arguments toward which a student might orient his/her *future* scholarship? While we bet on such a graduate field emerging, this was initially a leap of faith. Our syllabi for Irvine's first graduate world history seminars (circa 1998–2000) were mostly patched together from scholarship on regions or nations that gestured toward larger questions and could be placed side by side to suggest "global" hypotheses. But it worked. The seminars and the field soon became very popular; students found that, even if their dissertations remained anchored in one country's archives, they could be usefully informed by questions and sensibilities from world history; and it gradually became easier to fill a syllabus with high-quality works that had been written as world history. I should also emphasize that not having done world history in graduate school myself, it was through teaching that I solidified my own sense of the field. There were many foundational figures – William McNeill, Philip Curtin, Marshall Hodgson, Leften Stavrianos *et al.* – of whom I had read very little before I began teaching. I suspect this is true of much of my generation.

Institution-Building

Here my story begins to segue into the third area of most professors' careers: service, which in a new field means institution-building. I was not part of creating the first wave of world history institutions – the World History Association, the *Journal of World History*, etc. – but came along when building a world history presence at research-oriented institutions was becoming an increasingly central task. In many ways UC Irvine, and the University of California system more generally, was a good place to be for those purposes; and personally, I became self-conscious and strategic about building world history in the context of institutional work before I necessarily thought of my research or teaching through a world history lens. The case for building world history programs was first and foremost an intellectual one; but people think where they are, and the institutional setting at UC Irvine reinforced the intellectual arguments for world history in certain important ways.

One problem for the world history field was that the most prestigious institutions had little incentive to take it seriously. Their graduate students were doing reasonably well in a job market defined by national specialties, and they were well-equipped to continue recruiting top students in these fields. Among other things, size matters in history programs. Even if an individual professor at a less-prestigious institution is every bit as good as anyone at a more famous school, it is a gamble for a student to go where there may be the only professor in his/her field, and few if any fellow students with similar interests. Elite departments also faced fewer of the material pressures that made world history attractive to less prestigious programs (Pomeranz and Segal, 2013). But to have world history overwhelmingly associated with teaching institutions, or with graduate programs whose students were rarely competitive for the most coveted jobs, would just reinforce the field's marginality. In-between schools, such as the less prestigious UCs, were therefore critical for making world history an established field.

And for complementary reasons, world history made institutional sense for departments like UCI's. These were departments at institutions where research and graduate teaching were central concerns and with many faculty quite comparable to those at leading institutions – but unlikely, given size and funding, to be able to attract, train, and place many top students in strictly national histories. Here, too were departments that often faced a Catch-22 as they sought to expand (as was still happening in the 1990s and early 2000s) and diversify away from a heavy concentration on the United States and Western Europe. If you didn't already have a historian of, say, Africa, how would you persuade a dean that such a person would be able to train graduate students, unless the dean gave you two Africanist slots? How would you persuade the person him/herself that they would not simply be providing undergraduate "coverage" courses? The problem had many dimensions, but building graduate-level world history, at least as a second field, seemed like one important part of a solution. And at least at the University of California, cross-campus collaboration was another.

Others had already started this collaboration. In 1996, professors from various fields – though mostly sociology and history – began a funded series of workshops and conferences under the rubric "Modernity's Histories." Edmund ("Terry") Burke III, at UC Santa Cruz, William Hagen at UC Davis, and Ray Kea and Randolph Head, at UC Riverside, were the leading historians involved. The group met at Irvine in February 1997, and somebody asked me to present part of my research for what became *The Great Divergence*; I did, and discovered a group that shared many of my interests. Terry Burke was particularly important for bringing me further into world history. He was teaching a National Endowment for the Humanities Summer Seminar on the "Environment and World History" in 1998 and asked me to teach a unit on China; I agreed and began years of fruitful collaboration. (Some of these presentations became part of a coedited volume with the same title, published in 2009.) Through Terry and "Modernity's Histories," I met others who were interested in world history, including non-UC world historians such as John Richards – a South Asianist who did pioneering work on the global histories of topics ranging from deforestation to the circulation of precious metals – Ross Dunn, and David Christian.

As the group's funding neared its end in 1999, I applied for a new grant, this time for a multicampus research group explicitly devoted to world history. The proposal argued, along the lines laid out earlier, that world history represented an opportunity particularly suited to UC (and especially the smaller UC history departments); 5 years later, seeking renewal, we could submit a sheaf of letters from Ph.D.s saying that by helping them enter this emerging field, we had helped them get jobs. Eventually, the group ran for a dozen years and involved some people from every campus (though Irvine, Santa Cruz, Davis and Riverside remained the core). Our most ambitious plans – for example, for truly collaborative graduate advising – were never realized, but we ran many conferences, helped stimulate the founding of world history graduate fields on various campuses, helped many students develop dissertation topics (or think about how they might turn a dissertation framed in national terms into a more global book somewhere down the road), and nurtured other faculty and student projects. The group also had many positive spillovers. Having it in existence and headquartered at Irvine helped persuade UCI administrators that we were on to something: at least for a while, we got more resources and were able to hire in crucial fields (Africa, Middle East, South Asia, etc.) where we had never had a line before. A book series began at UC Press, with Terry and I as two of the editors; the first two books in the series (by John Richards (2003) and David Christian (2004)) both won prizes. Each initiative helped raise the profile of the others. We also built relationships with people in the California State University system – notably at Long Beach and San Diego – who were doing world history, and were in many ways out ahead of UC in doing so. Meanwhile, as we had both hoped and feared, some bigger and better-funded institutions had entered the field: Columbia, Penn, Brown, Duke, Rice, and others (Streets-Salter, 2012, p. 56, n. 26). (The UC campuses did not respond to this challenge by putting more resources behind their own world history programs, but perhaps that was too much to hope for.)

Conclusions

My relationship to world history continues to evolve, particularly now that I am at a very different sort of institution: the University of Chicago. But by this point it made sense to call me a world historian – I was doing research, teaching, and service in the field. So instead of continuing to tell my story, it seems more worthwhile to make a few points about what the story thus far may mean.

The importance of accident and coincidence stands out in my career – as I suspect it does for many world historians of my generation. Now that programs to train world historians exist, this may become less common: certainly people who start moving in the directions that attracted me should find a name for what interests them faster than I did. But many of our recruits will probably always arrive by circuitous paths: graduate programs remain unusual, and many people will probably enter the research ranks of world historians through their second book rather than their first.

A round-about path certainly has disadvantages. In my own case, having come to world history through comparative history meant that it took me a while to appreciate the possibilities of making trans-regional flows – of resources, people, technologies, ideas, species, disease, and so on – into central foci for historical investigation, even though my early exposure to international history should have sensitized me to that possibility. But this kind of path has its advantages as well. I suspect I have had an easier time than many of my world history colleagues in having what I did accepted as "real history" precisely because I also remained (and still remain) anchored in an "area studies" field. And I think it is only by combining comparisons and connections – and raising theoretical questions about what both those terms mean – that world history can have the full impact on the larger discipline that I think it ought to have. Either comparisons or connections alone leave area fields intact, with world history becoming another specialization alongside of them; combining comparisons and connections will pose greater epistemological challenges for ourselves and for our colleagues who are more satisfied within national and area fields. (For a fuller development of this argument, see Pomeranz and Segal, 2012.)

Second, because history curricula are much less standardized across universities than those for many other fields – both at the level of individual courses and at the level of the major – what it means to become involved in world history will also remain very varied. As I have tried to explain earlier, the institutional configuration at Irvine favored building a lower division world history survey, and, to some extent, a graduate program; where I am now, I doubt that a new survey course would attract much interest. On the other hand, we may be much better situated to develop upper-level undergraduate courses in world history – which has often been a real weakness in programs like Irvine's, where the pressures to maximize enrollment by offering immediately legible course topics are more intense, and there are fewer colleagues who can insure that your "home" area also gets covered as you teach more world history. More elite schools may therefore be a better vantage point from which to figure out what a history major not primarily assembled from national pieces might look like. Meanwhile, a graduate field that may need unusual amounts of language training, and/or may pay off more in people's second books than their first ones, may also be easier to consolidate at elite schools, even if it was easier to launch at less prestigious ones. While to some extent every subfield looks different on different campuses, I suspect it is particularly true of ours: it is not clear that the nature of, say, gender history or environmental history (to name two other relatively recent arrivals) need to be quite as strongly inflected by the kind of institution that one is at.

Third, world history also seems a more necessarily collective enterprise than many other historical fields. All fields are collective creations, of course. Still, we have viable models for how one might function as, say, a historian of gender in the nineteenth-century United States without having other gender historians in the department – such a person can even train Ph.D. students, as long as there are other Americanists around. It is harder to imagine how one could be the only world historian in a department – except, of course, through one's research, which is great but not, by itself, sufficient. My own story suggests that even publishing in world history would not have made me a world historian without both the personal interactions and the pressures to clarify one's goals that came from trying to build courses and programs with other people, and in response to specific institutional pressures and opportunities. It's nice to be called an "architect of world history," but I suspect that world history is not so much to be found in the houses any one of us has built as in the neighborhood created by their juxtaposition.

References

Abel, Wilhelm. 1980. *Agrarian Fluctuations in Europe from the 13th to the 20th Centuries*. New York: St. Martin's Press.

Allen, Robert. 2009a. *The British Industrial Revolution in Global Perspective*. Cambridge: Cambridge University Press.

Allen, Robert. 2009b. "Agricultural Productivity and Rural Incomes in England and the Yangtze Delta, ca. 1620–1820," *Economic History Review* 62/3: 525–550.

Arrighi, Giovanni. 2009. *Adam Smith in Beijing: Lineages of the Twenty-First Century*. London: Verso.

Bayly, C.A. 1989. *Imperial Meridian: The British Empire and the World, 1780–1830*. London: Longman's.

Brenner, Robert and Christopher Isett. 2002. "England's Divergence from China's Yangzi Delta: Property Relations, Microeconomics, and Patterns of Development," *Journal of Asian Studies* 61/2: 609–662.

Chaudhuri, K.N. 1985. *Trade and Civilization in the Indian Ocean: An Economic History from the Rise of Islam to 1750*. Cambridge: Cambridge University Press.

Chaudhuri, K.N. 1990. *Asia Before Europe: Economy and Civilization of the Indian Ocean from the Rise of Islam to 1750*. Cambridge: Cambridge University Press.

Christian, David. 2004. *Maps of Time: An Introduction to Big History*. Berkeley, CA: University of California Press.

Crosby, Alfred. 1986. *Ecological Imperialism: The Biological Expansion of Europe, 900–1900*. Cambridge: Cambridge University Press.

Crosby, Alfred. 2003. *The Columbian Exchange: Biological and Cultural Consequences of 1492*, 30th anniversary edition. New York: Praeger.

Elvin, Mark. 1973. *The Pattern of the Chinese Past*. Stanford, CA: Stanford University Press.

Flynn, Dennis. 1995. "Arbitrage, China, and World Trade in the Early Modern Period," *Journal of the Economic and Social History of the Orient* 38/4: 429–448.

Flynn, Dennis and Arturo Giraldez. 1996. "China and the Spanish Empire," *Revista de Historia Economica* 14/2: 309–338.

Goody, Jack. 2004. *Capitalism and Modernity: The Great Debate*. Cambridge: Polity.

Hoffmann, Philip. 2012. "Why Was It Europeans Who Conquered the World?," *The Journal of Economic History* 72/3: 601–633.

Huang, Philip. 2002. "Development or Involution in Eighteenth Century Britain and China?" *Journal of Asian Studies* 61/2: 501–538.

Jones, Eric. 1981. *The European Miracle: Environments, Economies, and Geopolitics in the History of Europe and Asia*. Cambridge: Cambridge University Press.

Kindleberger, Charles. 1990. "Spenders and Hoarders," in Charles Kindleberger, ed. *Historical Economics: Art or Science*. Berkeley, CA: University of California Press, pp. 35–85.

Kriedte, Peter, Hans Medick, and Jurgen Schlumbohm. 1981. *Industrialization Before Industrialization*. Cambridge: Cambridge University Press.

Levine, David. 1977. *Family Formation in an Age of Nascent Capitalism*. New York: Academic Press.

Li Bozhong and Jan Luiten van Zanden. 2012. "Before the Great Divergence: Comparing the Yangzi Delta and the Netherlands at the Beginning of the Nineteenth Century," *Journal of Economic History* 72/4: 956–989.

Mokyr, Joel. 1988. "Is There Life in the Pessimist Case? Consumption during the Industrial Revolution, 1790–1850," *Journal of Economic History* 48/1: 69–92.

Mokyr, Joel. 2002. *The Gifts of Athena: Historical Origins of the Knowledge Economy*. Princeton, NJ: Princeton University Press.

Mokyr, Joel. 2010. *The Enlightened Economy: An Economic History of Britain, 1700–1850*. New Haven, CT: Yale University Press.

Morris, Ian. 2010. *Why the West Rules – For Now. The Patterns of History and What They Reveal About the Future*. New York: Farrar, Strauss & Giroux.

O'Brien, Patrick K. 1982. "European Economic Development: The Contribution of the Periphery," *Economic History Review* 35/1: 1–18.

Phelps-Brown Henry, and Sheila V. Hopkins. 1981. *A Perspective of Wages and Prices*. London: Methuen.

Pomeranz, Kenneth. 1993. *The Making of a Hinterland: State, Society, and Economy in Inland North China, 1853–1937*. Berkeley, CA: University of California Press.

Pomeranz, Kenneth. 2000. *The Great Divergence: China, Europe, and the Making of the Modern World Economy*. Princeton, NJ: Princeton University Press.

Pomeranz, Kenneth. 2002. "Beyond the East–West Binary: Resituating Development Paths in the Eighteenth Century World," *Journal of Asian Studies* 61/2: 539–590.

Pomeranz, Kenneth. 2010. "Préface a l'édition française," in Kenneth Pomeranz, ed. *Une grande divergence* (trans. Nora Wang). Paris: Albin Michel, pp. 7–30.

Pomeranz, Kenneth. 2011a. "Ten Years After: Responses and Reconsiderations," response to a forum on the 10th anniversary of the publication of *The Great Divergence, Historically Speaking* 12/4: 20–25.

Pomeranz, Kenneth. 2011b. "How Big Should Historians Think? A Review Essay on Ian Morris' *Why the West Rules – for Now*," *Cliodynamics* 2/2: 304–329.

Pomeranz, Kenneth. 2012. "Repenser le changement économique de longue durée : la Chine, l'Europe, et l'historie comparée, in Jean Claude Daumas, ed. *L'histoire économique en mouvement: entre héritages et renouvellements*. Villieneuve d'Ascq: Presses universitaires du Septentrion, pp. 293–310.

Pomeranz, Kenneth. 2013. "Getting Right with Mr. Epstein," *Perspectives* 51/4 (April, 2013).

Pomeranz, Kenneth, and Daniel Segal. 2012. "World History: Departure and Variations," in Douglas Northrup, ed. *A Companion to World History*. Chichester: Wiley-Blackwell, pp. 15–31.

Richards, John. 2003. *The Unending Frontier: An Environmental History of the Early Modern World*. Berkeley, CA: University of California Press.

Rosenthal, Jean-Laurent, and R. Bin Wong. 2011. *Before and Beyond Divergence: The Politics of Economic Change in China and Europe*. Cambridge, MA: Harvard University Press.

Scheidel, Walter. 2007. "From the 'Great Convergence' to the 'First Great Divergence': Roman and Qin-Han State Formation and its Aftermath," *Princeton/Stanford Working Papers in Classics*, November, 2007.

Skinner, William G. 1964–65. "Marketing and Social Structure in Rural China," parts 1–3. *Journal of Asian Studies* 24/1 (November, 1964): 3–44; 24/2 (February, 1965): 195–228; 24/3 (May, 1965): 363–399.

Skinner, William G. 1971. "Chinese Peasants and the Closed Community: An Open and Shut Case," *Comparative Studies in Society and History* 13/3: 270–281.

Skinner, William G. 1977a. "Regional Urbanization in Nineteenth Century China," in G. William Skinner, ed. *The City in Late Imperial China*. Stanford, CA: Stanford University Press, pp. 211–249.

Skinner, William G. 1977b. "Cities and the Hierarchy of Local Systems," in G. William Skinner, ed. *The City in Late Imperial China*, Stanford, CA: Stanford University Press, pp. 275–351.

Streets-Salter, Heather. 2012. "Becoming a World Historian: The State of Graduate Training in World History and Placement in the Academic World," in Douglas Northrup, ed. *A Companion to World History*. Chichester: Wiley Blackwell, pp. 45–62.

Sanjay Subrahmanyam. 1990. *The Political Economy of Commerce: South India, 1500–1650*. Cambridge: Cambridge University Press.

Sanjay Subrahmanyam. 1993. *The Portuguese Empire in Asia, 1500–1700*. London: Longman.

Sugihara, Kaoru. 2003. "The East Asian Path of Economic Development: A Long-term Perspective," in Giovanni Arrighi, Takeshi Hamashita, and Mark Selden, eds. *The Resurgence of East Asia: 500, 150 and 50 Year Perspectives*. London: Routledge, pp. 78–123.

Tilly, Charles. 1972. "How Protest Modernized in France," in Wiliam Aydelotte, Allan Bogue, and Robert Fogel, eds. *The Dimensions of Quantitative Research in History*. Princeton, NJ: Princeton University Press, pp. 192–255.

Tilly, Charles. 1975. "Food Supply and Public Order in Modern Europe," in Charles Tilly, ed. *The Formation of National States in Western Europe*. Princeton, NJ: Princeton University Press, pp. 380–455.

Tilly, Charles. 1979. "Did the Cake of Custom Break?" in John Merriman, ed. *Consciousness and Class Experience in Nineteenth Century Europe*. New York: Holmes and Meier, pp. 17–44.

Tilly, Charles. 1985. "Retrieving European Lives," in Olivier Zunz, eds. *Reliving the Past: The Worlds of Social History*. Chapel Hill, NC: University of North Carolina Press, pp. 11–52.

Tilly, Charles. 1990. *Coercion, Capital, and European States, AD 990–1990*. London: Basil Blackwell.

Tilly, Charles, Louise Tilly and Richard Tilly. 1985. *The Rebellious Century*. Cambridge, MA: Harvard University Press.

Topik, Steven and Kenneth Pomeranz. *The World that Trade Created: Society, Culture and the World Economy, 1400 to the Present*. Armonk: M.E. Sharpe. 1997.

Van Zanden, Jan Luiten. 2009. "The Skill Premium and the 'Great Divergence'," *European Review of Economic History* 13/1: 121–153.

Von Glahn, Richard. 1996. *Fountain of Fortune: Money and Monetary Policy in China, 1000–1700*. Berkeley, CA: University of California Press.

Wallerstein, Immanuel. 1974. *Capitalist Agriculture and the Origins of the European World Economy*. New York: Academic Press.

Williams, Eric. 1944. *Capitalism and Slavery*. New York: Russell and Russell.

Wrigley, E. Anthony. 1988. *Continuity, Chance, and Change: The Character of the Industrial Revolution in England*. Cambridge: Cambridge University Press.

5

Cultural and Religious Exchanges

Dominic Sachsenmaier

Relating Chinese and European History to Each Other

During the early 1990s, when I entered the University of Freiburg/ Germany as a freshman, the history curriculum was basically a European one. The same had been true for my high school education, so the idea of exploring worldwide connections and global entanglements seemed to me a rather remote possibility, a dream that future historians eventually might be able to pursue. No one had ever pointed me to the rich and fascinating landscapes of world historical research that at that time were already well established in several countries. Certainly, I was well aware of the area studies such as sinology or indology, but it seemed very hard to bridge the gaps between these fields and European history.

In high school, I had acquired a rather solid educational background in European history. Moreover, I had studied English, French,

Architects of World History: Researching the Global Past, First Edition.
Edited by Kenneth R. Curtis and Jerry H. Bentley.

and Latin to quite advanced levels, which allowed me to read original texts in all three languages. During my first 2 years in college, I continued along those lines, taking medieval history as a major with the classics as one of my minors. But deep inside me there was a growing desire to widen my knowledge about other parts of the world and explore the connections between them. I felt that this would open many important and exciting intellectual opportunities, particularly in a period when intellectuals and politicians started ruminating about the age of "globalization," even though this term was often used in rather stereotyped ways.

Searching for wider intellectual horizons, I started auditing lectures in area studies and related fields such as cross-cultural religious studies or comparative politics. At the same time, I was looking out for new chances to gain more expertise in East Asia, which as a world region and historical realm had long fascinated me. I was fortunate enough to receive a fellowship from the German National Academic Foundation that allowed me to spend a year at the Mandarin Training Center at Shi-Ta University in Taipei. After 1 year of intensive language instruction, I reached an intermediate level of modern Mandarin, and I also started learning classical Chinese. At the same time, I gained many fascinating insights into key social, political, cultural, and other facets of the Chinese world. Reading intensely about China's global connections in the past and the present, I grew even more convinced that if I were to become a historian, my own area of expertise would need to transgress the boundaries of European history or area studies.

Given my new exposure to different parts of the world, it no longer seemed promising to continue studying medieval and ancient history after my return to Germany. This was particularly the case since as research fields they were even more limited to the European experience than the historiography of the modern period. Hence, I changed my major to modern history and chose sinology as my first minor. This meant that I could continue my language training in modern and classical Chinese while at the same time widening my knowledge base of both European and Chinese history.

Within the scope of my new major, I was particularly attracted to early modern history – a field that was more open to the study of global connections and in which nevertheless my previous background in medieval history and Latin still mattered. I was quite fortunate that early modern history was quite well represented in Freiburg and that Wolfgang Reinhard had joined the faculty just a few years earlier. Reinhard had a very strong reputation in European history with areas of research ranging from the early modern papacy to the history of ideas. At the same time, however, he was actually one of the very few German historians who were actively engaged in world historical scholarship. For example, his four-volume history of European expansions from antiquity to the twentieth century was, in the German context, commonly regarded as an unparalleled work covering all world regions while drawing on literature in several Western languages (Reinhard, 1983–1990).

In this and other works, Reinhard went against the stereotyped notion that European history could be largely understood as a process *sui generis*. Rather, he emphasized the wealth of transcultural entanglements and reverse influences that were underlying central facets of the so-called "rise of Europe." In a related step, Reinhard was quite critical of historical narratives that ascribed global historical agency solely to Western powers. Going against academic currents that were still rather strong during the mid-1990s, he emphasized that even colonial encounters needed to be seen as mutually conditioned forms of contact. Consequently, he argued, modern colonialism and imperialism should not be investigated solely from the perspectives of Western agents. Rather, one needed to take their counterparts in other parts of the world equally into account – which meant that it was necessary to study the historical backgrounds of other world regions with due diligence.

All these ideas resonated not only with my personal interests but also, increasingly, with my own educational background. I was hence glad that Wolfgang Reinhard accepted me as his doctoral student and that the German National Academic Foundation decided to award me with a 3-year stipend. Still, it seemed quite a challenge to find my exact research theme since I was just not sufficiently familiar with the most recent world historical scholarship as being able to readily identify a promising project. I knew that I wanted to work on Sino–European interactions during the early modern period – a field I felt passionate about. Furthermore, I was eager to explore such contacts primarily from the Chinese side, which I was also linguistically well equipped to do. In addition, I realized that my main areas of interest were less social and economic history but first and foremost intellectual and religious history.

Seventeenth-Century Chinese Christians and Their Global Contexts

Out of many possibilities, it was particularly the history of Jesuit missionaries and Chinese converts during the seventeenth and eighteenth centuries that drew my attention. I certainly was eager to better understand the various facets of this contact between learned individuals from China and Europe. After all, here Chinese and European, intellectual and religious history obviously overlapped with one another in multifarious ways, which triggered many fascinating encounters. For example, there were the sophisticated treatises through which Jesuits and Chinese Christians sought to merge Confucianism and Catholicism into an overarching framework – that later came to be referred to as the "accommodation method." There was also the staunch opposition of Jesuit missionaries to Buddhism and other facets of China's religious landscapes in which syncretism between different faith systems was rather common. Fascinating also were the perceptions of the Jesuits by their Chinese allies and foes, which particularly in the late Ming dynasty (1368–1644) generated a rather vivid body of intellectual debates as well as publications. It was also captivating to read about topics like the huge pressures the Jesuits had to face in Europe for aspects of their accommodation policy such as, for instance, their acceptance of certain Chinese rites like ancestor worship. They did not interpret as a pagan rite but rather as a legitimate way of honoring father and mother. Obviously the effort of weaving Christianity into the cultural fabrics of China posed not only many intellectual and linguistic challenges but also political ones. And it did so from both sides of the Sino–European encounter.

In my voyages through the scholarly literature surrounding topics of this nature, I became quite aware of some significant methodological changes this field of research had experienced during the previous one or two decades. Many of them were in line with the new world historical approaches and changes within the disciplinary cultures of historiography. It struck me that for a long time the study of Christianity in China had been dominated by Eurocentric or Christianity-centered approaches. For example, I was amazed that up until the 1960s a rather high proportion of rather influential academic publications had been openly based on the belief in Christianity as the only universal faith (e.g., Bettray, 1955).

Two or three decades later, the research landscape had changed, but quite a number of publications were still written from a very Jesuit-centered perspective and tended to portray China as a mere stage for their actions. There was still a clear tendency to overestimate the Jesuits' role in adapting Christianity to China's overall cultural, political, and social contexts. For example, many authors depicted Matteo Ricci (d. 1609) not only as the founder of the Jesuit mission in China but also as the main creator of the erudite philosophical and philological ruminations that mainly referred to the Confucian classics and constituted the basis of the accommodation method in China. Likewise, Ricci was also most frequently portrayed as the sole author of the *The True Meaning of the Lord of Heaven* (*Tianzhu shiyi*), a monograph that was published under his name in late Ming China (introduction to Ricci *et al.*, 1986).

Yet changes in the study of early modern Chinese Christianity were apparent, and many of them were related to the fact that previously marginal academic disciplines now became more important to the field. In many regards, it is adequate to state that around the 1980s or 1990s the center of research activities on Chinese Christianity shifted from theology to sinology (Mungello, 1999; Standaert, 2000). This meant that the academic community in Europe and the United States now paid far more attention to source materials in Chinese, which could range from pro-Christian books to anti-Christian pamphlets and from prayer manuals to scientific publications. Compared to many earlier historians in the field, most sinologists operated with a far more complex vision of China's social, political, religious, and scholarly patterns during the seventeenth century. Scholars like Erik Zürcher, Nicolas Standaert, and David Mungello started pointing to the wealth of highly disparate – and at times also rival – intellectual schools, religious movements, and political groupings during the late Ming dynasty (Zürcher, 1990; Mungello, 1994; Standaert and Yang, 1998). At the same time, a growing literature assessed more detailed facets of the religious and scholarly landscapes of Europe during that same period. Both efforts combined meant that many scholars were less inclined to investigate Sino–European relations as contacts between representatives of Chinese and European "civilizations" as monolithic cultural systems. Rather, the field grew more open to the idea of identifying particular networks of agents whose value systems, fears, and ambitions were compatible with the Jesuits' agenda without, however, ever becoming the same. A renowned exception was the French sinologist Jacques Gernet who in his research on Chinese critics of Christianity argued that Chinese culture was too incompatible with Christianity as to be possibly understood and appreciated by local literates (Gernet, 1985).

Nevertheless, the general shift away from thinking about Europe and China as monadic cultural systems was also related with efforts to rethink Jesuit agency during the late Ming dynasty, the time when the main conceptual pillars of the Confucian–Christian synthesis (i.e., the so-called "accommodation method") were being erected (Standaert, 1999). An increasing number of scholars grew convinced that important missionaries like Matteo Ricci or Giulio Aleni certainly mastered Chinese very well but could not possibly have reached a degree of proficiency necessary to compose books in such elegant Ming prose as the ones that appeared on the Chinese market under their names. Furthermore, one can safely assume that even after several decades in China, no European missionary would be able to singlehandedly construct the erudite references and fine allusions to the Confucian classics that characterized the bulk of pro-Christian texts published under Jesuit names.

As an alternative to the idea of European missionaries as the main shapers of seventeenth-century Christianity in China, a good number of scholars now began to conceptualize the accommodation method as the result of a joint effort between Jesuits and sympathetic Chinese scholars. This change of perspective also implied that it was necessary to pay great attention to the wealth of Late Ming concepts and schools that fed into the Confucian–Christian synthesis. Many elements of the latter, it turned out, were actually heavily influenced by contemporary Chinese currents.

This shift meant that the field now became more interested in different groups and types of Chinese Christianity. Scholars during the earlier period had been mainly attentive to the most upper echelons of Chinese Christianity, most notably the handful of individuals like Xu Guangqi or Li Zhizao who in the Chinese examination system had gained the highest degree (*jinshi*) and served as scholar-officials at the imperial level. However, the mere fact that by the 1640s Jesuit missionaries counted about 200,000 converts in China suggests that the vast majority of Christian life in China was far removed from the elite circles on which historical scholarship had focused thus far. In the less-privileged social layers, syncretism with Chinese popular religions played a major role, and so did belief in the power of magic, spells, and charms. In many cases, Christian sculptures, symbols, and elements of faith were merged with Buddhist and Taoist practices – which the small number of Jesuit missionaries in China could not accept but also could not control. The growing interest of recent scholarship in these complex worlds of faith implied conceptualizing Chinese converts as cocreators of new forms of Christianity that unfolded their own momentum (Zürcher *et al.*, 2007; Menegon, 2010).

I was greatly attracted to these new areas of research and at the same time slightly befuddled by the vast number of opportunities that the study of early modern Chinese Christianity apparently had to offer. For my own research project, I developed some rather vague ideas for possible directions; at the same time, I was quite aware of the fact that I still lacked an adequate overview of the relevant literature. Searching for a promising project, I thus contacted some leading scholars in the field, describing my plans and ambitions. I received several very kind and encouraging responses, but it was particularly a letter by David Mungello (Baylor University) that pointed me into a direction that I would follow for the years to come. He mentioned that while doing research for his own book *The Forgotten Christians of Hangzhou* he frequently encountered the name of a Christian convert, Zhu Zongyuan, who lived during the Ming-Qing transition period, that is, in the mid-seventeenth century. Zhu certainly belonged to the wealthier classes of his home town, the port city of Ningbo in Zhejiang province, but since he did not hold the highest official degree and mainly remained in his native region, his career was certainly not comparable to the upper crust of Chinese Christian circles during the late Ming period. In that sense, Zhu's writings promised great insight into segments of Chinese Christians that research still had not sufficiently illuminated and understood.

Yet there was a challenge: as David Mungello told me, Zhu's writings were probably scattered across various archives throughout the world and hard to get – for example, the significant collections of the former Jesuit Xujiahui library in Shanghai were still closed during the mid-1990s. One hope was the Bibliothèque nationale in Paris, which also held the collections of France's former royal library. Since during the seventeenth and eighteenth centuries many French kings systematically collected literature about other parts of the world and were also heavily involved in the China mission, there was at least a realistic chance that the library's collections would also contain Zhu's writings. My heart sank when in the old cart catalog for "oriental texts and manuscripts" there was not a single entry for Zhu Zongyuan. However, these cards were hand-written and may well have dated back to the early modern period when French librarians most probably did not have a strong command of Chinese. I thus checked under a different Chinese character, which is pronounced "wei" (未) and looks slightly similar to the Chinese last name "Zhu (朱)." And indeed, under "Wei Zongyuan," I found all the main works of Zhu

Zongyuan, most notably two books and two long essays, written in classical Chinese and first printed during the late Ming period. It is hard to describe the enthusiasm of a young doctoral student who had finally secured his main source materials and found a viable project – an enthusiasm that needed to be kept rather restrained due to the busy silence within the old walls of the Bibliothèque Nationale. That building itself dated back to the days of Richelieu who in turn was a contemporary of Zhu Zongyuan.

I managed to have these texts copied, and a first glance seemed to confirm my initial hypothesis that Zhu Zongyuan's works would indeed open up windows to various aspects of Christianity in late Ming China. On the one hand, Zhu wrote in a highly learned manner about themes ranging from science to the compatibility of Christian and classical Confucian concepts. On the other hand, his texts also reveal a belief in the miraculous power of Christian symbols or the healing force of substances such as the soil that allegedly had been scraped off the grounds of Mount Golgotha. On all these levels, Zhu not only connected with his local community but also with many European missionaries whose religious thought and practice was more far more diversified than it is often assumed. For example, while Jesuits figured as scientists and scholars conversing with Chinese elite circles, they also conducted exorcisms among the common populace.

From the beginning of my work on this project, I was resolved to attempt at more than a close reading and contextualization of Zhu Zongyuan's works. I definitely was less interested in situating Zhu's thought primarily within a Christian context. After all, this would have almost unavoidably implied the question if and in what regards his faith and value systems deviated from an ill-defined "European" spectrum of religiosity. Quite to the contrary, I was primarily drawn to the question of how Zhu Zongyuan's decidedly Christian works fit into the cultural, religious, and social landscapes of Late Ming China. Such a methodological step would shift my main emphasis away from a concern about Christian "originals" to the intellectual and even political interventions Zhu Zongyuan wanted to make in his own society.

Choosing a concrete analytical perspective, I decided to primarily investigate how contemporary Ming readers might have understood Zhu Zongyuan's texts. For this purpose, it was necessary to consider a wide range of discourses, prominent concepts and issues of contention in Chinese society during the Ming-Qing transition period. I was quite aware that I would need to consult a rather wide range of primary sources and secondary literature in several languages, and that the collections at the University of Freiburg did not suffice for my project. Hence, I decided to spend one semester at the University of Nanjing, where I worked closely with Professor Deng Rui. For the following 2 years, I had the opportunity to do research at the Harvard-Yenching Institute, where I could not only draw on excellent library collections but also on the expertise of scholars like Tu Wei-ming and Peter Bol. Moreover, I traveled to Leiden in the Netherlands and Leuven in Belgium and used these universities' substantial collections in the field of early modern Chinese Christianity. In Leuven, I got to know Nicolas Standaert, a leading figure in my field of study. For the years to come, I had the privilege of having him serve as my second adviser and commentator on all my chapters.

In my research for my doctoral dissertation, which lasted for about three and a half years, I applied a combination of semantic and historical perspectives in order to investigate the ways in which Zhu presented various European religious elements and philosophical concepts to the Chinese reader. In this context, I also considered various controversial issues and tensions that ended up shaping the translation of Christianity from one cultural context into another. Partly following other scholars, I argued that the overall framework of accommodating Confucianism with Christianity could pose significant sociopolitical challenges. Since the Jesuit approach in China faced significant opposition from other Catholic circles in Europe, the missionaries needed to particularly emphasize the purely secular character of this Chinese teaching. They interpreted ancient Confucianism as a philosophy that, like ancient Greek thought, had remained secular and hence was compatible with the revelation of God. Yet they also believed that Confucianism had in the meantime been infiltrated by Buddhism and other religious elements, which is why had lost its original ethos and needed to be freed from these later additions.

In principle, this resonated with the growing number of Chinese schools blaming the crisis of the Late Ming on strong Buddhist and other spiritual influences on a supposedly pristine Confucian tradition. Yet at the same time, the Christian association with Confucian "purist" movements weakened its potential support base. After all, not unlike Buddhist scholars with syncretic inclinations, many Christians also claimed to enrich the Confucian teaching by connecting it with their own religious system. In that sense, they violated the principles of their potential allies: *Confucian "purists"* who also professed to fight Buddhism in order to return Confucianism to its ancient glory.

As can be seen from these examples, I analyzed Zhu Zongyuan's writings primarily from within their late Ming contexts while at the same time showing that these texts were nevertheless related with Europe's intellectual, political, and philosophical landscape, which had its own struggles and patterns of control. From a similar angle, I also sketched Zhu Zongyuan's biography by situating his rather local life within a variety of overlapping contexts. This was only possible after a detective's work of putting together single pieces of information scattered across a wide range of Western and Chinese sources.

About 2 years after my thesis defense, a revised version of my dissertation was published in German as a monograph (Sachsenmaier, 2001). I am presently working on an English version of this book, which will also consider some of the latest research in the study of Chinese Christianity, as well as surrounding areas of inquiry. However, the book also reflects my changing horizons as a historian in the sense that it situates Zhu Zongyuan – his thinking, writing, and his zones of interaction – even more immediately within transregional and world historical contexts. For instance, I draw on new studies trying to situate seventeenth-century China within world historical frameworks (e.g., Waley-Cohen, 1999; Struve, 2004). Moreover, I provide an overview of the growing and diversifying literature assessing Eurasian contacts and entanglements during the early modern period. This can range from the debates surrounding the idea of Eurasia-wide early modern formations (Lieberman,

1997; Flynn and Giraldez, 2002; Darwin, 2008) to studies suggesting parallel political, social, and cultural centralization processes in Europe and (South-)East Asia during that same era (Lieberman, 2003–2004; Woodside, 2006). Furthermore, I draw on publications seeking to contextualize the global and local interactions underlying early modern global networks like the Jesuits (e.g., Alden, 1996; Brockey, 2007; Worcester, 2008) or other religious webs. For instance, during the same time period not only Christianity went through a period of enormous geographical expansion but also other religions: particularly Islam and, to a lesser extent, Buddhism. In many regards, the experience of a finite world and the challenge of negotiating cultural differences heavily impacted many religions and cultures during the early modern period (Subrahmanyam, 1998). In that sense, the Jesuit mission in China was only a small part of a global trend which in its scopes was much wider than the growing European presence in different parts of the world.

All these added contexts will further accentuate my main idea of assessing Zhu Zongyuan as a rather common member of the Ningbo elite who in his daily life and thinking was locally rooted yet at the same time globally connected. In my eyes, investigating individuals like him thus certainly means making a contribution to the field of world history at large. Studies of this kind can contribute to refining and decentering our understanding of global nexuses and transregional interactions during the early modern period.

Global History, Globally or World History as a Worldwide Endeavor

My current work on Zhu Zongyuan means actually a return to early modern history after about a decade-long hiatus. After the publication of my first book, I grew increasingly interested in the history of more recent global connections and interactions. After a brief venture into the business world, I returned to Harvard as a postdoctoral fellow in 2001. In Cambridge, Massachusetts, as well as in the entire Greater Boston Area, I attended many lectures and seminars on topics related to transnational, world, and global history. Especially during the late 1990s and early 2000s, there were frequent – at times ardent – debates on how to differentiate global history and world history from each other (e.g., Mazlish, 1998). However, in my eyes, the terms "world history" and "global history" do not connote monolithic areas of research but rather point to highly diversified landscapes of historical scholarship that each encompass a variety of subfields ranging from global economic history to global intellectual history. Since many scholars in the field tend to use both terms in a rather interchangeable way, I also do not draw a categorical distinction between them (Sachsenmaier, 2011, pp. 70–78).

In addition to coming into contact with many visiting scholars and lecturers from all over the world, I drew much inspiration from historians like Bruce Mazlish, longtime editor of *History and Theory*, and Akira Iriye who was the first Japanese citizen to ever become president of the *American Historical Association*. I learned much about new theories and topics in contemporary history where the debates on themes such as Eurocentrism or decentering our global visions were clearly more politically relevant and at times more emotionally charged than in the field of early modern history. In my own research, I first ventured into a variety of directions – for example, I initiated an international research project on the concept of "multiple modernities," which involved scholars from different disciplines like the historical sociologist Shmuel Eisenstadt, the economist Gordon Redding, and the China-historian Frederic Wakeman (Sachsenmaier, Riedel, and Eisenstadt, 2002).

Together with Sebastian Conrad, a global historian at the Free University of Berlin, I set up a trans-Atlantic research network exploring globally circulating visions of world order during the period between the 1880s and the 1930s. Here nine young European and American scholars with different regional expertise met five times over a 3-year period. Our goal was to produce a joint book publication whose single chapters would be methodologically and thematically more intertwined with one another than in the case of most edited volumes (Conrad and Sachsenmaier, 2007). Working toward this objective, our group engaged in many lively and thought-provoking methodological debates across field-specific boundaries. To all of us the relative lack of communication between geographically defined research areas became more obvious. Different academic communities like East Asianists and South Asianists apparently tended to conceptualize clearly related phenomena in modern history from rather different angles.

Yet at the same time, it was obvious that conceptual differences between single scholarly communities in the West were not the only divisions within the environments of transnational and world historical scholarship. As every single conference that I attended outside of the United States reminded me, historians in different world regions tended to approach global historical issues in rather different ways. For instance, in many Chinese books, research papers and theoretical contributions, the pair of concepts "modernity" and "modernization" was used as a way of describing important processes ranging from industrialization to the emergence of consumerism. By contrast, in the United States, a strong majority of historians had actually come to shun the notion of "modernization" as a tool to analyze changes at both a national and a transnational level.

It seemed hardly surprising to me that particularly in the socially and ethnically pluralizing landscapes of US universities, concepts such as "modernity" and "modernization" had come under strong attack in many academic disciplines. After all, the concept of "modernity" had long been related to world historical visions that identified the West as a civilization of uniquely global significance. Particularly from the 1970s, the intellectual wings of the civil rights movement and other academic developments such as the growing influence of postmodern thinking or the rising presence of postcolonial approaches, the cultures of US historiography were changing profoundly. In the field of world history, a mounting number of scholars were challenging hitherto prominent master narratives that in one way or another had defined the West as the center of world historical interactions (Sachsenmaier, 2011). As part of growing efforts to let the subaltern, the marginal speak in world history, also concepts such as "modernity" became the subjects of intellectual critique and scrutiny. The hegemonic connotations of such terms seemed to stand squarely against efforts to decenter world historical narratives and make them more inclusive. So within the American academic community there were certainly important reasons for abandoning the conceptual frameworks developed by such prominent theorists as Talcott Parsons or Walt Whitman Rostow. In their eyes, the concept of "modernization" was tied to a teleological understanding of history as a developing process that was spearheaded by the West (Latham, 2003).

At the same time, there were reasons why historians in China were much more ready to operate with the concept of "modernization" – despite the fact that they were well informed and influenced by many currents from the United States, including the postcolonial and subaltern studies schools (Xu and Chen, 1995; Sachsenmaier, 2007a; Wang, 2009). Yet in my view, these differences between the ways in which the majority of US-American and Chinese historians operated with the concept of "modernization" were less rooted in a lack of transnational academic contacts but more closely related to divergent sociopolitical contexts. In particular, the generational experiences of historians in both parts of the world were an important factor to be reckoned with. To put it in a nutshell, the personal stories of many Chinese scholars during the past 30 years were not too far apart from living through processes that some renowned modernization theorists had once described. Certainly, the picture of economic development in China since the 1980s has been rather uneven, and it certainly formed a pattern that was far too complex to sketch in a one-dimensional way. Yet for a significant number of people in cities such as Shanghai, Guangzhou, or Beijing, overall life circumstances had certainly changed from a preindustrial economy to a consumerist society. This particularly included the educated strata of society, including university professors and their wider families.

In addition, many intellectuals in China favored the term "modernization" for other reasons: this term was not only in line with the new official government rhetoric, which emphasized gradual reforms, but also opened up new possibilities of conceptualizing historical changes without having to resort to the revolutionary rhetoric of the Mao Period (1949–1976). In fact, in quite a number of Chinese historical accounts the term "modernization" was now used to connote more drawn-out, gradual historical transformations. In that sense, "modernization" became one of the more prominent concepts among those Chinese historians who questioned the alleged historical ruptures between imperial and twentieth-century China. Since a certain re-appreciation of the Chinese historical heritage is often an essential part of Chinese interpretations of "modernization," Chinese scholars certainly do not blindly follow modernization theory as it was being developed during the 1960s in the United States and some other Western countries (Xu, 1998; Schneider, 2001).

The concept of "modernization" and its usage among scholars in the United States and China was just one among many examples for the fascinating dissimilarities in world historical approaches in different parts of the world. Every time when I attended international conferences I was struck by such nuances and differences of world historical scholarship. Yet trying to come to terms with such local varieties in the sense of placing them in overlapping regional and global contexts posed significant methodological challenges. After all, it was obviously naïve and ill-informed to assume that the differences between Chinese, American, and other approaches to history were rooted in pristine and unbroken cultural traditions. As the example of the concept of "modernization" showed, it was certainly not the case that the vast majority of Chinese historians were primarily operating from within Confucian or other traditionalist parameters. In my eyes, the reasons for local specificities in world historical scholarship were related to an entire spectrum of factors ranging from institutional setups and funding structures to social conditions, forms of historical memory, and political constraints. Though it was hard to categorically deny the importance of particular intellectual and academic traditions anywhere in the world, these were obviously only a small part of miscellaneous local factors seasoning the ways in which communities of historians approached a variety of world historical topics.

Yet the picture grew even more complex when trying to define or even sketch the contours of such local historiographical cultures. After all, it seemed clear that historiographical cultures anywhere in the world were internally extremely diverse and hence could not be easily be sketched and put side by side. Moreover, in each society, different groups of scholars interacted with their colleagues in other parts of the world, and they did so in multifarious ways. And yet despite all entanglements of this kind, locally conditioned differences in key concepts, methodologies, and dominant narratives did clearly exist. The challenge was to compare Chinese, US-American, and other landscapes of global and world historical research while at the same time paying a due amount of attention to transnational academic connections.

For this purpose, it was necessary to consider the global academic landscapes framing the exchanges between world historians in different countries and regions. One added complexity was that these exchanges have not been arranged on the principles of a flat world; rather, they have long been decidedly hierarchical in nature. Local differences were not equal variations of global academic discourse, since on the global stage some voices spoke more loudly than others. For example, whereas Anglophone historians could rather easily afford to ignore scholarship produced in other languages, the equivalent was clearly not the case in other parts of the world. It was quite obvious that in many societies ranging from Chile to Japan, no historian was able to build a career in his or her field of study while not even considering the most relevant literature produce in the United States or Britain, either through translations or by reading relevant texts in English. On the other side, not many scholars in the West were paying attention to new world historical approaches emerging from the Chinese, Japanese, Arabic, or other academic systems. Actually, in many conversations with world historians I encountered echoes of such global hierarchies of knowledge. For example, even quite a few critical scholars in the United States and Germany evidently assumed that the differences between Western and Chinese approaches to world history were rooted in the fact that the latter were several decades "behind." Such an answer struck me more as part of the problem of international hierarchies of knowledge, and thus as an impediment to envisioning both deeper and broader forms of scholarly collaboration on a global level.

All this made me feel that many crucial questions surrounding the local, national, and regional differences within the field (as well as the hierarchies between them) had not yet been sufficiently accounted for. Certainly, the literature coming out of schools such as postcolonialism and subaltern studies had made important contributions to problematizing facets of Eurocentrismin the field of historiography (Majumdar, 2010), and in that sense it had also influenced my own thinking. In addition, some world historians produced a number of important edited volumes assessing the status quo of their field, with some chapters providing an account of activities in particular societies or world regions (e.g., Manning, 2008; now also Northrop, 2012). While I benefited tremendously from publications of this kind, these volumes typically did not tackle the multifarious problems surrounding the apparent inequalities between different languages and academic systems.

Trying to assess the landscapes of current global and world historical scholarship with a particular eye on hierarchies of knowledge and locally specific patterns struck me as a both fascinating and challenging intellectual project. Most importantly, I felt it was more than timely for world historians to start debating questions of this kind more thoroughly and more extensively. After all, as a research field situated at the intersection of many academic communities and fields of inquiry, world history can potentially play a very important role in international and interdisciplinary dialogues. I grew convinced that our landscapes of historiography were actually not fully prepared to actualize all the intellectual and public possibilities of world history. As I pointed out in an article, it was not sufficient for global historians in the West to talk increasingly *about* the world; rather, it was necessary to find new and better ways of talking *with* the world *about* the world (Sachsenmaier, 2007b). In other words, I grew convinced that only if there were sustained efforts to break through the current global hierarchies of knowledge could global debates on topics such as the heritage of colonialism or Eurocentrism truly unfold their full potential. And only then could world historical scholarship hope to significantly contribute to forums and public spheres that – somewhat optimistically – might be viewed as facets of a global civil society in the offing.

During my time as an assistant professor of global history at the University of California, Santa Barbara, I grew increasingly attached to the idea of writing a monograph on this topic. Several years later, when I was working as an assistant professor of Chinese and transcultural history at Duke University, I completed my work on this book, *Global Perspectives on Global History. Theories and Approaches in a Connected World* (Sachsenmaier, 2011). From the very beginning, it was obvious to me that I would not be able to cover global historical scholarship all over the world equally and unequivocally. I thus decided to dedicate three long case studies to the scholarly communities I was most familiar with: Germany, the United States, and China. For my work on each chapter, I consulted a wide range of literature in these respective languages and interviewed a good number of scholars in each country. For each case, I tried to outline the development of research areas in a variety of academic disciplines that have proven relevant for the study of world history and related areas of research. I also addressed important changes in the overall sociopolitical environments that in my view certainly left an imprint in the contours of transnational and world historical scholarship. In this context, I dealt with themes such as, for instance, the impact of changing migration patterns on academic life in Germany and the United States or the debates on changing world orders in China.

Needless to say, it would have been possible to add many additional case studies to my analysis. However, my primary aim was not to provide an international historiographical overview of the field. Instead, my book is meant to contribute to opening a debate on the problems and potentials inherent in the current international and transnational academic structures in world history and adjacent areas of research. For this reason, I also chose national academic systems as the main, roughly defined units of my case studies. Certainly, it would have also been possible to focus on Anglophone, Francophone, and Sinophone publications that are being produced across a wide variety of political boundaries, academic communities, and economic systems. Yet I did not want to neglect the lasting influence of the nation state on historical scholarship. After all, not only public funding structures and foundation policies but also public debates (many of which still follow largely national parameters) continue to be a shaping force in the ways in which world historical scholarship unfolds.

While my book certainly pays due attention to the nation state as a force to be reckoned with when reflecting upon historiography in its current state, I also discuss several transregional and global aspects of historical scholarship. For instance, in a long chapter I examine the spread of historiography as a university-based field in different parts of the world. In addition to epistemological questions, I also view historiography from social historical perspectives in order to be able to assess more comprehensively a range of problems reaching from Eurocentrism to the aforementioned hierarchies in the global landscapes of the field. I conclude that more recent forms of global and world historical scholarship can make an important intervention, particularly by challenging conceptions of space that have long dominated academic historiography almost all over the globe. In many countries and world regions, much of historical scholarship has long been based on nation-centered visions of the past, and these were usually tied to rather Western-centric interpretations of global interactions.

In that sense I believe that world historical scholarship has already turned into an important forum for cross-disciplinary exchanges. For example, in the United States, the barriers between the historiography of Europe and the United States on the one side and the former area studies on the other side have become far more permeable than before, and in this rapprochement world history figured as an important meeting point. In China, many university departments and even school boards have started taking active steps toward lowering the institutional divides between Chinese history and world history. Here developments of this kind further encouraged new studies trying to view facets of Chinese history from transnational perspectives or seeking to rethink important world historical narratives by viewing them from East Asian angles.

Certainly, some of these currents are embedded within unabashedly nationalistic outlooks, but many historians are far more concerned to complexify their visions of China and the world, as well as the multifaceted interrelationships between the two.

Particularly in an age in which many political, cultural, and religious identities may again be drifting again into jingoistic and intolerant directions, world historical scholarship can contribute not only to academic research and education but can also make significant interventions within the wider public in many countries and world regions. If written and taught in an open-minded way, world history can help promote skills and values such as multiperspectivity, tolerance, and appreciation of otherness. Along those lines, it can also foster notions of joint responsibilities for a shared world. These goals can gain much significance if scholars increasingly work on actively changing the institutional and collaborative structures of their field. There are many reasons to assume that nowadays the field has come somewhat closer to a role envisioned by William McNeill during the 1980s (McNeill, 1986).

Still, the cultures of academic historiography are still very much based on solitary work which, moreover, primarily speaks to national or regional academic communities. Yet the traditions of disciplinary communication that are either explicitly or implicitly shared by many historians have definitely started to change. As an overall trend, this is partly related to transformations such as the revolution in communication technology as well as the greatly reduced fares (compared to a generation ago) for international travel. Transnational study programs, international conferences, and faculty exchange programs have been rising in number, which in turn had an impact on many local communities of world historians.

For this reason, I deeply respect the lifework of scholars like Jerry Bentley, who not only contributed much to shaping the intellectual contours of world historical scholarship but also to strengthening its transnational structures. Among many other activities, he was a key figure in founding the *Journal of World History* as well as in further developing the World History Association, both of which have grown into important enabling frameworks for transnational academic exchanges in the field. In my eyes, it is remarkable that the World History Association decided to hold one in three of its annual meetings on different continents, which in the past has already fostered much dialogue with scholars in East Asia, Africa, and other parts of the world.

Thus far, I also tried adding my own modest share to making the structures of world historical scholarship less hierarchical and more transnationally interactive. For example, together with Sven Beckert, I established a Harvard-Duke conference project entitled *Global History, Globally*. Here leading world and global historians from virtually all continents met four times in order to discuss the pathways, challenges, and opportunities of their field, both on a local and a global level. In this project, it again became apparent how important it is to consider the current global academic landscapes and hierarchies of knowledge when reflecting upon world historical issues.

Projects of this kind will certainly be an important part of my own professional activities in the future, in addition to my own research and writing. My own home base has now moved closer to where I had grown up: After having spent more than 10 years in the United States, I returned to Germany, where I accepted a professorship at Jacobs University in Bremen. Here I initiated a program that allows Chinese scholars in the humanities and social sciences to come to Germany as visiting professors. In addition to maintaining rather close ties with the US academic system, I am currently teaching as a recurrent visiting chair at Global History Center at Capital Normal University in Beijing. Like my own studies, my own professional life continues to move mainly between Germany, China, and the United States. On such rather interactive bases, I will hopefully be able to conduct much of my own work in the future.

Acknowledgment

Relevant research for this project was supported by an Academy of Korean Studies grant (AKS-2010-DZZ-3103).

References

Alden, Dauril. 1996. *The Making of an Enterprise: The Society of Jesus in Portugal, Its Empire, and Beyond, 1540–1750*. Stanford, CA: Stanford University Press.

Bettray, Johannes. 1955. *Die Akkommodationsmethode des P. Matteo Ricci S.J. in China*. Rome: Universitas Gregoriana.

Brockey, Liam M. 2007. *Journey to the East: The Jesuit Mission to China, 1579–1724*. Cambridge, MA: Belknap.

Conrad, Sebastian and Sachsenmaier, Dominic. 2007. *Competing Visions of World Order. Global Moments and Movements, 1880–1935*, Paperback edition 2012. New York: Palgrave.

Darwin, John. 2008. *After Tamerlane: The Global History of Empire Since 1405*. New York: Bloomsbury Press.

Flynn, Dennis and Arturo Giraldez. 2002. "Cycles of Silver: Global Economic Unity through the Mid-Eighteenth Century," *Journal of World History* 13/2: 391–427.

Gernet, Jacques. 1985. *China and the Christian Impact. A Conflict of Cultures*. Cambridge: Cambridge University Press.

Latham, David. 2003. *Mandarins of the Future: Modernization Theory in Cold War America*. Baltimore, MD: Johns Hopkins University Press.

Lieberman, Victor B., ed. 1997. *Beyond Binary Histories: Reimagining Eurasia to c. 1830*. Ann Arbor, MI: University of Michigan Press, pp. 289–315.

Lieberman, Victor B. 2003. *Strange Parallels: Southeast Asia in Global Context. c. 800–1830*, 2 vols. Cambridge: Cambridge University Press.

Majumdar, Rochona. 2010. *Writing Postcolonial History*. New York: Bloomsbury.

Manning, Patrick, ed. 2008. *Global Practice in World History: Advances Worldwide*. Princeton, NJ: Markus Wiener Publishers.

Mazlish, Bruce. 1998. "Comparing Global History to World History," *Journal of Interdisciplinary History* 28/3: 385–395.

McNeill, William. 1986. "Mythistory, or Truth, Myth, History, and Historians," *American Historical Review* 91/1: 1–10.

Menegon, Eugenio. 2010. *Ancestors, Virgins, and Friars. Christianity as a Local Religion in Late Imperial China*. Cambridge, MA: Harvard University Press.

Mungello, David E. 1994. *The Forgotten Christians of Hangzhou*. Honolulu, HI: University of Hawaii Press.

Mungello, David. 1999. *The Great Encounter of China and the West 1550–1800*. Lanham, MD: Rowman & Littlefield.

Northrop, Douglas. 2012. *A Companion to World History*. Hoboken, NJ: Wiley-Blackwell.

Reinhard, Wolfgang. 1983–1990. *Geschichte der europäischen Expansion*, 4 vols. Stuttgart: Kohlhammer.

Ricci, Matteo S., Douglas Lancashire, Kuo-chen Hu, and Edward Malatesta. 1986. *The True Meaning of the Lord of Heaven*. San Francisco, CA: Institute of Jesuit Sources.

Sachsenmaier, Dominic. 2001. Die Aufnahme europäischer Inhalte in die chinesische Kultur durch Zhu Zongyuan (ca. 1616–1660) [Zhu Zongyuan's Integration of Western Elements into Chinese Culture]. *Monumenta Serica Monograph Series*, Vol. 46. Nettetal: Steyler.

Sachsenmaier, Dominic. 2007a. "Debates on World History and Global History – The Neglected Parameters of Chinese Approaches," *Traverse. Zeitschrift für Geschichte – Revue d'histoire* 40/3: 67–84.

Sachsenmaier, Dominic. 2007b. "World History as Ecumenical History?," *Journal of World History* 18/4: 465–490.

Sachsenmaier, Dominic. 2011. *Global Perspectives on Global History. Theories and Approaches in a Connected World*. New York: Cambridge University Press.

Sachsenmaier, Dominic, Riedel, Jens, and Eisenstadt, Shmuel. 2002. *Reflections on Multiple Modernities: European, Chinese, and Other Approaches*. Leiden: Brill.

Schneider, Axel. 2001. "Bridging the Gap: Attempts at Constructing a 'New' Historical–Cultural Identity in the People's Republic of China." *East Asian History* 22: 129–143.

Standaert, Nicolas. 1999. "Jesuit Corporate Culture as Shaped by the Chinese," in John W. O'Malley, Gauvin Alexander Bailey, Steven J. Harris, and T. Frank Kennedy, eds. *The Jesuits: Cultures, Sciences, and The Arts, 1540–1773*. Toronto: University of Toronto Press, pp. 352–363.

Standaert, Nicolas. 2000. *Handbook of Christianity in China*, vol. 1. Leiden: Brill, pp. 635–1800.

Standaert, Nicolas and Yang, Tingyun. 1998. *Confucian and Christian in Late Ming China: His Life and Thought*. Leiden: Brill.

Struve, Lynn. 2004. *The Qing Formation in World-Historical Time*. Cambridge, MA: Harvard University Press.

Subrahmanyam, Sanjay. 1998. "Hearing Voices: Vignettes of Early Modernity in South Asia, 1400–1750," *Daedalus* 127/3: 99–100.

Waley-Cohen, Joanna. 1999. *The Sextants of Beijing: Global Currents in Chinese History*. New York: Norton.
Wang, Q. Edward, ed. 2009. "Modernization Theory in/of China." *Chinese Studies of History* 43/1: 3–7
Woodside, Alexander. 2006. *Lost Modernities: China, Vietnam, Korea, and the Hazards of World History*. Cambridge, MA: Harvard University Press.
Worcester, Thomas, ed. 2008. *The Cambridge Companion to the Jesuits*. Cambridge: Cambridge University Press.
Xu, Ben. 1998. "From Modernity to 'Chineseness': The Rise of Nativist Cultural Theory in Post-1989 China," *Positions* 6/1: 203–237.
Xu, Jilin, and Chen, Dakai. 1995. "Zhongguo xiandaihua de qidong leixing yu fanying xingzhi [The Initializing Patterns and Reacting Natures of Chinese Modernization]," in Jilin Xu and Chen Dakai, eds. *Zhongguo xiandaihua shi 1800–1949 [History of Modernization in China, 1800–1949]*. Shanghai: Sanlian shudian, pp. 1–5.
Zürcher, Erik. 1990. *Bouddhisme, Christianisme et société chinoise*. Paris: Julliard.
Zürcher, Erik, Jiubiao Li, and Richao Kouduo. 2007. *Li Jiubiao's Diary of Oral Admonitions: A Late Ming Christian Journal*. Nettetal: Steyler.

Further Reading

Appleby, Joyce O., Lynn Hunt, and Margaret C. Jacob. 1995. *Telling the Truth About History*. New York: W.W. Norton.
Bentley, Jerry H. 2005. "Myths, Wagers, and Some Moral Implications of World History," *Journal of World History* 16/1: 51–82.
Eisenstadt, Shmuel. 2005. *Comparative Civilizations and Multiple Modernities*. Leiden: Brill.
Iggers, Georg G., Wang, Edward Q., and Mukherjee, Supriya. 2008. *A Global History of Modern Historiography*. Harlow: Pearson Longman.
Manning, Patrick, ed. 2008. *Global Practice in World History: Advances Worldwide*. Princeton, NJ: Markus Wiener Publishers.
Mignolo, Walter D. 2000. *Global Histories/Local Designs: Coloniality, Subaltern Knowledges, and Border Thinking*. Princeton, NJ: Princeton University Press.
Mungello, David. 1999. *The Great Encounter of China and the West 1550–1800*. Lanham, MD: Rowman & Littlefield.

Northrop, Douglas. 2012. *A Companion to World History*. Hoboken, NJ: Wiley-Blackwell.

Sachsenmaier, Dominic. 2011. *Global Perspectives on Global History. Theories and Approaches in a Connected World*. New York: Cambridge University Press.

Standaert, Nicolas. 2000. *Handbook of Christianity in China*, vol. 1. Leiden: Brill, pp. 635–1800.

Subrahmanyam, Sanjay. 1998. "Hearing Voices: Vignettes of Early Modernity in South Asia, 1400–1750," *Daedalus* 127/3: 99–100.

Waley-Cohen, Joanna. 1999. *The Sextants of Beijing: Global Currents in Chinese History*. New York: Norton.

Wang, Q. Edward. 2003. "Encountering the World: China and Its Other(s) in Historical Narratives, 1949–89." *Journal of World History* 14/3: 327–358.

Woolf, Daniel R. 2011. *A Global History of History: The Making of Clio's Empire from Antiquity to the Present*. Cambridge: Cambridge University Press.

Xu, Luo. 2007. "Reconstructing World History in the People's Republic of China Since the 1980s." *Journal of World History* 18/3: 325–350.

6

Law and World History

Lauren Benton

Law is hardly an obvious subject for world historians. The study of law has mainly been framed by national histories, except for the history of international law, which until recently centered resolutely on Europe. Subjects such as colonial legal politics, transregional legal cultures, and the formation of global legal regimes have developed on the margins of legal history. The chronological and geographic limitations of the field made the marriage of law and world history a union both difficult and late.

Yet, despite such constraints, a field of global legal history is now taking shape at record speed. It draws strength from new studies of law in colonial settings and from attempts to craft new narratives of the formation of polities and relations among them. The move within world history to highlight both empires and small states, and to question the story of a smooth development of an international system of nation-states, has gained momentum. Older narratives about the evolution of international law have been challenged as

Architects of World History: Researching the Global Past, First Edition.
Edited by Kenneth R. Curtis and Jerry H. Bentley.

historians have uncovered and analyzed jurists' and political theorists' persistent preoccupation with divergent trends and phenomena, including divisible sovereignty, legal pluralism, and interimperial legalities. A world history of law that is more than a collection of national legal histories is now clearly in view.

How did we get here? The origins of the study of law and world history extend back in several different directions, to legal anthropology, comparative constitutional law, and the history of a broader set of "transnational" legal forces such as natural law, the *ius gentium*, religious law, and the legal regulation of trading companies and diasporas. In recent years, the goal of illuminating global patterns of law has become explicit, resulting in a boom in studies of colonial crime and punishment, conquest, imperial sovereignty, and the nature of authority in imperial and colonial states. Subthemes such as jurisdictional politics, imperial constitutionalism, and imperial internationalism compose rich perspectives for new studies linking legal cultures and local conflicts with institutional world history.

Rather than attempt a grand narrative of such developments, this essay tells the story of my own engagement with world history and law. In offering the metaphor of "architect," the editors of this volume generously label my efforts as the results of self-conscious acts of design and planning. The better metaphor is vernacular architecture, a collective practice in which accumulating knowledge develops ahead of individual insight and coherent planning. As the following account will show, my participation in the emerging field of world legal history was prompted, inspired, and enabled at every turn by the work and words of other scholars. The context for my intellectual choices transforms my own story into one that reflects and illustrates the development of the broader field.

Three insights or approaches stand at the center of much of my own work, and of the work by many of my colleagues writing about law and world history. This chapter in part follows the thread of these ideas through several decades of my own intellectual trajectory, illuminating one strand running through the field's untidy landscape. A first idea centers on the notion of jurisdictional politics, a concept that captures historical actors' strategies in relation to one or another legal authority. The analysis of jurisdictional politics has proven powerful in comparative and world history. Legal formations across the globe are jurisdictionally plural, and clusters of conflicts over jurisdictional boundaries have structured key institutional and political transformations. A second insight reflects the flexibility and wide-ranging influence of legal cultures. Grasping the fluidity of legal cultures opens new ways of understanding cross-cultural legal encounters. A third idea refers to the processes by which law and legal practices constructed regional and global continuities. The concept of a global (or regional) legal regime in which different kinds of polities recognize continuities in law neatly merges legal and world history. To some degree, all three insights are key to understanding the way attention to law has the potential to alter periodization in world history and to inform new narratives of legal ordering over large spaces and long spans of time. These themes have been central to my scholarship and to my own sense of the challenges and joys of writing global legal history.

Law and the History of Capitalism

As a rather self-absorbed and intellectually restless undergraduate in the mid-1970s, I took a year-long course in comparative economic history as a senior at Harvard. I used to call it the "talk show course" because it was taught by four professors, three of whom sat at a table on stage while a fourth lectured. David Landes, the historian of the industrial revolution, was one of the professors, and since at the time I considered myself a budding Marxist, I stirred fitfully during his long, dry lectures on the cultural advantages of Protestant Europeans in creating capitalist economies. Henry Rosovsky, an expert on the Japanese economy, seemed less triumphalist about the capitalist past, a sign of prescient restraint on his part since at the time the Japanese economy was being touted as an unadulterated capitalist success story and had yet to enter into its long phase of painfully slow growth. When he noticed me at all hovering in the back row, Rosovsky, too, had little patience for my occasional carping about the need for greater attention among historians to production, global capitalist crises, and the structural tendency to inequality in the world economy.

Inspiration comes from odd sources. After an especially frustrating exchange in class one day, I headed directly to Widener Library in search of another perspective. Surely someone, I thought, must be writing about the history of the global economy in a way that would follow Marxist precepts and place labor at the center of the analysis. I was not starting my search entirely from scratch. I had already come across formative studies of peasant revolutions by Eric Wolf (1969) and Jeffrey Paige (1975), and my love affair with the work of E.P. Thompson on the history of the English working class was well under way. I was also taking a course taught by William Lazonick, a maverick professor in the Economics Department who was writing about inequalities at the heart of business and shop-floor practices. I was looking specifically for a historical work that would highlight agrarian labor within a narrative of the growth of the capitalist world economy.

Flipping through the card catalogue in Widener – a now ancient practice – I came across an entry for the first and then only volume of Immanual Wallerstein's *The Modern World-System* (Wallerstein, 1974). The book, subtitled *Capitalist Agriculture and the Origins of the European World-Economy in the Sixteenth Century*, was miraculously in the stacks, and I cradled it eagerly back to my garret on Chauncey Street to read that night. Even with its mass of footnotes and inflated claims, I found the book oddly thrilling. To my undergraduate eyes, it opened a new vista, entirely different from the one I was learning about in the "talk show course." I was intrigued by Wallerstein's argument that three zones with different configurations of labor and state power encompassed a single "world-economy." I noticed with curiosity that the book left Asia out of this "global" formation, and it sidelined Africa – an especially peculiar choice for Wallerstein, a historical sociologist who had cut his teeth on African topics. But the book's ambitious thesis and its scope were irresistible. It was my first taste of world history.

Reading Wallerstein led me in two very different directions. As anyone who has even perused the book will remember, the notes are strewn with references to Fernand Braudel. Lured by Wallerstein's references to Braudel's claims about the geographic and cultural continuities that made the Mediterranean a unified region, I bought both volumes of Braudel's *The Mediterranean World in the Age of Phillip II* and put them aside, promising myself I would read them cover to cover – a pledge that I waited three more years to keep (Braudel, 1949). My *idée fixe* that agrarian labor held the key to economic history also led me to pick up a copy of Sidney Mintz's *Worker in the Cane* (1960). That book I read right away, in part also because I had Puerto Rico on my mind. I had recently spent a summer there, and I had briefly visited the sugar region in the south and the coffee lands of the central region. The visit had not been a very extensive or deep introduction to the Caribbean, but it was enough to make me want to know more about the history of sugar, and its place in the economic and social history of the world.

Graduate students in Atlantic or Caribbean history still read Sidney Mintz's *Sweetness and Power* (1985), but it has been a long time since I have met a student who has picked up *Worker in the Cane*. In that book, Mintz explored the life and labors of a cane worker, Anastacio Zayas Alvarado (Don Taso), across several decades. It was a micro-history written before the term was fashionable – as Mintz put it, a "look down the corridor of time through which a man had walked" (Mintz, 1960, p. 5). The knowledge Mintz gained in his year with Don Taso in 1948 formed the basis for everything he subsequently wrote about the history of sugar production in the Caribbean. Reading the book did not instantly make me want to be an anthropologist – though I would end up going to graduate school in anthropology, in part to study with Mintz – but the book did convince me of the power of small narratives in illuminating bigger stories and trends. The richness of Mintz's case study made me think about Wallerstein's work in a different way. Few individual agents cluttered Wallterstein's book; labor was present, but no laborers. I began to think that if I ever pursued my interest in world economic history, one objective would be to balance the two approaches by interweaving small stories with broader theoretical interventions.

Three years later, after an interlude that included a series of odd jobs and a decidedly un-Braudelian view of the Mediterranean from the galley of a yacht where I worked as a very bad cook, I had plans to enter a doctoral program to study anthropology at Johns Hopkins. It was then, in the summer before I began graduate school, that I read both volumes of Braudel's master work. I still have the heavily underlined copies that I carried all over New York that summer. The marginalia include wavy lines, school-girl exclamation points, funny little arrows, and the occasional question mark. In the backs of the volumes I penciled urgent questions, some of which puzzle me even now and seem to reflect my undergraduate courses in economics: "What was the role of interest rates in the Atlantic economy? Why couldn't creditors hedge against inflation of money on account by adjusting interest?" The material that had inspired Wallerstein weaves through the book, of course – he must have his own heavily underlined copy somewhere. The second volume, a page-turning account of the struggle between the Spanish crown and the Ottoman Empire, was in many ways the better read, but the first volume made a deeper impression with its exegesis of the longue durée – Braudel's term for the framework of slow historical change – and its startling images. I particularly loved the inverted map of the Mediterranean in which Braudel shows the Mediterranean, and Africa beyond, on the European horizon. The Sahara, Braudel's "waterless sea," (too empty, African historians would now tell us) dominates Europe's near horizon. It was perhaps gazing at that map that I came to understand that my subject would be the movement of Europeans into those other worlds. Judging from my marginal notes, I might have followed my interests to become an economic historian if I had not, soon after, had a close encounter with a book out of a very different scholarly tradition.

The History of Power

When I arrived at Johns Hopkins, the history and anthropology departments were experiencing what turned out to be a golden era of collaboration. The colonial American historian Jack Greene had secured a grant from the Rockefeller Foundation to develop studies in Atlantic history and culture, and in addition to the seminar in which all history doctoral students tremblingly presented their first-year research papers, an Atlantic World seminar was meeting every week, hosting a series of visiting historians and anthropologists who were shaping the emergent field. In the first week, I visited the offices of various faculty members and pointed to a line in the Hopkins brochure saying that it was possible to do a joint Ph.D. in anthropology and history. No student had done it before, but everyone on the faculty seemed willing to have me try. I began studying anthropology with Sidney Mintz and Katherine Verdery, and working closely with two historians, John Russell-Wood and Philip Curtin.

Philip Curtin did not strike me, or anyone else, as much of an intellectual guru. He was a slightly stocky, unprepossessing man with unfashionable glasses and a habit of pulling up his belt with both hands, even while he was sitting down. He was taciturn and only very rarely eloquent. His teaching style involved giving a group of graduate students plenty to read and sending us to the library to listen to the taped lectures of an undergraduate course he taught, "The World and the West." We would then convene in his office, and he would ask us one or two questions, and then become very quiet. We flailed around to find the answers; every once in a while he would inject an encouraging word, but not often. My Marxist enthusiasms still intact, I complained to friends throughout the first semester that Curtin had no "theoretical vision," and I made plans to drop the course. But I slogged onward, gradually gaining appreciation for the sheer volume of new material I was learning and beginning to detect the outlines of a valuable framework beneath.

Curtin's approach to world history was to trace the engagements of Europeans with other world regions. It was Wallerstein on steroids. I learned a history of European imperial ventures in Asia that was entirely new to me, I read about what Curtin called the South Atlantic system, and I immersed myself in the analytical power of placing such phenomena as serfdom and slavery, or the fur trade in New France and Russia, or political organization in Central Asia and Southern Africa, in comparative perspective. In the Hopkins library basement, a small group of fellow students and I listened to tapes of Curtin's lectures about a rich array of topics, from the Portuguese trading post empire to the history of Jesuits in empire, the Columbian exchange, Spanish scholasticism, English pirates, Dutch and Xhosa interactions, Ottoman janissaries, Muslims in the Russian Empire, and on and on. As I got my first real education in world history, I began to glimpse not so much a theoretical vision as a perspective. Curtin was a world historian interested mainly in the shifting relationship between culture and trade. The scaffold of his course on Europe and the world consisted loosely of commercial patterns: the trade in fish, silver, captives, fur, hides, gold, coffee, opium, and wheat. But he was an economic historian peculiarly drawn to the illumination of cultural and political phenomena. While he was then best known for his startlingly ambitious census of the Atlantic slave trade, his first book, *Two Jamaicas* (1955), had relied on literary and legal sources to try to reconstruct the cultural life of freed blacks on the island and their place in the evolving political order. If I had any doubt about Curtin's inclinations toward a kind of history that married economic and cultural questions, they vanished when he gave us the manuscript of the book he was then writing, a world history of trade diasporas that emphasized patterns of long-distance trade made possible by relations of kinship and religion (Curtin, 1984).

After taking in as much as I could of the history of Europe's engagement with the world, I went into Philip Curtin's office one afternoon and asked him if he would supervise my preparation of comprehensive examinations in history. An account of that conversation appears in the first paragraph of the preface of my book *Law and Colonial Cultures* (2002, p. xi):

> After I explained that I was interested in the history of Iberian empires, he asked, "Why not world history?" I suggested broadening my studies to include West Africa. "World history would be better," he urged. I offered to label my interests Atlantic history and culture. "Study world history," he insisted.

And so began my formal training in world history. The fact that I fought so hard to define the scope of my studies in a different, narrower way speaks volumes about the marginal recognition of world history as a research field at the time. I was afraid that nobody would take me seriously if I declared that my field of history was so vast. When it was time to enter the title in my record, I asked the department to list "Comparative Social and Economic History." World history sounded boastful and preposterous, I thought.

Curtin knew better. He had been part of an all-star faculty at the University of Wisconsin that began defining their field as "Comparative History of the Tropics" and then migrated as a group toward a world history rubric. Many key figures in world history, such as Michael Adas and Patrick Manning, came through Wisconsin, some during and some after Curtin's time there. One of the core contributions that Curtin made was to insist on fully integrating African history in world history (Curtin, 1964, 1969). Another was his willingness to try different methods and explore novel topics; after finishing his book on diasporas in world history, he was beginning work on a history of Europeans' experience of disease in West Africa in what was then a novel attempt to bring together the history of medicine with the infant field of environmental history (Curtin, 1998).

As quietly influential as my readings with Curtin were becoming, two other encounters shaped my intellectual trajectory more urgently around the same time. The very first graduate student essay I wrote was on E.P. Thompson's *Whigs and Hunters* (1975). I had already read Thompson's greatest hits: *The Making of the English Working Class* (1963) and the essays on the moral economy, time, and the actions of the crowd that would later be gathered in the volume *Customs in Common* (1991). Having tracked down Roberto Unger's books after hearing him lecture brilliantly at Harvard, I already had an inkling about the power of questions about law within social theory. My inchoate interests in these topics and approaches were given a more robust form by my reading of *Whigs and Hunters*, in particular its riveting last chapter, in which Thompson presents a defense of the rule of law. The book analyzes the passage of the Black Act in England, an event marking the conversion of a long list of practices of the commons into capital crimes.

For Thompson, the legal story made no sense without an understanding of the broad context of the encounter between foresters' moral economy and the interests of the improving gentry. It was a tale of two grids, a capitalist grid descending on a grid of custom, in a clash of vernacular power and state authority.

While many of Thompson's Marxist followers criticized him for failing to represent the law as a mere tool of the most powerful class in England, the book seemed to me both exemplary in its methods and flawed in other, more subtle ways. Thompson had not gone far enough to undo his own rigid scaffolding of a grid of capitalist property rights descending on the moral economy of the forest. The essay I wrote about the book pushed me to begin to imagine a fluid, jurisdictionally complex world in which people might energetically oppose the interests most often protected by legal authorities while still recognizing their legitimacy. While Curtin was calling my attention to transregional practices, Thompson inspired me to study jurisdictional conflicts. I began to shape an idea of combining these subjects.

At the same time as I was wading into the waters of law-focused social history, I was being introduced to the administrative history of empire by one of its masters, John Russell-Wood. Like Philip Curtin, John Russell-Wood was little drawn to theory, but he had a distinctive perspective that channeled his wide-ranging curiosity about the Portuguese empire as a global project. He had written important works about slaves and freed communities in Brazil, women in the Portuguese empire, Atlantic migration, and municipal administration as a key organizing construct of Iberian expansion (Russell-Wood, 1982, 1992). Russell-Wood was following his mentor Charles Boxer in developing imperial administrative history; although Boxer is typically regarded as a generalist, much of the material for his influential surveys of the Dutch and Portuguese empires derived from legal records and described administrative arrangements and crises (e.g., Boxer, 1965, 1969). At the time that I was reading colonial Latin American history with John Russell-Wood, he was also beginning work on a global history of Portuguese migrations that would seek to connect, through the movement of

Portuguese sailors, merchants, and officials, imperial spheres in the Indian and Atlantic Oceans (Russell-Wood, 1993). His was an early vision of world history through the lens of the history of empires.

John Russell-Wood was also, it must be said, an intellectually generous man who could appear formal and distant but had a thinly disguised warmth and a soft spot for struggling students. He taught me about the Portuguese empire and colonial Latin America while letting me know that he could see that I was casting about rather wildly for a topic and approach to call my own. My ambition to write about the Atlantic economy had unraveled, and I had nothing to replace it. I now understood more than I ever had about imperial strategies and about the vastness and often incoherence of imperial projects. I knew that I probably would not be able to write like Thompson, but I wanted at least to think about the same problems he was addressing. I was also not ready to give up my interest in researching economic history from a different perspective than the one I had been introduced to as an undergraduate. Russell-Wood urged me to follow my instincts and suggested that I canvass the Latin Americanists in other departments at Hopkins to help find my way.

Thus began the longest detour of my career, a series of years investigating and writing about the informal sector, or the underground economy, and industrial development in Spain and Latin America. I began to study and collaborate with the sociologist Alejandro Portes, and I wrote my dissertation on a topic very distant from imperial, world, and legal history. The work seemed to take me well away from my intellectual roots, but I always maintained a connection to Thompsonian "bottom-up" social history and an interest in questions about the integration of local economies into global markets. I got to indulge fully, at last, my interest in labor, investigating the lives of people working off the books in sweatshops in Alicante and make-shift industrial parks on the outskirts of Madrid. In recent years, that distant topic has roared back as the latest global economic crisis has exposed again the structural weaknesses that I observed in the Spanish economy in the mid-1980s, problems that had disappeared from view during the intervening boom years. Almost as soon as the ink was dry on the resulting book, *Invisible Factories* (1990), I felt a restless urge to return to comparative and global history.

I had in mind writing a book about law in world history. Legal history was still taught largely as a discipline contained within national histories, and many social and cultural historians still avoided the law, while others merely used legal records as sources or complex narratives rather than a subject of its own. Historians such as Natalie Zemon Davis (1983) and Carlo Ginzburg (1980) had drawn attention to the value of legal sources as the bases of micro-histories, but they were not mainly interested in the law. Even the Annales school, the name of the influential set of French scholars who had built on Braudel's work to explore various dimensions of social and cultural history, had left the law largely to one side, except as a source of documents revealing social patterns and cultural mindsets, or *mentalité*. But if one defined legal history broadly to include the sorts of conflicts that I knew drew colonial subjects everywhere into fierce conflicts, the topic had to be understood as central to the construction of global narratives. The key was to figure out how to connect the study of legal conflicts within polities to the evolving framework for interactions across polities. I decided, privately, that if I was going to remain an academic, I would work on this big problem. When I resigned from my tenure-track position in the Department of Urban Studies and Planning at M.I.T. and began to redefine myself as a world historian studying law rather than as an economic anthropologist with interests in history, some of my friends and colleagues suspected that I had gone mad.

A Global Legal Regime

Luckily, I would soon meet new muses. I first encountered the always-smiling Jerry Bentley at a World History Association conference where I was presenting a paper in honor of Philip Curtin. I already knew Jerry as the efficient and encouraging editor of the *Journal of World History*. The journal had published an article of mine the year before reassessing world-systems analysis by juxtaposing it to institutional economics (1996). The article argued for the study of something I was calling "institutional world history" (a phrase I still like but that never attracted many followers). Jerry had a steady editorial hand – the relatively new journal published high-quality articles – and he was not risk averse. He was willing to publish an essay making claims about a new direction in world history without yet much empirical support. Calm and cheerful in correspondence and in person, he gave the impression of someone who was genuinely hoping that he would be surprised and who delighted in new ideas.

That attitude was nurturing. A few years after placing my first article with the *Journal of World History*, I turned to Jerry Bentley again with an article based on a chapter of the book on law in world history (Benton, 2000). I was now fully engaged in imagining a global history of legal pluralism. The article outlined the main elements of the perspective I was developing about the emergence and nature of a "global legal regime." I argued that patterns of jurisdictional complexity in European, African, and American societies were broadly similar across polities in ways that created possibilities for the transregional movement of people and goods. Going back to the lessons learned from John Russell-Wood, I could see that the Portuguese, for example, approached commerce and raiding in West Africa with clear assumptions about, and even an explicit understanding of, the expectations of African host polities with regard to law. As in the trading diasporas studied by Philip Curtin, the Portuguese settled into relationships with African polities by reproducing a pattern of legal pluralism that was as familiar to the Africans as it was to Iberians; both societies had long recognized the authority of minority religious or merchant diasporas to regulate petty conflicts within their own communities, referring only the matters considered especially serious, mainly those that could trigger capital sentences, to local sovereigns. Once again, Jerry Bentley published the article and also encouraged me to forge ahead with the book project. Of course, he never claimed to have had a hand in the book or its ideas when it came out. But *Law and Colonial Cultures* (2002) would have been a different, and lesser, book without his editorial guidance at a critical stage.

Also rather by accident, I encountered another scholarly muse around the same time. Early in the project, I had the great good fortune to come across James Muldoon's *Popes, Lawyers, and Infidels* (1979). As had happened with Wallerstein's work, I simply found the book in the library – this time at Rutgers, where I was then teaching. Muldoon's extraordinary monograph was a revelation. *Popes, Lawyers, and Infidels* explains the medieval roots of the core jurisdictional tensions of European law, the struggle between secular and religious legal authority. Like Harold Berman's magisterial *Law and Revolution* (1983), Muldoon's book exposes the pervasive and acute nature of this tension, and then he goes further, examining the ways that jurisdictional conflicts played out not only in creating a pan-Christian legal order but also in shaping interactions on the edges of Europe: to the east, with diplomatic forays into Russia, and to the south and west, as Iberians began their halting and contentious push to claim and settle the Atlantic islands. Reading Muldoon's brilliant book, I could begin to understand the thrust of what I began to call "jurisdictional politics" in European empires across the centuries, and in the Ottoman Empire, too. When I finally met James Muldoon on a visit to the John Carter Brown Library, I found that, like Jerry Bentley, he was willing to read and critique my work while also urging me to continue with the project. Together with Bentley, Muldoon had banished the doubts I had that a world history of law in empire was beyond anyone's reach.

Law and Colonial Cultures is a book with one perspective and two arguments. The perspective is the one I have already described: in the multicentric legal orders we call empires, jurisdictional politics engaged legal actors and drove structural and institutional changes. The first of two arguments was that the process generated continuities across polities in the early modern world. People from a wide variety of world regions recognized how to maneuver within the legal systems of foreign empires. They understood legal orders to be composed of many parallel jurisdictions. Merchants, for example, positioned themselves inside host polities as members of legal communities that retained partial jurisdiction over their own affairs. Expanding empires, meanwhile, set up jurisdictionally complex legal orders that recognized a degree of jurisdictional autonomy for conquered communities. The similar structures of multicentric legal orders provided the underpinning for transregional contact and exchanges in the early modern world. The second argument of the book was that the jurisdictional conflicts that emerged in such complex plural legal orders helped to give rise to the colonial state. The book traced sharpening claims to state legal hegemony over the long nineteenth century, a process that featured struggles over the definition of the legal status of a wide variety of imperial subjects. In this account of "jurisdictional politics" as the medium for the formation of state authority, the interstate order of the late nineteenth century emerged from colonial politics and world history, not from circulating European models of statecraft and sovereignty. Put differently, imperial legal conflicts were guiding widespread patterns of institutional change.

The second argument about the shift to state legal hegemony was less well fleshed out than the first argument about pervasive legal pluralism. There was also a subtle tension between the two arguments because strong state legal authority was consistent with continued jurisdictional complexity and ambiguity. Authors usually know better than anyone else on finishing a project where the loose ends lie. I thought that my next project should try to refine understandings of sovereignty by approaching the topic from another angle. I originally conceived the next book as an investigation of the late and contingent development of territorial sovereignty. As I waded into the new project, I did so in the company of a new set of colleagues. At New York University, I was for the first time since my tenure as a graduate student at Johns Hopkins in close proximity to an impressive group of historians working on transregional and transnational history.

NYU historians were already approaching the history of empires from fresh angles. Jane Burbank and Frederick Cooper had moved to NYU from the University of Michigan, bringing with them a broad-ranging course on the comparative history of empires. We began to coteach a year-long graduate course on empires in world history, an opportunity meant not only getting to shape students' thinking about empire as a framework for analysis as well as to learn from one another. As Jane Burbank completed an elegant study of Russian peasants and law (2004) and as Frederick Cooper embarked on an ambitious project to rewrite the history of French imperial citizenship, I began to probe the possibilities of writing a book about geography and law in European empires.

Several faculty members at NYU Law School were, meanwhile, helping to guide my way into legal history as an academic discipline. Even before coming to NYU as a faculty member, I had participated in the NYU Legal History Colloquium, and I now also joined a year-long reading group organized around the theme of empire and law. The group brought together a diverse set of scholars looking for new ways to think about imperial law and the history of international law. This stimulating forum included the intellectual historians David Armitage and Jennifer Pitts, as well as the international law scholar Benedict Kingsbury. The group introduced me to the work of Charles Alexandrowicz, whose writings from the 1960s had garnered relatively little attention but who had sought to liberate the history of international law from its endemic Eurocentrism, together with the writings of Carl Schmitt, the Weimar theorist whose controversial ideas about the nature of sovereignty were then capturing the imagination of an interdisciplinary audience (e.g., Alexandrowizc, 1967; Schmitt, 2003).

As with most books, *A Search for Sovereignty* (2010) took a direction that surprised me. I began with a relatively straightforward set of questions: When and how did territorial control become integral to understandings of sovereignty? What sorts of practices and discourses characterized Europeans' legal imagination about the geographies of empires? How did empires claim control of territory, and why? I thought such questions would lead to interesting and new insights about the intersection of geographic discourse and legal practices in empires. And they did. I discovered a deep preoccupation with rivers matching a grammar of imperial claims and anxieties about marking membership in colonial political communities. I traced the merger of understandings of sea routes and representations of maritime jurisdiction, a relation easiest to see by studying the legal strategies of pirates, who turned out to be not antiauthoritarian rogues but sophisticated consumers and producers of legal rationales. I charted a late-eighteenth-century fixation on islands as sites of strong imperial authority. And I probed a nearly Braudelian idea of mountains as places of primitive sovereignty and slow political change, an element of geographic and legal imagination that resurfaced forcefully in the context of late-imperial debates about the quasi-sovereignty, or partial sovereignty, of the Indian princely states and other polities inside imperial spheres (cf, Scott, 2010).

In the process, I discovered that what I was writing was a book about layered sovereignty in empires, particularly the interweaving of legal practices related to subjecthood and delegated legal authority. The legal geography of empires was best described as a congeries of enclaves and corridors, a composite of jumbled spaces that contrasted sharply with the familiar maps of evenly colored expanses of imperial territories. The uneven spatial patterns of empires corresponded to a persistent understanding of sovereignty as divisible and incomplete. The book became an analysis of imperial rule over territory as variegated and interrupted, a collection of "anomalous legal zones" (Benton, 2010, p. 6).

The project taught me that writing new global histories of law encompassed the possibility of revising the history of international law and advancing constitutional history. Whereas such goals had appeared remote 10 years before, it now became possible for me to join with other scholars in questioning some of the standard and long-accepted tenets of international law and thought. I joined colleagues such as David Armitage (2007), Daniel Hulsebosch (2005; Golove and Hulsebosch, 2010), and Sudipta Sen (2002) in considering sovereignty and constitutions in global perspective; historians such as Uday Singh Mehta (1999), Jennifer Pitts (2005), and Christopher Bayly (2012) in blending the study of the imperial constitution with analysis of the global origins of liberalism; and a varied group of other innovative scholars in seeking new legal perspectives on colonial and imperial history, including Ken MacMillan (2011) writing on the English acquisition of empire and the early imperial constitution; Kerry Ward (2009) on the Dutch empire as a matrix of coerced labor movements; Jenny

Pulsipher (2005) on English and Indian interactions in the context of imperial and monarchical politics; Malick Ghachem (2012) and Rebecca Scott (Scott and Hébrard, 2012) on the continuities of the law of slavery; Miranda Spieler (2012) on the legal exceptionalism of French penal colonies; Nasser Hussain (2003) and Rande Kostal (2005) on the colonial law of emergency; and Lisa Ford (2010) on the origins of sovereignty in settler colonies. In contrast to my perceived solitude only a decade before in writing *Law and Colonial Cultures*, I now found myself happily surrounded by fellow-travelers – historians writing the global history of law.

Looking Back, Looking Forward

If we extend the metaphor of vernacular architecture, we find ourselves in a pleasantly chaotic and impressively eclectic assemblage of constructions. Does the collection add up to a style or a school? The outlines of several major projects with significance for world history are certainly clear. We have yet to take the measure of recent legal histories with regard to periodization in world history. We can notice the definite outlines of an effective and interesting approach to legal cultures. A broad agenda – rewriting the history of international law as encompassing the world beyond Europe – may ultimately be built on these foundations.

The glimpse of the promise of new periodization is still partial. Much of the research on empires and law in world history has focused on the period after 1500, when growing long-distance trade was bringing world regions into closer contact, and when legal processes were operating alongside other forces to structure frameworks for trade, conquest, and rule. How and in response to what influences were legal orders in distant parts of the world developing? The problem of synchronism – the simultaneous emergence of similar phenomena – still haunts global legal history as a research field. It is difficult or impossible to explain conjunctures such as newly robust claims to state legal command as the result of the circulation of ideas or practices. In part, broad shifts in the law may be explained in relation to forces such as intensifying trade and cross-regional investment. In part, such shifts were responding to similar jurisdictional tensions, for example, the reconfiguration of empires as more clearly hierarchically organized, if still internally diverse, structures of rule. In an effort to understand the impulse for extensive imperial legal reform in the early nineteenth century, I turned my attention to the reconstitution of the British colonial magistracy (Benton, 2011; Benton and Ford, 2013) and sought to place the subject of legal pluralism in comparative context (Benton and Ross, 2013). Questions about the nature, structure, and timing of global legal transformations remain.

Another fertile area for research centers on legal cultures. We now know that across very different kinds of societies and contexts, historical agents have consistently displayed the ability to adjust legal strategies quickly. One of the signal contributions of recent studies of fluid and flexible legal strategies is to pose new questions about the relation between legal practice, broadly defined, and institutional trends. For example, in studying the legal behavior of pirates, I have found that the approach reveals something about pirates as political subjects (rather than stateless rogues) as well as about their place within the maritime regulatory order (Benton, 2005). Other historians have developed nuanced ways of interpreting categories of difference, proposing that historical actors' expectations about law shaped their reading of cultural encounters and political systems (Burbank, 2004; Owensby, 2011). A blending of institutional and legal cultural analysis has produced new findings about transregional processes structuring labor, slavery, extraterritoriality, and rights (Tomlins, 2010; Moyn, 2011; Cassel, 2012; Rushforth, 2012).

Rather than favoring a vague and capacious study of legal culture, we can produce especially significant findings by focusing on the exercise, recognition, or legitimacy of legal authority. In analyzing legal *authority* in all its varieties, world and comparative histories have moved away from an alternative perspective, one that privileges *norms* or *rules* as objects of study. Norms are not easily knowable, in part because historical actors treat them as reference points rather than as fixed constraints. In contrast, legal conflicts can be studied because participants produce and leave documentary trails, while the conflicts tend to correspond to larger patterns of strategic action resulting in changes in law. Debates about the evolution of legal forums, such as criminal courts; controversies about punishment (e.g., imprisonment or flogging); struggles over the status and persecution of religious groups; and tensions over the exercise of legal authority within social and cultural spheres such as families – such topics open windows into social and political processes that in turn shape world history.

If the study of law and world history has nurtured the nuanced interpretation of legal cultures and strategies, it has also opened a vast and still underdeveloped field of the study of inter-polity law. I choose the term "inter-polity" carefully. As I have discussed, the history of international law has been marked by an emphasis on European jurisprudence, European perspectives on natural and positive law, European definitions of sovereign states, and European criteria for membership in the international legal community. Comparative and global histories of law have forcefully proposed the need to understand the role of empires in the evolution of the global legal order. They have, less explicitly, also opened the question of how to understand law in relations among political communities unmediated by imperial (including European) power. A small group of legal scholars has begun to sketch a capacious frame for the history of international law that would include inter-polity relations of all varieties and regions (Anghie, 2004; Belmessous, 2012; Benton, 2012). Such efforts promise a reconceptualization of European international thought that places empires at the center (Kingsbury and Straumann, 2011; Armitage, 2013; Benton and Ross, 2013).

As in all fields of world history, the list of research challenges is longer than that of accomplishments. Yet the remarkable pace at which a research field has developed out of disconnected endeavors is also impressive. The "global history of law" is a phrase that makes sense now but might have sounded odd or even delusional only a decade ago. The transformation would not have been possible without an equally swift development of world history research on migration, labor, trade, and other phenomena that composed regulatory regimes and legal institutions. As part of the field's vernacular architecture, the study of global law and legal cultures is now clearly visible, and may even prove enduring, within the landscape of world history.

References

Alexandrowicz, Charles Henry. 1967. *An Introduction to the History of the Law of Nations in the East Indies: 16th, 17th and 18th Centuries*. Oxford: Clarendon.

Anghie, Antony. 2004. *Imperialism, Sovereignty, and the Making of International Law*. Cambridge: Cambridge University Press.

Armitage, David. 2007. *The Declaration of Independence: A Global History*. Cambridge, MA: Harvard University Press.

Armitage, David. 2013. *Foundations of Modern International Thought*. New York: Cambridge University Press.

Bayly, C.A. 2012. *Recovering Liberties: Indian Thought in the Age of Liberalism and Empire*. Cambridge: Cambridge University Press.

Belmessous, Saliha, ed. 2012. *Native Claims: Indigenous Law Against Empire, 1500–1920*. Cambridge: Oxford University Press.

Benton, Lauren. 1990. *Invisible Factories: The Informal Economy and Industrial Development in Spain*. Albany, NY: State University of New York Press.

Benton, Lauren. 1996. "From the World Systems Perspective to Institutional World History: Culture and Economy in Global Theory," *Journal of World History* 7/2: 261–289.

Benton, Lauren. 2000. "The Legal Regime of the South Atlantic World: Jurisdictional Politics as Institutional Order," *Journal of World History* 11/1: 27–56.

Benton, Lauren. 2002. *Law and Colonial Cultures: Legal Regimes in World History, 1400–1900*. Cambridge: Cambridge University Press.

Benton, Lauren. 2005. "Legal Spaces of Empire: Piracy and the Origins of Ocean Regionalism," *Comparative Studies in Society and History* 47/4: 700–724.

Benton, Lauren. 2010. *A Search for Sovereignty: Law and Geography in European Empires, 1400–1900*. Cambridge: Cambridge University Press.

Benton, Lauren. 2011. "Abolition and Imperial Law, 1780–1820," *Journal of Commonwealth and Imperial History* 39/3: 355.

Benton, Lauren. 2012. "Possessing Empire: Iberian Claims and Interpolity Law," in Saliha Belmessous, ed. *Native Claims: Indigenous Law Against Empire, 1500–1920*. Cambridge: Oxford University Press, pp. 19–40.

Benton, Lauren and Lisa Ford. 2013. "Magistrates in Empire: Convicts, Slaves, and the Remaking of the Plural Legal Order in the British Empire," in Lauren Benton and Richard J. Ross, eds. *Legal Pluralism and Empires. 1500–1800*. New York: New York University Press, pp. 173–198.

Benton, Lauren and Richard Ross, eds. 2013. *Legal Pluralism and Empires, 1500–1850*. New York: New York University Press.

Berman, Harold J. 1983. *Law and Revolution: The Formation of the Western Legal Tradition*. Cambridge, MA: Harvard University Press.

Boxer, Charles. 1965. *The Dutch Seaborne Empire, 1600–1800*. London: Hutchinson.

Boxer, Charles. 1969. *The Portuguese Seaborne Empire, 1415–1825*. New York: A.A. Knopf.

Braudel, Fernand. 1949. *The Mediterranean and the Mediterranean World in the Age of Philip II*, vols. I and II. Berkeley, CA: University of California Press.

Burbank, Jane. 2004. *Russian Peasants Go to Court: Legal Culture in the Countryside, 1905–1917*. Bloomington, IN: Indiana University Press.

Cassel, Pär Kristoffer. 2012. *Grounds of Judgment: Extraterritoriality and Imperial Power in Nineteenth-Century China and Japan*. Oxford: Oxford University Press.

Curtin, Philip D. 1955. *Two Jamaicas: The Role of Ideas in a Tropical Colony, 1830–1865*. Cambridge, MA: Harvard University Press.

Curtin, Philip D. 1964. *The Image of Africa: British Ideas and Action, 1780–1850*, vol. 2. Madison, WI: The University of Wisconsin Press.

Curtin, Philip D. 1969. *The Atlantic Slave Trade: A Census*. Madison, WI: The University of Wisconsin Press.

Curtin, Philip D. 1984. *Cross-Cultural Trade in World History*. Cambridge: Cambridge University Press.

Curtin, Philip D. 1998. *Disease and Empire: The Health of European Troops and the Conquest of Africa*. Cambridge: Cambridge University Press.

Davis, Natalie Zemon. 1983. *The Return of Martin Guerre*. Cambridge, MA: Harvard University Press.

Ford, Lisa. 2010. *Settler Sovereignty: Jurisdiction and Indigenous People in America and Australia, 1788–1836*. Cambridge, MA: Harvard University Press.

Ghachem, Malick W. 2012. *The Old Regime and the Haitian Revolution*. Cambridge: Cambridge University Press.

Ginzburg, Carlo. 1980. *The Cheese and the Worms: The Cosmos of a Sixteenth-Century Miller*. Baltimore: The John Hopkins University Press.

Golove, David M. and Daniel J. Hulsebosch. 2010. "A Civilized Nation: The Early American Constitution, the Law of Nations, and the Pursuit of International Recognition." *New York University Law Review*, Public Law Research Paper No. 10-58.

Hulsebosch, Daniel J. 2005. *Constituting Empire: New York and the Transformation of Constitutionalism in the Atlantic World, 1664–1830*. Chapel Hill, NC: University of North Carolina Press.

Hussain, Nasser. 2003. *The Jurisprudence of Emergency: Colonialism and the Rule of Law*. Ann Arbor, MI: University of Michigan Press.

Kingsbury, Benedict and Benjamin Straumann, 2011. *The Roman Foundations of the Law of Nations: Alberico Gentili and the Justice of Empire*, New York: Oxford University Press.

Kostal, R.W. 2005. *A Jurisprudence of Power: Victorian Empire and the Rule of Law*. Oxford: Oxford University Press.

MacMillan, Ken. 2011. *The Atlantic Imperial Constitution: Center and Periphery in the English Atlantic World*. New York: Palgrave Macmillan.

Mehta, Uday Singh. 1999. *Liberalism and Empire: A Study in Nineteenth-Century British Imperial Thought*. Chicago, IL: The University of Chicago Press.

Mintz, Sidney W. 1960. *Worker in the Cane: A Puerto Rican Life History*. New York: W.W. Norton.

Mintz, Sidney W. 1985. *Sweetness and Power: The Place of Sugar in Modern History*. New York: Penguin Group.

Moyn, Samuel. 2011. *The Last Utopia: Human Rights in History*. New York: Belknap Press.

Muldoon, James. 1979. *Popes, Lawyers, and Infidels: The Church and the Non-Christian World, 1250–1550 (The Middle Ages)*. Philadelphia, PA: University of Pennsylvania Press.

Owensby, Brian. 2011. *Empire of Law and Indian Justice in Colonial Mexico*. Stanford, CA: Stanford University Press.

Paige, Jeffery M. 1975. *Agrarian Revolution*. New York: MacMillan Publishing Co., Inc.

Pitts, Jennifer. 2005. *A Turn to Empire: The Rise of Imperial Liberalism in Britain and France*. Princeton, NJ: Princeton University Press.

Pulsipher, Jenny Hale. 2005. *Subjects Unto the Same King: Indians, English, and the Contest for Authority in Colonial New England*. Philadelphia, PA: Pennsylvania Press.

Rushforth, Brett. 2012. *Bonds of Alliance: Indigenous and Atlantic Slaveries in New France*. Chapel Hill, NC: University of North Carolina Press.

Russell-Wood, A.J.R. 1982. *The Black Man in Slavery and Freedom in Colonial Brazil*, New York: Palgrave Macmillan.
Russell-Wood, A.J.R. 1992. *Society and Government in Colonial Brazil, 1500–1822*. New York: Variorum.
Russell-Wood, A.J.R. 1993. *The World on the Move: The Portuguese in Africa, Asia, and America, 1415–1808*. New York: St. Martin's Press.
Schmitt, Carl. 2003. *The Nomos of the Earth in the International Law of the Jus Publicum Eurepeaum*. New York: Telos Press.
Scott, James C. 2010. *The Art of Not Being Governed: Anarchist History of Upland Southeast Asia*. New Haven, CT: Yale University Press.
Scott, Rebecca and Jean M. Hébrard. 2012. *Freedom Papers: An Atlantic Odyssey in the Age of Emancipation*. Cambridge, MA: Harvard University Press.
Sen, Sudipta. 2002. *Distant Sovereignty: National Imperialism and the Origins of British India*. New York: Routledge.
Spieler, Miranda Frances. 2012. *Empire and Underworld: Captivity in French Guiana*. Cambridge, MA: Harvard University Press.
Thompson, E.P. 1963. *The Making of the English Working Class*. New York: Vintage Books.
Thompson, E.P. 1975. *Whigs and Hunters: The Origin of the Black Act*. New York: Pantheon Books.
Thompson, E.P. 1991. *Customs in Common*. New York: New Press.
Tomlins, Christopher. 2010. *Freedom Bound: Law, Labor, and Civic Identity in Colonizing English America*. Cambridge: Cambridge University Press.
Wallerstein, Immanuel. 1974. *The Modern World-System I: Capitalist Agriculture and the Origins of the European World-Economy in the Sixteenth Century*. Berkeley, CA: University of California Press.
Ward, Kerry. 2009. *Networks of Empire: Forced Migration in the Dutch East India Company*. Cambridge: Cambridge University Press.
Wolf, Eric R. 1969. *Peasant Wars of the Twentieth Century*. New York: Harper & Row.

Further Reading

Anghie, Antony. 2004. *Imperialism, Sovereignty, and the Making of International Law*. Cambridge: Cambridge University Press.
Armitage, David. 2013. *Foundations of Modern International Thought*. New York: Cambridge University Press.

Belmessous, Saliha, ed. 2012. *Native Claims: Indigenous Law Against Empire, 1500–1920*. Cambridge: Oxford University Press.
Benton, Lauren. 2002. *Law and Colonial Cultures: Legal Regimes in World History, 1400–1900*. Cambridge: Cambridge University Press.
Benton, Lauren. 2010. *A Search for Sovereignty: Law and Geography in European Empires, 1400–1900*. Cambridge: Cambridge University Press.
Benton, Lauren and Richard Ross. 2013. *Legal Pluralism and Empires, 1500–1850*. New York: New York University Press.
Ford, Lisa. 2010. *Settler Sovereignty: Jurisdiction and Indigenous People in America and Australia, 1788–1836*. Cambridge, MA: Harvard University Press.
MacMillan, Ken. 2011. *The Atlantic Imperial Constitution: Center and Periphery in the English Atlantic World*. New York: Palgrave Macmillan.
Moyn, Samuel. 2011. *The Last Utopia: Human Rights in History*. New York: Belknap Press.
Muldoon, James. 1979. *Popes, Lawyers, and Infidels: The Church and the Non-Christian World, 1250–1550 (The Middle Ages)*. Philadelphia, PA: University of Pennsylvania Press.

7

Africa in the World: From National Histories to Global Connections

Kerry Ward

When I first heard the infamous assertion by Sir Hugh Trevor-Roper that "there is only the history of Europe in Africa. The rest is darkness …" I was a freshman at Adelaide University in South Australia and I interpreted his comment as an example of hopelessly antiquated prejudice that had long been consigned to the dustbin of history. Trevor-Roper not only painted the African past as "the unrewarding gyrations of barbarous tribes in picturesque but irrelevant corners of the globe" but also wrote off the possibility of an inclusive world history by stereotyping all non-Eurasian societies as static and outside the purview of history that, in his view, was the close examination of the written record to illuminate human progress.

Trevor-Roper was not, however, writing off comparative history. He believed that this method had to be based in developing expertise through specialization before engaging in generalization. "In other words, the historian is amphibious: he must live some part of

Architects of World History: Researching the Global Past, First Edition.
Edited by Kenneth R. Curtis and Jerry H. Bentley.

his time below the surface in order that, on emerging, he can usefully survey it from above. The historian who has specialized all his life may end as an antiquarian. The historian who has never specialized at all will end as a mere blower of froth" (Trevor-Roper, 1969, p. 16). Ironically, if one ignores the outrageous and outdated chauvinism of his earlier statements, this quote from Trevor-Roper is not a too far-fetched formula of current debates on graduate education in world history (Streets-Salter, 2012). It also points to the current evolution of world history scholarship, in which most practitioners begin training as area specialists and then expand conceptually into world history. Historians of Africa have been foundational in these developments and have remained prominent in world history debates in the last few decades (Gilbert and Reynolds, 2012). Along with historians of other areas primarily shaped by European colonialism, Africanists are trained to read widely in fields out of their specific areas of research and to synthesize multiple historiographies. More recently, one of the most influential fields of writing Africa into world history has been to take literally Trevor-Roper's amphibian metaphor by embracing Atlantic and Indian ocean histories as an alternative regional or comparative framework of historical analysis.

This chapter explores the roots of African history as world history and the ways in which there has been a constant interplay between the local and the global in the evolution of African historiography. Generationally, the evolution of African studies as a distinct field of research within the evolution of area studies from the 1950s coincided with the era of global decolonization and the emergence of postcolonial states. This provided the inspiration for the proliferation of national histories rooted in precolonial pasts while simultaneously stimulating debates on the coherence of the units of analysis for area studies. But African history as the history of the continent and people of African descent in the New World had a long pan-African tradition. More recently, scholarship linking Africa to the Indian Ocean and Asia has gained momentum and my book *Networks of Empire: Forced Migration in the Dutch East India Company* (Ward, 2009) is part of this trend.

Old Societies and New States: Africa and the Emergence of the Modern World

My encounter with Africa started young, through the mid-1960s American children's television drama *Daktari* (Swahili for doctor) about a research veterinarian and his young daughter living in East Africa. I envied the girl's fabulously adventurous life with her cross-eyed lion and chimpanzee companions and even now remember the distinctive Afro-jazz theme music. The mid-1960s was a particularly innovative time in Australian education and I attended an experimental state school. A central pedagogical component of the school was the promotion of the United Nations. Each class chose and studied a nation for the entire year as we learned history, culture, geography, music, and art through the medium of our chosen country. In 1972, our class chose Africa. Upon reflection, this now strikes me as odd and invokes the "Africa is not a country" response that Africanists still have to insist upon far too often. Another year my class studied Jamaica – not the West Indies or the Caribbean – but when it came to Africa we uncritically embraced the whole continent in a pan-Africanist fashion. Yet our costumes for United Nations Day were tie-dyed sarongs, beads, and bare feet. Only the boys chosen to be David Livingstone and Henry Morton Stanley got to wear regular clothes – homemade safari suits.

Africa was not an integral part of the school curriculum in Australia in the 1960s and by the 1970s Asia increasingly occupied greater attention not only through the Vietnam War but the postwar shift in Australian foreign policy. It was not until I began a B.A. degree at Adelaide University in 1980 that I again encountered Africa through the cotaught introductory History Department course "Old Societies and New States" that, having become a staple of the curriculum, was known affectionately as "old socs" (Harvey *et al.*, 2012). As an 18 year old, I did not recognize the title of the course came from Clifford Geertz's classic edited volume *Old Societies, New States: The Quest for Modernity in Asia and Africa* (1963). The range of essays was broadly comparative and Geertz argued that the "primordial" attachments of ethnicity, nation, language, and religion were a threat to the integrative politics of emergent independent states in the postcolonial era. The class was organized around a series of case study lectures by area studies experts, including the Pacific Islands, Japan, China, India, Indonesia, and Africa. The specificity of some case studies being nation-based and others being regional still reflects the challenges of specificity and generalization in world history text books and survey courses today.

The first set of lectures outlined the structure of traditional societies, the second focused on transformations brought about by imperialism and colonialism, and the third the transformation to modern independent states. Our first essay was to write a critique of Barrington Moore's *Social Origins of Dictatorship and Democracy* (1966), a foundational text for comparative historical analysis in sociology. Moore compared the modernization in England, France, America, China, Japan, and India, with further comparisons between revolutions in China and Russia and the emergence of fascism in Japan and Germany. It has only been upon reflection, many years later, that I realized that "old socs" was an introduction to world history although it was not conceived as a world history course.

In the second major part of the course, students were allocated to tutorials run by each of the area studies specialists. I chose to study South Africa with Norman Etherington. Having been primed implicitly by Geertz and explicitly by Barrington Moore, I compared the evolution of South Africa as a racially based capitalist industrial powerhouse in southern Africa alongside the emergence of newly independent states struggling with their colonial legacies of underdevelopment in the region. Australians are raised to barrack for the underdog and so I wrote my final paper on the insidious bullying of South African foreign policy in destabilizing the valiant social revolutions of postcolonial states in southern Africa. It was a David and Goliath story gone wrong – Goliath seemed to be winning. I was not particularly politically aware nor well informed as a teenager, instead, youthful indignation and a sense of global justice fired my first foray into examining the horrors of apartheid as a system of white supremacy that oppressed the black majority in South Africa.

To my surprise, my essay was published in the History Department's *Little Magazine* of best student essays. I have to admit it was quite heady stuff to see my name in print but the thought of actually doing this kind of thing for a living never occurred to me.

African History in the World

I continued to take a variety of courses in what could be broadly termed "third world" studies in the Departments of History and Politics. These courses were generally taught through critical approach to Marxist analytical frameworks of modes of production and the examination of class formation and struggle in the transition from traditional society to contemporary states. Our classes focused on the critiques of modernization theory (Rostow, 1960) by the "development of underdevelopment" theorists (Frank, 1966) and world systems analysis (Wallerstein, 1974), which I would revisit again in graduate school at the University of Michigan in the mid-1990s.

Norman Etherington organized an academic exchange with Christopher Saunders from the University of Cape Town (UCT) in 1981, and a postgraduate student, Patricia Sumerling, gave the visiting academic my published freshman essay to read. I was amazed when Saunders suggested I think about pursuing postgraduate studies at UCT. What was no doubt a kind but casual bit of encouragement to a shy undergrad opened up to me the possibility of exploring the world as a student rather than a tourist. When Etherington returned to Adelaide, I jumped at the chance to take his senior seminar in African history. Reading the evocative critiques of colonialism and its legacies by Rodney (1972) and Fanon (1961), Etherington also shared with us his work-in-progress on theories of imperialism (Etherington, 1984) alongside the foundations of African historiography. Jan Vansina's *Oral Tradition* (1965) and its critiques placed African historiography at the forefront of the study of the precolonial past and interdisciplinary methodologies, including archeology and anthropology. We also read selectively from the classic grand narratives of pan-African history (Davidson, 1964; Oliver and Atmore, 1967) in juxtaposition with the emergence of national histories in postcolonial states (Denoon and Kuper, 1970). Focusing on the continent, we were introduced to the debates surrounding the consequences of the trans-Atlantic slave trade for African societies and the persistence of slavery and forms of unfree labor under colonialism (Curtin, 1972; Cooper, 1977, 1980).

Etherington's generation of Africanists came mostly out of Yale, London, and Oxbridge (including a fairly large cohort of South African-born Rhodes scholars). They sparked the materialist critique of liberal Africanist interpretations of South African history exemplified by Wilson and Thompson's *Oxford History of South Africa* (1971) that emphasized race and politics over class and economics (Saunders, 1988). Materialist "radical" scholarship recast large-scale interpretations of the emergence of racial domination, clearly linking the development of the regional economy to the diamond and gold mineral revolution that fueled industrial capitalism and the transformation of African societies starting from the 1870s. Colin Bundy's research (Bundy, 1979) had established that African peasants responded positively to the market opportunities provided by the mineral revolution but were ultimately undermined by capitalist production on white farms and the insatiable demand for black labor on the mines. Shula Marks' intellectual collaborations presented alternative materialist explanations for the transformation of social relations in African societies with the emergence of capitalism in the region (Marks and Atmore, 1980; Marks and Rathbone, 1982). South African historiography of this era also celebrated the emergence of African states. Alongside this reading, we were introduced to the concept of the *Mfecane* and the rise of the Zulu empire, naively embracing Shaka as the heroic black Napoleon he was made out to be in this celebratory literature (Omer-Cooper, 1966).

The books on South African history I remember most evocatively from this period directly challenged the liberal narrative represented by the Oxford History by making black South Africans the center of class based analysis of race in the evolution of South African society

(Roux, 1967; Simon and Simon, 1969; Saul and Gelb, 1981). George Frederickson's *White Supremacy: A Comparative Study in American and South African History* (1981) was intriguing as an introduction to comparative historical analysis, although it reinforced both American and South African "exceptionalism" narratives in the evolution of racial segregation.

I was personally interested in the emergence of a black urbanized working class and organized labor in South Africa. Drawing on whatever I could find in the Adelaide libraries, I wrote essays on the charismatic figure of Clements Kadalie and the first mass black worker's movement, the Industrial and Commercial Union in the 1920s, and the organization of racially divided trade union congresses since the 1960s. I had continued corresponding with Christopher Saunders at the University of Cape Town, sending him copies of my essays not realizing that my bibliography was filled with books and articles banned by the South African government (although still available to researchers there through special permission). With Christopher's and Norman's encouragement, I applied for a scholarship to study for my B.A. Honours degree at UCT, much to the ambivalence of my family and friends who could not understand my fascination with South African politics and thought that after a few months in Africa I'd end up in London on a working holiday like generations of Australian youth.

African Studies in South Africa

I enrolled for a B.A. Honours degree in African Studies at the University of Cape Town in 1984, where I was the first foreign student in the interdisciplinary honours degree coordinated by the multidisciplinary research unit, the Centre for African Studies. Student politics made me more intensely aware of the inclusion of academics in the anti-apartheid cultural boycott of South Africa. In Adelaide, I had attended a public talk by Oliver Tambo, Nelson Mandela's ex-law firm partner and the exiled leader of the African National Congress. He would have been tried for treason had he returned to his homeland. Being in South Africa and immersed in a political situation where protests against the state resulted in arrest and violence was eye-opening. Student organizations at UCT linked protests about education issues with the broader political struggle. In 1984, they set up a "squatter camp" outside the main campus hall in protest against racially segregated student residences resulting in their de-segregation. They also protested in solidarity with black students who suffered violent state and homeland security force oppression in black homeland universities. Students led the "end conscription" movement by young white South African men refusing to serve in the military and resulting in long prison terms. Although the police did not conduct raids on the UCT campus, student protesters risked detention by the security forces once they were off campus.

The UCT African Studies Honours program was self-directed, I could enroll for any courses for which I gained permission, and so I took courses in history, politics, economics, and urban and regional planning, as well as beginning studies in Afrikaans. I was fortunate to arrive at UCT not long after Hermann Giliomee, the Afrikaner historian and intellectual who had decamped from the politically conservative University of Stellenbosch. Giliomee's South African politics honours seminar was attended by faculty and doctoral students and generated intense discussions on the current South African "crisis". I'm pretty sure this is where we furthered reading on the comparative histories of white settler colonialism on a global scale drawing on Fredrickson's *White Supremacy* alongside Lamar and Thompson's *The Frontier in History* (1981), Denoon's *Settler Capitalism* (1983), Cell's *The Highest Stage of White Supremacy* (1982), and Greenberg's *Race and State in Capitalist Development* (1980).

Not surprisingly, my intellectual focus shifted to contemporary politics and I sought inspiration for research topics by spending a lot of time reading in the Southern Africa Labour and Development Research Unit (SALDRU) that conducted empirical microeconomic research on labor issues and social policy. However, I was hopelessly unrealistic about the kind of empirical research on labor organization and resistance I could conduct in the context of the intensifying political situation. The United Democratic Front (UDF) had emerged in 1983 in response to continued state repression of anti-apartheid activism and to challenge the legitimacy of constitutional changes by the South African state to entrench racially divided political representation and "independence" for black homelands.

One of the momentous political events during my first months at UCT was the signing of the Nkomati Accord, a nonaggression pact between Mozambique and South Africa on March 16, 1984. South Africa's policy of destabilization in Southern Africa coupled with diplomatic overtures – "carrot and stick" politics – had finally borne fruit in the capitulation of Samora Machel's FRELIMO socialist government to South African demands to stop supporting the African National Congress (ANC) in exchange for South Africa withdrawing support from RENAMO insurgents who focused on terrorizing rural communities and sabotaging infrastructure. I wrote my honors thesis analyzing the background and content of the Nkomati Accord as part of South Africa's foreign policy and critiquing the support of the Reagan and Thatcher governments' policies. In Cape Town, I saw Chester Crocker, Assistant Secretary of State for African Affairs under President Ronald Reagan and one of the architects of the "constructive engagement" policy that focused on incentives rather than economic sanctions and divestment to encourage the South African government to end apartheid. I was struck by the moral dissonance between constructive engagement with its call for the relaxation of the arms embargo and the violent preemptive strikes by the South African military and special forces against both neighboring states and internal protesters. I completed my thesis around the time of the declaration of the First State of Emergency in July 1985 and declined my supervisor's invitation to revise it for publication because I was uncertain of the implications for my student visa. Although this was probably an overly cautious response, it was not unreasonable given the increased targeting of state harassment and detention without trial of individual students (including some of my friends) who were politically active.

Throughout 1985, the apartheid state dug in its heals and redoubled its repressive and violent policies against the emergence of widespread dissent, strikes, boycotts, and armed struggle in what had clearly become a civil war. By the end of November, the Congress of South African Trade Unions (COSATU) was formed with a membership of half a million workers aimed at ending apartheid discrimination and the complete transformation of the state.

I left South Africa within weeks of the apartheid regime's declaration of a national State of Emergency in June 1986 that would last until the year after my return at the beginning of 1989. In the interim, I finally embarked on the working holiday in London my parents had encouraged me to consider in 1983, but by the end of 1988, I was making plans to go back to the University of Cape Town for my M.A. in history.

"People's History" and the History of Slavery and Emancipation in South Africa

My friends from Cape Town pursued divergent careers, only a few of us persisted with doctorates. At the University of Michigan, Pamela Scully wrote the first gender-based analysis of slave emancipation in South Africa (Scully, 1997). With her help, I devised a master's research proposal on rural–urban migration in the post-emancipation Western Cape, intending to work with Colin Bundy. Instead, I was taken on by Nigel Worden, widely acknowledged as the most influential scholar of slavery, emancipation, and colonialism in pre-twentieth-century Western Cape history not only because of his broad ranging scholarship but because he is a superlative mentor, teacher, organizer, and collaborator. At the time, *The Shaping of South African Society* (1989) had just been published. The excitement at UCT around the chronological and thematic revision of early colonial South African history was palpable as historians of the Cape argued that the pre-mineral revolution and pre-industrialization period in South African colonialism set the foundation of legal status groups based on race that was extended into all subsequent colonial encounters in the region. The volume significantly bridged the Dutch and British colonial periods and extended the analysis through the period of slave emancipation. Building on this insight, Nigel Worden and Clifton Crais were collaborating on a project to examine postemancipation society in South Africa and my archival research into the transformation of mission stations in the southwestern Cape through emancipation and increasing rural–urban migration became part of their project *Breaking the Chains: Slavery and its Legacy in the Nineteenth-Century Cape Colony* (1995).

While Worden encouraged me to read deeply in the historiography of slavery and emancipation in South Africa, Africa, and the Atlantic World; Crais handed me a copy of the recently published book by David W. Cohen and E. S. Atieno Odhiambo, *Siyaya: The Historical Anthropology of an African Landscape* (1989), and suggested I read Rhys Isaac's *The Transformation of Virginia* (1982). I also caught up on Benedict Anderson's *Imagined Communities* (1983) and the influential edited collection by Hobsbawm and Ranger *The Invention of Tradition* (1983). The theoretical insights from this broader reading outside South African historiography helped to shape my ideas around the creation of identity among people who were designated as "Coloured" under apartheid and who lived in mission stations in the Western Cape that had been founded during the era of slavery and transformed by emancipation and increasing rural–urban mobility in the late nineteenth century. Ironically, one of the essays in Hobsbawm and Ranger collection that stayed in my mind was Hugh Trevor-Roper's "The Invention of Tradition: The Highland Tradition of Scotland," which was a superbly documented and witty critique of tartans and kilts as ancient expressions of clan identity (Trevor-Roper in Hobsbawm and Ranger, 1983). While the "invention of tradition" paradigm has been criticized for over-emphasizing the distinction between invented and authentic traditions by presuming the inflexibility of the latter, the invocation of "ancient traditions" as one of the foundations of modern nationalism has remained a powerful idea, particularly in world history.

Nigel Worden (1985), Robert Ross (1983), Robert Shell (1994), Clifton Crais (1992), and Pamela Scully were among the South Africanists at the forefront of bringing the history of slavery and early colonial Cape society into comparative perspective by drawing directly on the expanded literature on the Atlantic World, comparative slavery in the Americas and Caribbean, comparative colonialism and imperialism, feminist and postcolonial theory, and on global historical approaches to slavery as pioneered by Orlando Patterson's *Slavery and Social Death* (1982). Worden and his colleagues extended these insights into undergraduate teaching at UCT by designing a cotaught course that integrated South Africa into "Atlantic World" history. As one of the collaborators in designing and tutoring this course, I can attest to the resonance it had with South African undergraduates schooled in conservative nationalist history who were excited to compare their own history with the United States through the history of slavery, emancipation, black cultural innovation, and civil rights struggles.

The University of Cape Town as an institution was looking for new ways to address the transformation of South African society through the current struggles of the Mass Democratic Movement (MDM) and looking ahead to shaping postapartheid education policies. Several conferences and workshops were held at UCT (and other South African universities) to address these pressing issues, recognizing that the transformation of the education system from preschool to university would be foundational to a more equitable and democratic society. UCT also responded through the Center for African Studies initiative Community Education Resources (CER) that sought to transform research praxis through accountable research methodologies whereby university-based researchers collaborated with communities and organizations to jointly design and implement projects that would both contribute to the production of knowledge in the academy and in communities. In terms of community history projects, this involved collaborative research design and sharing results instead of the more common extractive model of considering interviewees as mere informants and sources of information for writing academic history. This was part of the larger "education for liberation" movement and, more specifically within the discipline of history, the "People's History" movement that had been challenging the received historical narratives of state endorsed history curriculums in the education system, as well as empowering local communities to "write their own" histories (Witz, 1988).

Through recruiting cohorts of multidisciplinary master's students, CER sought to train academics during their formative years in the theories and practice of accountable research, education, and writing. My cohort included students in history, English and linguistics, mathematics, politics, and economics. Each of us developed a collaborative research project with a specific organization or community wherein we would both share our research methodologies and the results we produced in various mediums. One of the challenges for CER as a project embedded institutionally in the university was that a number of the students used their training to become full-time activists instead of completing their degrees. This was not surprising given the political urgency of the time, but it did undermine one of the foundational purposes of the project, which was to train a new generation of academics steeped in critical pedagogy and research praxis. My research with the Mamre community, a village founded as a Moravian mission station in 1818 that had evolved into a dormitory town for Cape Town and the surrounding rural and peri-urban ecomony, resulted in an oral history project, a youth group history and fund-raising project, and people's history fair in the village, as well as my M.A. thesis "The Road to Mamre: Migration, Memory and the Meaning of Community, circa 1900–1992" (1992). One of my primary intellectual inspirations was *Siaya* as Cohen and Odhiambo explored the fluidity of place, movement, and imagination in constructing community identity and notions of home.

CER was one of the few pedagogical initiatives at university level that sought to directly address the issue of accountable research as a core mission of the production of knowledge in the academy. It was certainly the only one of its kind at the elite universities in South Africa at the time. CER involved an extensive critique of and innovate on the methodologies of Paulo Freire's "education for liberation." Catherine Kell, who codirected CER through its three cohorts of master's students, was grounded in the theories and practice of Freirian methodologies as they applied to teaching adult literacy. Freire's *Pedagogy of the*

Oppressed (1970) had been influenced by Fanon (1961) in seeking to change the consciousness of the oppressed so that they could liberate themselves from their oppressors instead of seeking to emulate them within the confines of existing social structures. Within the anti-apartheid movement, this methodology was a powerful tool; Freire's books were influential in the Black Consciousness movement and subsequently banned by the South African state.

The MDM Defiance Campaign launched in August 1989 challenged the state of emergency through coordinated local and national civil disobedience campaigns that challenged segregation, established the right of peaceful mass protest and directly defied state authority through parallel structures of authority in African townships. It was clear that apartheid's days were numbered, but the struggle over shaping the transformation of post-apartheid society intensified by both the state and the liberation movements. In response to internal and external pressures, President F.W. de Klerk announced the unbanning of all political parties and the release of political prisoners at the opening of parliament in early 1990. I was among the estimated 80,000 people who packed the Cape Town parade grounds on the hot summer's morning of February 11, 1990, and one of the fewer thousands who waited until the late evening to hear Nelson Mandela give his first public speech in 27 years and to sing with him *Nkosi Sikelel' iAfrika* (God Bless Africa), the nineteenth-century Xhosa hymn by Enoch Sontonga that had become a pan-African liberation anthem and was incorporated into the post-apartheid national anthem of South Africa.

Comparative and Connective Histories

By the early 1990s, with apartheid in its violent death throes, the transformation of liberation organizations into political parties, and the reintegration of political and intellectual exiles back into South Africa, I decided to pursue my doctorate in Australia or the United States. Nigel Worden and I discussed that one of the largest gaps in Cape slave historiography was an analysis of connections between

Southeast Asia and South Africa during the Dutch colonial period because the Dutch East India Company headquarters was in Batavia (modern Jakarta) on the island of Java. For political reasons, no South African historian had conducted research in the colonial archives in Jakarta since the 1920s.

I designed a doctoral research project on slavery and forced migration in the Dutch East India Company period focusing on the links between Batavia and the Cape. This would require multiarchival research trips to The Hague, Jakarta, and Cape Town. I was recruited to the University of Michigan by David Cohen with whom I had been corresponding about my M.A. thesis and potential Ph.D. topic. The combination of Africanists David Cohen and Frederick Cooper; Southeast Asianists Victor Lieberman, Rudolf Mrazek, and Ann Stoler; and Julia Adams, an historical sociologist whose research on patrimonialism and evolution of the early modern Dutch state, offered the opportunity to engage in the perfect multi-area specialization and language training in Dutch and Indonesian for my intended project.

There was no course in "world history" at Michigan in the early 1990s, not even at undergraduate level. But there was incredible excitement around the Doctoral Program in Anthropology and History, which drew faculty and students from a wide variety of area studies and theoretical perspectives into a joint seminar program. I declined to formally register in the dual degree, preferring to participate selectively as part of my doctoral program in History, although I did participate in the "retrospective" collective *Anthrohistory* (2011). Area Studies at Michigan was under review and restructuring with the foundation of the International Institute under the direction of David Cohen. Graduate students were simultaneously recruited into area studies programs and encouraged to think beyond these boundaries and envisage connections across historiographies, theoretical approaches, and areas of research.

From among the many exciting collaborations of that period, four stand out for me in terms of my evolution as a "world historian" even though I never heard nor used that phrase once in graduate school. One was participating in Southeast Asian history seminars with Victor Lieberman and John Whitmore at the time when Lieberman was developing his "Eurasian analogies" ideas transcending east–west dichotomies that would result in his collaborative project *Beyond Binary Histories* (1999). His rethinking of the foundations of Southeast Asian history as comparative world history within the framework of Eurasia continued with the publication of his two-volume magnum opus, *Strange Parallels* (2003 and 2009). The second was having the unique opportunity to read and discuss early modern history and social theory and historical sociology with Julia Adams while she was writing *The Familial State* (2005), which sought to explain state formation and empire in early modern Europe through examining patrimonialism and patriarchy in the Dutch Republic in comparison with France and England. It was with Julia that I finally digested Wallerstein and his critics, oftentimes over an evening meal at an Ann Arbor eatery. The third was participating in Frederick Cooper and Jane Burbank's "Empires" advanced seminar at the International Institute, which planted the seed that would eventually bear fruit in their *Empires in World History* (2010). The fourth was working closely with David Cohen and his large cohort of graduate students as we engaged with each other's intellectual journeys such as my close colleague Lynn Thomas' dissertation on gender, reproduction, and the state in modern Kenya (Thomas, 2003). Although none of the aforementioned academics would call themselves "world historians," it is no coincidence that their work has been recognized as making a contribution to the field. In the last few years, particularly under the inspiration of Douglas Northrop, this recognition of Michigan's potential to develop the field of world history has resulted in new curricula initiatives at undergraduate and graduate level, as well as in his edited collection *Companion to World History* (2012) for which I wrote the chapter "People in Motion."

My original intention with my dissertation research was to incorporate an empirical analysis of the slave trade into the spectrum of forced migration of the Dutch East India Company. Although historians, particularly Robert Shell, had already established the broad patterns of the origins of slaves to the Cape and argued that the nature of the archival sources made it extremely difficult to enumerate the slave trade, I thought I would be able to overcome the challenges of the fractured nature of archival sources. I was wrong. It quickly became apparent that unless I had a decade to devote to archival research I would need to rethink the parameters of my project. Beginning with the criminal records of the Cape, available in the Cape archives, I began compiling a database of criminals (including slaves) who had been sentenced to penal transportation from other Dutch East India Company settlements. A pattern emerged whereby penal transportation emanated from Batavia as the imperial capital. I then proceeded to the Dutch East India Company archives in The Hague to follow up with the Batavian criminal records to match individual names to their original criminal cases to figure out the details of their crimes leading to a sentence of penal transportation. I was hoping this would be a relatively simple archival exercise. But I was wrong again. It was akin to looking for a needle in a haystack because it was a rare moment, sometimes only once or twice in a full week of archival research, that I found someone I recognized from my Cape based list of names. However, looking at the topic from the perspective of Batavia criminal records, I realized that the Cape was just one place of penal transportation. When I returned to the archives to revise my dissertation for the book, I began to build up a database of cases that included all destinations of penal transportation in the Company realm and thereby to extend my original analysis.

My research in the National Archives in Jakarta during 1998 did not take place under ideal research conditions as it coincided with the collapse of the Suharto government that had been in power since a military coup in 1965. The *Reformasi* (reform) movement to democratize Indonesia combined with the social pressure generated by the economic crisis of the late 1990s that hit Southeast Asia's "tiger economies" particularly hard resulted in Suharto succumbing to demands for his resignation. Some of the urban violence that accompanied this period resulted in the evacuation of foreign nationals, while many wealthy Indonesians, particularly ethnic Chinese-Indonesians whose communities were targeted for violence, fled to Singapore. Nevertheless, the archivists at the National Archives were extremely helpful when the archives were open. Because the archival files were organized by geographical space rather than topic or bureaucratic division, I was able to find some sources that would have remained "hidden" through the organization of Dutch East India Company archives in the Netherlands and South Africa (Ward, 2011b).

During the period of my dissertation, the Dutch government funded an innovative program to digitize, catalog, and share Dutch colonial archives, as well as train local researchers and archivists from areas where there are major holdings of Dutch colonial archives. This has changed the potential for multi-area research in Dutch colonial history. One of the challenges remains the acquisition of languages for research. The archives that I used were all in seventeenth- and eighteenth-century Dutch. I used my Indonesian language training for reading the modern historiography of Indonesian history. Other historians of Dutch–Asian relations often tend to focus on one region because there were so many different Asian languages and scripts in the region and gaining research competence in one language, for example Javanese, does not mean that one can read other regional languages that have their own scripts. Considering that I was focusing on a broad comparative project, I decided to concentrate on the Dutch sources and rely on assistance from other experts in the field if I needed translation of an Asian-language source from the seventeenth or eighteenth century. One of the challenges of my multi-site archival project was reading "across the archives" not only in terms of organization but in terms of shifting perspective and world view from one place to another. That is what I set out to achieve in my dissertation "The Bounds of Bondage: Forced Migration from Batavia to the Cape of Good Hope in the Dutch East India Company (VOC) Period, 1652–1795" (2002).

Becoming a World Historian

No graduate student in the last 20 years needs to be told about the vagaries and serendipities of the academic job market. What was interesting in terms of area studies training was that I was shortlisted for jobs in African and early modern history but not in Southeast Asian or Asian history. Martha Chaiklin, my doctoral student colleague in Dutch–Japanese cultural history at Leiden University, pointed out an advertisement for an assistant professorship in world history at Rice University. Having never thought of myself as a world historian, I went about crafting an application letter that set out my training and my willingness to engage in this "new paradigm." When invited to campus, I had several intense conversations with faculty about how my research connected to world history, particularly Gale Stokes, the Dean of Humanities, who had cowritten a Western civilizations textbook (Hollister, McGee, and Stokes, 1999). I was utterly astonished and delighted when I was offered the position and upon my arrival at Rice in 2001, as promised, I set about making myself into a world historian.

Just as I was completing my dissertation in 2002, Lauren Benton published *Law and Colonial Cultures: Legal Regimes in World History* (2002). I cannot overestimate how influential Benton's work was in helping me to think more broadly about the formation of sovereignty and the rule of law in the context of empire in preparation for writing my book. Timothy Coates' book on the Portuguese empire *Convicts and Orphans* (2001) likewise provided a comparative model for conceptualizing a spectrum of free and forced migration in an imperial context. It was through these books and the growing literature on networks that I began mapping out my book. However, it was through ongoing intellectual collaborations, especially with my graduate colleague from Michigan, Colleen O'Neal, that I was able to articulate the model of imperial networks that provides the foundation of my book, *Networks of Empire: Forced Migration in the Dutch East India Company* (2009). I was excited to have the book included in the Cambridge University Press "Studies in Comparative World History" series founded by Philip Curtin that included his seminal work *Cross Cultural Trade in World History* (1984), as well as the books by Lieberman and Benton already mentioned.

Simultaneously, my friend and fellow Cape colonial historian, Laura Mitchell, was busy making herself into an Africanist-world historian at UC Irvine to continue this trajectory. Our different institutional settings created differing demands. While Mitchell developed world history survey and African history lecture courses, the much smaller class sizes at Rice allowed me to focus on specialized thematic world history seminar courses on forced migration, comparative slavery, comparative imperial and colonial history, and Indian Ocean history. We both found our feet through participation in the World History Association where senior scholars, notably Jerry Bentley, editor of the *Journal of World History*, and Patrick Manning, then head of the World History Center at Northeastern University, were generous and encouraging to younger scholars. Listing all the senior world historians and my contemporaries who have been creatively engaged in world history would take up more space than my editor, fellow Africanist and world historian Ken Curtis, will allow, so I will focus below on books that I think have made significant contributions to "Africa in world history."

The main methodological point I want to make here is that I believe collaborative projects have made some of the most innovative contributions to world history as a field but because of the merit structures of the academy this form of knowledge production is not valued as highly as single authored monographs. Given the methodological challenges of world history – multiple area specializations, research languages, and archival expertise – it is a general trend that senior historians (Victor Lieberman is a case in point here) write synthetic world history books. Graduate students conceptualizing their dissertations or junior scholars working on their first books instead produce research monographs that contribute to world history conceptually by pushing the boundaries of their primary fields or demonstrating explicitly that world history approaches contribute to these fields. It was after I started my appointment in world history at Rice that I finished my dissertation and then reconceptualized it as a contribution to world history while revising it for publication.

African History and Oceanic History

I conceptualized *Networks of Empire* as intersecting debates in oceanic world history around the themes of forced migration and diasporas, connective histories and networks, comparative empires, and biographies. *Networks of Empire* shifted the focus of slavery in early colonial South Africa from comparisons with the Atlantic World to connections with the Indian Ocean while expanding the analysis of slavery into multiple forms of bondage including penal transportation and religious and political exile.

Foundational works in Atlantic History (Curtin, 1972; Miller, 1988; Thornton, 1992) reconceptualized African history as integral to the making of the Atlantic world and by extension of world history. Historians of early colonialism in South Africa drew upon these debates in Atlantic studies to situate the Cape of Good Hope within these frameworks. Cape slavery historians had identified the origins and approximate numbers of slaves from around the Indian Ocean but had drawn their comparative examples from the Atlantic rather than examining how the slave trade to the Cape had evolved within existing Indian Ocean networks and comparing Cape slavery to forms of indigenous and colonial slavery in the slaves' regions of origin. By the time I was writing *Networks of Empire*, the field of Indian Ocean studies was growing rapidly particularly through the collaborative energy of Ned Alpers at UCLA and also Gwyn Campbell at Avignon, who later founded the Indian Ocean World Centre at McGill University in 2004. These projects resulted in a significant extension of African history and its connections to slavery and bondage in the Indian Ocean world connecting Africa and Asia through the multibook series *Studies in Slave and Post-Slave Societies and Cultures* edited by Campbell and various colleagues. This is not to argue that African history did not previously connect to the Indian Ocean, the long established literature on the Swahili Coast, especially the work of Abdul Sheriff (2010) and of linking the western Indian Ocean islands and archipelagos to Africa and these regions to the Arabian peninsula have been a core part of African history. William Gervase Clarence-Smith's work on the economics of the Indian Ocean slave trade (1989) was an early contribution to this field, and studies of the African diaspora in the Indian Ocean have proliferated recently (De Silva Jayasuriya and Pankhurst, 2003). But extending these debates into a reconsideration of the Indian Ocean itself has been relatively new given that the foundational histories of the

Indian Ocean like Chaudhuri 's *Trade and Civilization in the Indian Ocean* (1985) only mentions Africa in passing. The South Asianist, Michael Pearson, soon made up for Chaudhuri's omissions with his study of the Swahili Coast, *Port Cities and Intruders* (1998).

The elaboration of these "oceanic worlds" of the Atlantic and Indian Oceans has developed in parallel with a rethinking of region that transcends the older area studies frameworks in three ways, first by considering the ocean itself as a connective region, second by challenging the bounded notions of "Africa" or "Asia", and third by examining the global flows and movements of people as categories, and increasingly, as individuals in a renaissance of biographical writing that exemplifies one of the new directions of world history. Michael Pearson's Indian Ocean history (2003) set the agenda of writing history from the sea rather than from the land. Jerry Bentley, Renate Bridenthal, and Kären Wigen's *Seascapes* (2007) conceptualized their project as moving beyond area studies to transregional and global historical analyses bringing together "ocean-oriented" scholars through exploring categories of oceanic constructs, transmarine empires, maritime sociologies, and maritime subversives. My chapter on the Cape as a transoceanic "tavern of the seas" in *Seascapes* (Ward, 2007) sought to cross over the conceptualization of Atlantic and Indian Ocean worlds.

Finishing a book sometimes means saying "no" to the siren song of invitations to collaborate in fascinating projects. One of these, conceptualized by Atlantic historians Emma Christopher, Cassandra Pybus, and Marcus Rediker, resulted in *Many Middle Passages: Forced Migration and the Making of the Modern World* (2007), which pushed my thinking about the spectrums of forced migration that I was articulating in *Networks of Empire*. The concept of "middle passage" as articulated in the history of the Atlantic slave trade as a "threefold process of violence, resistance, and creativity," was extended to examine a range of coercive migrations that involved oceanic voyages in a variety of contexts. These insights were carried further by Clare Anderson who conceptualized the project on "Marginal Centers" (2011) that extended the reach of middle passages to individual life journeys. My contribution to Anderson's project, "Bloodties: Exile, Family, and Inheritance across the Indian Ocean in the Early Nineteenth Century," extended the narrative of *Networks of Empire* into the British Empire (Ward, 2011a). I think Anderson eloquently articulates one of the most exciting new methodological directions of world history in the digital age, even though she is commenting explicitly on Indian Ocean history.

> Methodologically, this makes us take seriously the implications of crossing geographical and imperial borders and thus national archives and languages ... If writing life histories in the Indian Ocean suggests a different pay of producing historical knowledge – and producing new types of history – collaboratively, so does the changing nature of history within and beyond the academy ... [G]rowing academic interest in biography has emerged at least partly out of a broader social interest in family history ... Indeed it would not be an exaggeration to say that without respecting non-academic historians as producers of knowledge in their own right, and the heritage industry, much of our research would have been impossible. (Anderson, 2011, pp. 338–339)

I find these trends exciting in connecting Africa to world history. Biography and oceanic history (Anderson, 2012) has opened up the space for new contributions to African history, including the perennial student favorite, Ross Dunn's *The Adventures of Ibn Battuta* (1987) and the reworking of the story of Leo Africanus by Natalie Zemon Davis (2007). Taking this methodology further into family history, Linda Colley's biography of Elizabeth Marsh (2007), Rebecca Scott's *Freedom Papers* (2012), and James Sweet's *Domingos Alvares* (2011) explore the meanings of freedom, gender, and racial identity connecting living in Africa to broader world experiences.

And finally, the decades long collaboration project *Voyages: The Trans-Atlantic Slave Trade Data Base* (www.slavevoyages.org) under the direction of David Richardson and David Eltis exemplifies Anderson's claim that the boundaries of producing history have changed in the digital age. Although the database was conceived as a scholarly project to build on Philip Curtin's initial attempts to enumerate the numbers of Africans in the trans-Atlantic slave trade, the

Voyages Database includes detailed information on almost 35,000 slaving voyages from in the Atlantic and Indian Oceans. It has become an educational tool for schools (with provided materials) and individuals seeking to do their own historical research and even to correct errors and add information to the database.

My next project will draw on the *Voyages Database* to unpack the forced migration of Africans after the formal end of the slave trade and to examine the expansion of the British Empire through the antislavery projects of the nineteenth century. But the larger question I want to explore is about why there was such a concentration of economic and diplomatic resources by the British on suppressing the trade in African slaves in the western Indian Ocean while there was little systematic effort to suppress forced migration in the eastern Indian Ocean, particularly the networks that were linked to the Straits Settlements. Many discussions with Eric Tagliacozzo while he was writing his book on illicit trade across Southeast Asian maritime frontiers alerted me to this discrepancy in British antislavery projects (Tagliacozzo, 2005). Within this larger Indian Ocean framework, I am exploring a specific thread of Anglo-American connections in the nineteenth century, particularly around the period of the American Civil War. The extent of American shipping, capital, and diplomacy in the Indian Ocean has not been well researched and I think that these questions might contribute to bridging the divide between the "oceanic worlds" of the Atlantic and Indian Oceans. Such global research projects are increasingly viable because of the massive expansion of online archival resources. I am fascinated to engage with the next generation of historians trained in world history who are connecting African history to global frameworks that move beyond established area studies divides.

But as an historian of slavery and forced migration I have also become increasingly aware of the emergence of political and cultural discourses on "global human trafficking." With my colonial Americanist colleague James Sidbury, I codirected a year-long Rice Seminar on *Human Trafficking Past and Present: Crossing Disciplines, Crossing Borders* bringing together a multidisciplinary group of scholars to explore how the current emergence of human trafficking discourses draws on a limited understanding of historical slavery and to read across the contemporary and historical debates to gain new insights into our respective fields of scholarship. This brought us back to debates framed by Orlando Patterson (1982) on slavery and social death to consider whether contemporary forms of unfreedom constitute what Sidbury has called "civic death." In bridging the historical to the contemporary we are connecting to antitrafficking initiatives in Houston to encourage further engagement between the academy and our community bringing the global to the local. In some way, this is an extension of my training and scholarship in CER in South Africa. As a member of "Historians against Slavery," I believe that scholars have a role to play in bringing to the fore historical antecedents of contemporary social issues to extend critical public awareness of our world.

References

Adams, Julia. 2005. *The Familial State: Ruling Families and Merchant Capitalism in Early Modern Europe*. Ithaca, NY/London: Cornell University Press.

Anderson, B. 1983. *Imagined Communities: Reflections on the Origin and Spread of Nationalism*. London: Verso.

Anderson, Clare. 2011. "Introduction to Marginal Centers: Writing Life Histories in the Indian Ocean World," *Journal of Social History* 45/2: 335–344.

Anderson, Clare. 2012. *Subaltern Lives: Biographies of Colonialism in the Indian Ocean World, 1790–1920*. Cambridge: Cambridge University Press.

Bentley, J., R. Bridenthal, and K. Wigen, eds. 2007. *Seascapes: Maritime Histories, Littoral Cultures, and Transoceanic Exchanges*. Honolulu, HI: Hawaii University Press.

Benton, Lauren. 2002. *Law and Colonial Cultures: Legal Regimes in World History*. New York: Cambridge University Press.

Bundy, Colin. 1979. *The Rise and Fall of the South African Peasantry*. London: Heineman Press.

Campbell, G., S. Miers, and J. Miller, eds. 2008. *Women in Slavery. Vol. 2: The Modern Atlantic*. Athens, OH: Ohio University Press.

Cell, John. 1982. *The Highest Stage of White Supremacy: The Origins of Segregation in South Africa and the American South*. Cambridge: Cambridge University Press.

Chaudhuri, K. N. 1985. *Trade and Civilization in the Indian Ocean: An Economic History from the Rise of Islam to 1750*. Cambridge: Cambridge University Press.

Christopher, E., C. Pybus, and M. Rediker, eds. 2007. *Many Middle Passages: Forced Migration and the Making of the Modern World*. Berkeley, CA: University of California Press.

Clarence-Smith, W.G., ed. 1989. *The Economics of the Indian Ocean Slave Trade in the 19th Century*. London: Frank Cass and Company.

Coates, T. 2001. *Convicts and Orphans: Forced Migration and State-sponsored Colonizers in the Portuguese empire, 1550–1775*. Palo Alto, CA: Stanford University Press.

Cohen, D.W. and E.S. Atieno Odhiambo. 1989. *Siyaya: The Historical Anthropology of an African Landscape*. Athens, OH: Ohio University Press; London: James Currey.

Colley, L. 2007. *The Ordeal of Elizabeth Marsh: A Woman in World History*. New York: Anchor Press.

Cooper, F. 1977. *Plantation Slavery on the East Coast of Africa*. New Haven, CT: Yale University Press.

Cooper, F. 1980. *From Slaves to Squatters: Plantation Labor and Agriculture in Zanzibar and Coastal Kenya 1890–1925*. New Haven, CT: Yale University Press.

Cooper, F. and J. Burbank. 2010. *Empires in World History: Power and the Politics of Difference*. Princeton, NJ/Oxford: Princeton University Press.

Crais, Clifton. 1992. *White Supremacy and Black Resistance in Pre-Industrial South Africa: The Making of the Colonial Order in the Eastern Cape, 1770–1865*. Cambridge: Cambridge University Press; Johannesburg: Witwatersrand University Press.

Curtin, P. 1972. *The Atlantic Slave Trade: A Census*. Madison, WI: University of Wisconsin Press.

Curtin, P. 1984. *Cross Cultural Trade in World History*. Cambridge: Cambridge University Press.

David, Eltis and Martin Halbert. *Voyages: The Trans-Atlantic Slave Trade Data Base*. www.slavevoyages.org. Accessed on October 26, 2013.

Davidson, B. 1964. *The African Past: Chronicles from Antiquity to Modern Times*. London: Longmans.

De Silva Jayasuriya, S and R. Pankhurst, eds. 2003. *The African Diaspora in the Indian Ocean*. Trenton, NJ: Africa World Press.

Denoon, D. 1983. *Settler Capitalism: The Dynamics of Dependent Development in the Southern Hemisphere*. Oxford: Clarendon Press.

Denoon, D. and A. Kuper. 1970. "Nationalist Historians in Search of a Nation: The 'New Historiography' in Dar es Salaam." *African Affairs* 69/277: 329–349.
Dunn, R. 1987. *The Adventures of Ibn Battuta: A Muslim Traveler of the Fourteenth Century*. Berkeley, CA: University of California Press.
Elphick, R. and H. Giliomee, eds. 1989. *The Shaping of South African Society, 1652–1840*. Cape Town: Maskew Miller Longman.
Etherington, N. 1984. *Theories of Imperialism: War, Conquest and Capital*. Beckenham: Croom Helm Ltd.
Fanon F. 1961. *The Wretched of the Earth*. New York: Grove Press.
Frank A. G. 1966. *The Development of Underdevelopment*. London: Monthly Review Press.
Frederickson, G. 1981. *White Supremacy: A Comparative Study in American and South African History*. Oxford: Oxford University Press.
Freire, P. 1970. *Pedagogy of the Oppressed*. New York/London: Continuum International Publishing Group.
Geertz, C. 1963. *Old Societies and New States: The Quest for Modernity in Asia and Africa*. New York: Free Press.
Gilbert, E. and J. Reynolds. 2012. *Africa in World History*, 3rd edition. Upper Saddle River, NJ: Pearson Education.
Greenberg, S. 1980. *Race and State in Capitalist Development*. New Haven, CT: Yale University Press.
Harvey, N., Nick Harvey, Jean Fornasiero, Greg McCarthy, Clem Macintyre, and Carl Crossin, eds. 2012. *A History of the Faculty of Arts at the University of Adelaide, 1876–2012*. Adelaide: Adelaide University Press.
Hobsbawm, E. and T. Ranger, eds. 1983. *The Invention of Tradition*. Cambridge: Cambridge University Press.
Hollister, W., S. McGee and G. Stokes. 1999. *The West Transformed: A History of Western Civilization*. Belmont, CA: Wadsworth Publishing.
Isaac, R. 1982. *The Transformation of Virginia, 1740–1790*. Williamsburg, VA. Omohundro Institute of Early American History and Culture.
Lamar, H. and L. Thompson. 1981. *The Frontier in History: North America and Southern Africa Compared*. New Haven, CT: Yale University Press.
Lieberman, V., ed. 1999. *Beyond Binary Histories: Re-imagining Eurasia to c. 1830*.Ann Arbor, MI: University of Michigan Press.
Lieberman, V. 2003. *Strange Parallels: Southeast Asia in Global Context, c. 800–1830, vol. 1: Integration on the Mainland*. New York: Cambridge University Press.

Lieberman, V. 2009. *Strange Parallels: Southeast Asia in Global Context, c. 800–1830, vol. 2: Mainland Mirrors: Europe, Japan, China, South Asia, and the Islands*. Cambridge: Cambridge University Press.

Marks, S. and A. Atmore, eds. 1980. *Economy and Society in Pre-Industrial South Africa*. London: Longman Publishing Group.

Marks, S. and R. Rathbone, eds. 1982. *Industrialisation and Social Change in South Africa*. London: Longman Publishing Group.

Miller, J. 1988. *Way of Death: Merchant Capitalism and the Angolan Slave Trade, 1730–1850*. Madison, WI: University of Wisconsin Press.

Moore, B. Jr. 1966. *Social Origins of Dictatorship and Democracy: Lord and Peasant in the Making of the Modern World*. Boston, MA: Beacon Press.

Northrop, D., ed. 2012. *A Companion to World History*. Hoboken, NJ: Wiley-Blackwell.

Oliver, R. and A. Atmore. 1967. *Africa Since 1800*, 1st edition. Cambridge: Cambridge University Press.

Omer-Cooper, J. 1966. *The Zulu Aftermath: A Nineteenth Century Revolution in Bantu Africa*. London: Longman Publishing Group.

Patterson, O. 1982. *Slavery and Social Death: A Comparative Study*. Cambridge, MA: Harvard University Press.

Pearson, M. 1998. *Port Cities and Intruders: The Swahili Coast, India and the Portuguese in the Early Modern Period*. Baltimore, MD/London: The John Hopkins University Press.

Pearson, M. 2003. *The Indian Ocean*. London: Routledge.

Rodney, W. 1972. *How Europe Underdeveloped Africa*. London: Bogle-L'Overture Publications.

Ross, R. 1983. *Cape of Torments: Slavery and Resistance in South Africa*. London: Routledge, Chapman and Hall Inc.

Rostow, W.W. 1960. *Stages of Economic Growth: A Non-Communist Manifesto*. Cambridge: Cambridge University Press.

Roux, E. 1967. *Time Longer than Rope: A History of the Black Man's Struggle for Freedom in South Africa*. Madison, WI: University of Wisconsin Press.

Saul, J. and S. Gelb. 1981. *The Crisis in South Africa*. New York: Monthly Review Press.

Saunders, C. 1988. *The Making of the South African Past: Major Historians on Race and Class*. Cape Town: David Philip Publishers.

Scott, R. 2012. *Freedom Papers: An Atlantic Odyssey in the Age of Emancipation*. Cambridge, MA: Harvard University Press.

Scully, P. 1997. *Liberating the Family? Gender and British Slave Emancipation in the Rural Western Cape, South Africa, 1823–1853*. Portsmouth, NH: Heinemann.

Shell, R.C-H. 1994. *Children of Bondage: A Social History of the Slave Society at the Cape of Good Hope, 1652–1838*. Hanover, NH: University Press of New England.

Sheriff, A. 2010. *Dhow Cultures in the Indian Ocean: Cosmopolitanism, Commerce, and Islam*. New York: Columbia University Press.

Simon, H. J. and R.E. Simon. 1969. *Class and Colour in South Africa, 1850–1950*. Baltimore, MD: Penguin Books.

Streets-Salter, H. 2012. "Becoming a World Historian: The State of Graduate Training in World History and Placement in the Academic World," in D. Northrop, ed. *A Companion to World History*. Chichester: Wiley-Blackwell.

Sweet, J. 2011. *Domingos Alvares, African Healing and the Intellectual History of the Atlantic World*. Chapel Hill, NC: University of North Carolina Press.

Tagliacozzo, E. 2005. *Secret Trades, Porous Borders: Smuggling and States Along a Southeast Asian Frontier, 1865–1915*. New Haven, CT: Yale University Press.

Thomas, L. 2003. *Politics of the Womb: Women, Reproduction, and the State in Kenya*. Berkeley, CA: University of California Press.

Thornton, J. 1992. *Africa and Africans in the Making of the Atlantic World, 1400–1650*. Cambridge: Cambridge University Press.

Trevor-Roper, H. 1969. "The Past and the Present: History and Sociology." *Past and Present* 42: 3–17.

Vansina, J. 1965. *Oral Tradition: A Study in Historical Methodology*. Chicago, IL: Aldine Publishing Company.

Wallerstein, I. 1974. *The Modern World System: Capitalist Agriculture and the Origins of the European World Economy in the Sixteenth Century*. New York: Academic Press.

Ward, K. 1992. "The Road to Mamre: Migration, Memory and the Meaning of Community, c1900–1992." Unpublished MA thesis, University of Cape Town.

Ward, K. 1994. "The Making of Mamre: Community, Identity and Migration in a Western Cape Village, c1838–1938," in N Worden and C Crais, eds. *Breaking the Chains: Slavery and Emancipation in South Africa*. Johannesburg: Witwatersrand University Press.

Ward, K. 2002. "The Bounds of Bondage: Forced Migration from Batavia to the Cape of Good Hope in the Dutch East India Company (VOC) Period, 1652–1795." Unpublished PhD dissertation, University of Michigan, Ann Arbor.

Ward, K. 2007. "'Tavern of the Seas?' The Cape of Good Hope as an Oceanic Crossroads During the Seventeenth and Eighteenth Centuries," in Bentley, J., R. Bridenthal, and K. Wigen, eds. *Seascapes: Maritime Histories, Littoral Cultures, and Transoceanic Exchanges*. Honolulu, HI: University of Hawaii Press.

Ward, K. 2009. *Networks of Empire: Forced Migration in the Dutch East India Company*. Studies in Comparative World History. New York: Cambridge University Press. Cambridge Africa Collection. Cape Town: Cambridge University Press (paperback edition).

Ward, K. 2011a. "The Politics of Burial in Post-Apartheid South Africa," in Chandra D. Bhimull, David William Cohen, and Fernando Coronil, Julie Skurski, Edward L. Murphy, and Monica Patterson, eds. *Anthrohistory: Unsettling Knowledge and the Question of Discipline*. Ann Arbor, MI: University of Michigan Press.

Ward, K. 2011b. "Blood Ties: Exile, Family and Inheritance Across the Indian Ocean in the Early Nineteenth Century," *Journal of Social History* 45/2: 436–454.

Ward, K. 2012. "People in Motion," in Douglas Northrop, ed. *A Companion to World History*. Hoboken, NJ: Wiley Blackwell.

Wilson, M. and L. Thompson. 1971. *Oxford History of South Africa*, 2 vols. Oxford: The Clarendon Press.

Witz, L. 1988. *Write Your Own History*. Johannesburg: Sached Trust, Raven Press.

Worden, N. 1985. *Slavery in Dutch South Africa*. Cambridge: Cambridge University Press.

Worden, N. and C. Crais, eds. 1995. *Breaking the Chains: Slavery and its Legacy in the Nineteenth-Century Cape Colony*. Johannesburg: Witwatersrand University Press.

Zemon Davis, N. 2007. *Trickster Travels: A Sixteenth-Century Muslim Between Worlds*. New York: Hill and Wang.

Further Reading

Anderson, Clare. 2012. *Subaltern Lives: Biographies of Colonialism in the Indian Ocean World, 1790–1920*. Cambridge: Cambridge University Press.

Bentley, J., R. Bridenthal and K. Wigen, eds. 2007. *Seascapes: Maritime Histories, Littoral Cultures, and Transoceanic Exchanges*. Honolulu, HI: Hawaii University Press.

Benton, Lauren. 2002. *Law and Colonial Cultures: Legal Regimes in World History*. New York: Cambridge University Press.

Campbell, G., ed. 2003. *The Structure of Slavery in Indian Ocean Africa and Asia*. London: Routledge.

Campbell, G., ed. 2005. *Abolition and Its Aftermath in Indian Ocean Africa and Asia*. London: Routledge.

Campbell, G., E. Alpers, and M. Salmon, eds. 2005. *Slavery and Resistance in Africa and Asia*. London: Routledge.

Campbell, G., E. Alpers, and M. Salmon, eds. 2006. *Resisting Bondage in Indian Ocean Africa and Asia*. London: Routledge.

Campbell, G., S. Miers, and J. Miller, eds. 2007. *Women in Slavery. Vol. 1: Africa, the Indian Ocean World, and the Medieval North Atlantic*. Athens, OH: Ohio University Press.

Christopher, E., C. Pybus, and M. Rediker, eds. 2007. *Many Middle Passages: Forced Migration and the Making of the Modern World*. Berkeley, CA: University of California Press.

Colley, L. 2007. *The Ordeal of Elizabeth Marsh: A Woman in World History*. New York: Anchor Press.

Cooper, F. and A. Stoler, eds. 1997. *Tensions of Empire: Colonial Cultures in a Bourgeois World*. Berkeley, CA: University of California Press.

Fanon, F. 1967. *Black Skin, White Masks*, 1st English edition. New York: Grove Press.

Northrop, D., ed. 2012. *A Companion to World History*. Hoboken, NJ: Wiley-Blackwell.

Tagliacozzo, E. 2005. *Secret Trades, Porous Borders: Smuggling and States Along a Southeast Asian Frontier, 1865–1915*. New Haven, CT: Yale University Press.

Ward, K. 2009. *Networks of Empire: Forced Migration in the Dutch East India Company*. Studies in Comparative World History. New York: Cambridge University Press.

8

Big History

David Christian

What Is Big History?

Big history is the transdisciplinary study of the entire past – not just of humanity or even the earth, but of the entire universe. It studies the past on all possible scales in time and space. By doing so, it combines into a single coherent narrative the stories told within many different scholarly disciplines, all of which study the past. So all face the same basic challenge: how best to understand a vanished past from the random clues left to the present. The website of the International Big History Association (IBHA, 2010) describes big history as "the attempt to understand, in a unified, interdisciplinary way, the history of Cosmos, Earth, Life, and Humanity."

Big history shares much with world history. But it differs from world history because it crosses so many disciplinary borders and takes you well beyond the conventional borders of the history discipline. It surveys some 13.8 billion years, in contrast to the 10,000 years or so of

Architects of World History: Researching the Global Past, First Edition.
Edited by Kenneth R. Curtis and Jerry H. Bentley.

many world history courses. To put this in perspective, if the universe had been created 13 years ago instead of 13 billion years ago, the standard world history course would begin just two and a half minutes ago. To study earlier periods, you have to enter the domains of archaeology, of biology, of geology, and eventually cosmology. So the fact that most big history courses inhabit history departments is really an institutional accident. Future big history courses will settle as comfortably within archeology or biology or astronomy departments as within departments of history.

Their scale ensures that all big history courses must bridge the gulf between the humanities and the natural sciences. So big history faces the complex but fascinating challenge of finding a place for human history within the larger histories of the biosphere, the planet and the universe as a whole. Big history attempts to link human history and the natural sciences, in the belief that doing this can enhance our understanding both of our own species and of the planet and the universe we inhabit.

In the second decade of the twenty-first century, most educators and researchers still find big history an unfamiliar and perhaps discomfiting approach to the past. So I will start this essay by describing my own path from history to big history. Then I will describe some of the central ideas of big history as it is practiced today. Then I will try to place big history within the evolution of historical thought in general. Finally, I will discuss how big history may evolve in the near future, both as a form of education and as a form of research.

A Personal Pathway to Big History

I believe I moved toward big history because I am, by instinct, a "framework" thinker.

Framework Thinking: For many students of history, the details are numinous, engaging, and endlessly fascinating. Take a historical event such as the assassination of the Archduke Franz Ferdinand, heir to the Austrian throne, on June 28, 1914, in the Bosnian city of Sarajevo. Why did the Archduke visit Sarajevo? Why did the first two attempts to assassinate him fail? Why was a third assassin, Gavrilo Princip, ready, even though the Archduke changed his route? What did the assassins hope to achieve? The questions are endless and absorbing. They are also important because the assassination set off the political and military avalanche that started World War I, the largest and most destructive war the world had ever seen.

But for some students of the past, the details make little sense until they can be placed within a larger framework, and seen as parts of a larger story. These are "framework" learners. I was an extreme "framework learner." Faced with an event like the assassination of Archduke Franz Ferdinand I had to place it within a larger framework. What was the deeper "meaning" of the assassination? What can it tell us about nationalism? Why was the war on such a huge scale? Why do humans fight wars anyway? Do animals fight wars? If not, why not?

The danger of thinking like this was that I could easily lose sight of the details. So, though I was reasonably good at assembling historical *arguments*, I had to work much harder at tests that required me to remember dates and details. I often felt that good historians should have a better grip on the details than I had. Indeed, for historians, it is particularly important to feel comfortable with the details. As the philosopher of science, Thomas Kuhn, argued in his classic study, *The Structure of Scientific Revolutions*, history lacks a "paradigm"; it lacks the sort of overarching theoretical framework that natural selection provides for biologists or plate tectonics for geologists or big bang cosmology for astronomers (Kuhn, 1970). Without a paradigm you simply have to feel comfortable handling and interpreting a lot of detailed information if you are to make sense of complex changes or detect significant patterns.

Despite my limitations, I ended up as a professional historian. But my habits of framework thinking kept pushing me toward large framing questions. That may explain why, as a young historian, I was attracted to Marxist historiography and particularly to the work of the great English Marxist historians of the mid-twentieth century, such as Eric Hobsbawm or E.P. Thompson or the American anthropologist, Eric Wolf. I felt that they managed to balance detail and high theory much better than most of the historians I read. I was also attracted to the historians of the French *Annales* school, perhaps because they tried to place human history in a larger geographical and chronological frame. For me, Fernand Braudel's magisterial volumes on the Mediterranean were an inspiring exemplar of this approach (Braudel, 1972).

I think my instinct for framework thinking pushed me toward big history. After all, big history provides the largest possible framework for thinking about the past.

From the History of Russia to the History of the Universe: I had a pretty orthodox training as a historian, with an undergraduate degree at Oxford in "Modern History" (very Anglo- and Euro-centric), an M.A. at the University of Western Ontario in London, Ontario (on Lenin's views of history, though I spent most of my time acting), and then a doctorate (back at Oxford) in Russian history. My dissertation examined an unsuccessful 2-year-long discussion of constitutional reform early in the reign of Tsar Alexander I (1801–1825). I studied these discussions using the Bodleian library in Oxford, and archival sources in the old Senate building in Leningrad (St. Petersburg), near the famous statue of Peter the Great. I remember one document particularly clearly. Its pages were held together by a gorgeous, ivory-headed pin, which means it was almost certainly studied by Catherine the Great.

Alexander grew up in St. Petersburg during the French Revolution and imbibed radical ideas from his Swiss tutor, Frederic La Harpe. When his tyrannical father, Paul I, was assassinated in 1801, Alexander became Tsar. He surrounded himself with aristocratic radicals like himself, and they began to discuss plans for constitutional reforms, but the realities of Russia's feudal, serf-based social structure and warfare with Napoleonic France ensured that these plans were soon shelved. Autocracy and serfdom would outlast Alexander. Even partial constitutional reforms would have to wait for a century, before being reversed again after the October Revolution. Even today, the international NGO, Freedom House, classifies the Russian Federation as "unfree" (Freedom House, 2012). Did Alexander and his friends miss a great opportunity to reform Russia? Or were they political dilettantes, idly playing with the idea of reform? Such questions were good for me. They kept my head down, and my eyes on the details of early nineteenth-century Russian political history, so I completed my dissertation.

On the strength of my doctorate I secured a lectureship in Russian history at Macquarie University in Sydney. But so narrow was my research that I spent my first few years as a lecturer learning about Russian history. Thrown into the classroom utterly unprepared, I was appalled at my own ignorance, and sometimes I think I have spent the rest of my career trying to escape the trap of hyperspecialization.

I learnt quickly that teaching is a wonderful way of learning! Eventually, I wrote a short introductory history of modern Russia (Christian, 1997), which has been used in schools in the Australian state of New South Wales for more than 20 years.

My research took a new direction. Inspired by Fernand Braudel and the *Annales* school, I began researching the material lives of the nineteenth-century peasantry. Eventually, with R.E.F. Smith of Birmingham University, I coauthored a history of food and drink in pre-Soviet Russia (Smith and Christian, 1984). Then I wrote a book on the role of vodka in nineteenth-century Russia (Christian, 1990). That turned out to be a surprisingly interesting and broad-ranging topic. Vodka was not just Russia's main ceremonial and ritual drink; it also generated almost 40% of government revenues in the nineteenth-century. In other words, the Russian government paid for most of the costs of its massive army by taxing the consumption of a mind-altering substance. If Russians had stopped drinking vodka, the Russian government would have come close to collapse. And on one memorable occasion in 1859, when peasants started boycotting vodka sales because prices were too high and quality was too low, the government panicked, and bureaucrats started dreaming up schemes to force peasants to start drinking vodka again. (That fascinating episode generated an entire chapter in my book, and a separate article (Christian, 1991a).)

I enjoyed teaching and researching Russian history. And during the Cold War, teaching Russian and Soviet history seemed important. But I also had the nagging feeling that even Russian history was too specialized. In an increasingly globalized world, didn't my students need to know about the history of humanity as a whole? Wasn't I, as a Russian historian, teaching the dangerous subliminal message that humans will always be divided into competing tribes? What was the larger framework of which Russian history was just one component?

I had no good answers to these questions. Like most historians based outside of the United States, I was unaware of the rapid evolution of world history in the United States. I had not even read the work of pioneer world historians such as William McNeill or Leften Stavrianos or Marshall Hodgson.

But I couldn't shake off the idea of a nontribal history of humanity, so I tried to figure out what such a course might look like. The prospect was daunting. To teach the history of humanity I would have to survey not just 200 years (as I did in my Russian history courses), but 200,000 years. And to do it properly, I would have to discuss the evolution of human beings, which meant introducing some biology. After all, you can't really understand humans without comparing them to other animals. So where did these questions end? Was there a point beyond which larger and larger frameworks ceased to yield new and interesting questions? If there was, I couldn't find it. To *really* understand human evolution, I realized I would have to study the evolution of other species, which would take me back 3.8 billion years to the origins of life on earth. That scale would help me understand the place of humans within the history of life on earth. But to understand the history of life wouldn't I also have to study geology and the history of the earth, and wouldn't that lead me to astronomy and, heaven help me, to cosmology?

Despite a sense of intellectual vertigo, I found these questions exhilarating. And eventually I realized that the regress was not infinite. The story had a clear starting point at the "big bang," the spectacular moment, 13.8 billion years ago, when our universe appeared out of nothingness in a tiny exploding fireball. Before that point we had no evidence for anything, so that was where our story would have to start.

Was it possible (or sensible) to try to teach a history course covering all of this material? The idea seemed doolally. But I wanted to try. After all, I reasoned, if you really wanted to understand how history works, shouldn't you try at least once in your career to get a sense of the whole damn thing? In biology programs, introductory surveys looked over the entire field; why not in history, too? Besides, as someone who had always read good popular science, I knew that some scientists had attempted coherent histories of the universe, though they often skimped on the human history part. I had read Isaac Asimov's popular introductions to science, I knew of Carl Sagan's "Cosmos" series, and I loved John Gribbin's superb universal history, *Genesis* (Gribbin, 1981). So it was mainly the work of scientists that persuaded me to try teaching a history course that placed human history within the largest possible context: the history of the universe. If history is indeed about context (as I had read many times), why not go for broke!

Embedding Human History in the History of the Universe

In 1988, our history department decided that it needed a new first-year course. Keen to try out my "history of everything," I volunteered, and my colleagues (God bless them!) let me try. That decision launched me on an astonishing, exciting, and sometimes terrifying intellectual journey.

A First Course in Big History: At first, I and my historian colleagues had little idea what we were doing. I invited colleagues from the astronomy department, the geology department, the biology department, and the departments of anthropology and ancient history to lecture in our "history of everything." Naively, I imagined that those of us teaching the new course would sit in on the lectures, learn about the different disciplines, put the different stories together, and end up with a coherent history of everything. And, to my surprise and delight, that's more or less what happened, though it proved a more complex task than I had expected. I found very generous allies in other departments and with their help we cobbled together a syllabus. I heard some wonderful lectures that provided just enough material for those of us teaching in the course to glimpse a larger story. Sitting through those lectures, reading around them, and trying to make sense of them in class was my personal apprenticeship in big history. And the questions my students asked kept me focused on the big questions as well as the technical details of the story.

Some of the lectures were spectacularly good. David Allen, an infrared astronomer who worked with the Anglo-Australian Observatory (whose main telescope is based near Coonabarabran, in New South Wales), gave gripping lectures on the Big bang, that were accessible even for audiences with no scientific background at all. I can still remember the entranced silence as an entire lecture theatre followed David's account of how a universe appeared from nothing. A biologist, David Briscoe, gave absorbing and sometimes very funny lectures on evolution. He loved helping students appreciate the complexity of tiny organisms; but he also warned them of the dangers of Social Darwinism. An eminent Australian paleontologist, Mike Archer, gave some of the funniest lectures I have ever heard on our close anatomical similarities with chimps. Michael also helped us understand the severe limitations of so-called "Creation Science." Annette Hamilton, Bob Norton, and Ian Bedford helped me and my students see big history from the unique perspectives of anthropology. Meanwhile, I and my historian colleagues struggled to integrate the complex and contested narratives of human history into the larger narrative of big history, as we talked with real students in real classrooms.

Working with colleagues from so many different disciplines taught me a lot about the strengths and weaknesses of modern universities. I saw more clearly the astonishing range of expertise they warehouse. But I also saw how the disciplinary silos limit the sharing of expertise, knowledge, and insights. For historians, it was baffling and intimidating when a biologist referred in passing to alleles, or a geologist assumed you knew the dates of the Ordovician period. Each of us seemed to peer far too intently at our own patch of a vast scholarly garden. Standing on the shoulders of others to see the whole garden did not come naturally to any of us.

I realized how difficult it was to talk across disciplines. But I also realized how important it was, as I started glimpsing some of the intellectual synergies waiting for those willing to swap ideas across the discipline borders. Scientists generally appreciated these possibilities better than scholars in the humanities. After all, they had seen the astonishing synergies that linked cosmology (the science of the very large) and nuclear physics (the science of the very small) in big bang cosmology, or the many unexpected synergies that have emerged between biochemistry, genetics, natural selection, paleontology, and ecology. C.P. Snow lamented the divide between the cultures of the humanities and the sciences precisely because he knew how many insights were left stranded in a no-man's-land between the two "cultures" (Snow, 1971). The biologist E.O. Wilson has devoted an entire book to the challenge of "consilience" (Wilson, 1998). And over the years I have come to realize that big history can play an important role in such transdisciplinary conversations by developing a shared vocabulary and identifying common themes and concepts. Can we compare the complexity of human societies to that of galaxies or planetary systems? Is information the same thing whether used by computers or crustaceans or corporations?

Developing a Coherent Narrative: Despite the links we forged between departments, for several years, I feared we were creating an intellectual patchwork. Geologists talked about granites and basalts; biologists talked about cells and amino acids. What could hold such a ramshackle story together? Was there more to the story than a shared chronology?

At first, I had no answers. What kept us going was the enthusiasm of our students. Our first students understood that big history was a pedagogical experiment and that we, the teachers, didn't really understand the story we were trying to teach. But that didn't seem to matter. What clearly pleased them was our willingness to raise the large, unifying questions that many students were dying to ask but could not pursue in most other university courses. The sheer scale of our course, its attempt to embrace the entire past and the entire cosmos, meant that students could use it to explore fundamental questions about their place in the universe. How big is our universe? How did it appear? Why did life appear? Does the universe have meaning? What makes humans different? Like all large maps, big history offered a sense of orientation because our sense of meaning is so close to our sense of place (see Swain, 1993).

Besides, teaching big history was fun. I loved to brag that we covered 13 billion years in 13 weeks and traveled more or less seamlessly from astronomy to geology to biology to anthropology and on to human history. I felt that teaching big history was as near as I would ever get to the exhilaration of riding a fast motorbike at top speed along winding, cliff-side roads!

Gradually, though, the big history story came into focus and acquired coherence. That was even more exciting. We began to see links between different parts of the story and the story as a whole began to acquire shape and structure.

My wife, Chardi, who has read widely in Jungian psychology, offered a profound insight into what we were doing. She pointed out that we were teaching an origin story. Like all origin stories, our course assembled many different stories into a universal map of time and space. Like the Genesis story or indigenous Australian dreamtime stories, it was helping us and our students find our place in the cosmos. By doing so, we were pursuing questions that cannot even be asked clearly within the disciplinary silos of modern education. (I later came across a superb essay by William McNeill on history and myth that pursued similar themes (McNeill, 1986).)

We also began to see the many benefits of linking the humanities and the natural sciences. Students scared by the technical drills of science classes found they could make sense of topics such as the big bang or plate tectonics when they encountered them as parts of a larger story. And students who preferred the sciences suddenly found that human history made more sense if they could link it to the history of the biosphere. Big history built a natural bridge between the sciences and humanities by treating them as parts of a single complex but coherent narrative.

There was one more delightful surprise: big history taught us to think about the future. During the first 2 years of teaching big history, my colleagues and I simply stopped when we got to the present day. Like most historians, I felt my dealings were with the past, not the future. Hadn't R.G. Collingwood once said that "The historian's business is to know the past, not to know the future, and whenever historians claim to be able to determine the future in advance of its happening, we may know with certainty that something has gone wrong with their fundamental conception of history" (Collingwood, 1994, p. 54).

But after the final lecture in our second year of teaching, a student came up to me and said that she had really enjoyed the course but was disappointed that we hadn't discussed the future. After all, she said, you've covered 13 billion years and you're looking at some big trends, many of which will continue for decades. Besides, she said, having seen how human history has evolved and how the pace of change has accelerated, it is vital to think seriously about where it is all going. After all, we'll be living through it! She was clearly right. Big history provided the ideal launch pad for serious discussion of the future. From then on, with my colleague, David Briscoe, I began lecturing on possible futures for humanity, the earth and the universe as a whole. David and I tossed a coin at the start of the lecture to figure out who would play the optimist and who would play the pessimist.

All in all, teaching big history turned out to be more exciting and more doable than I had ever imagined. In 1991, Jerry Bentley, the editor of the *Journal of World History*, asked me to write a short essay on big history because he felt that other world historians might find it intriguing. There was, after all, a natural affinity between world history and big history because both were pushing the boundaries of the history discipline. While writing that essay, I coined the phrase "big history" (Christian, 1991b). I meant it as an ironic joke, but, for better or worse, the name has stuck!

Key Themes in Big History: Over the years, I started to give more of the lectures in our freshman course as guest lecturers dropped out. The course lost something in expertise, but it gained in coherence, because I could point out links, contrasts, and continuities between different parts of the course. I began to see big history as a fractal, a complex pattern that revealed eerie similarities at different scales. The energies that power stars have also nourished dinosaurs and fed civilizations and empires; and the atoms forged inside dying stars live in the cells of our bodies.

Writing lectures on big history was the first step toward writing a book, *Maps of Time* (Christian, 2004). In lectures and classes, I searched for new, vivid, engaging, and rigorous ways of explaining complex and unfamiliar ideas, and often it was in the course of teaching, or in response to students" questions, that I had the mini revelations that helped refine and deepen my understanding of big history.

At about the same time I started my own course, John Mears launched a similar course at the Southern Methodist University in Dallas. Even earlier, a Boston astronomer, Eric Chaisson, had started teaching what he called "The Epic of Evolution." Chaisson developed what would turn out to be one of the most powerful of all the unifying themes in big history: the idea of increasing complexity.

Chaisson showed that as the universe has evolved over 13.8 billion years, the upper levels of complexity seem to have increased. That is not necessarily "good" or "bad," of course; there is nothing intrinsically superior about complex things, and they are usually more fragile than simpler things. But if you are human, it is hard not to be intrigued by complexity, and to wonder how complex things such as ourselves have arisen. What made the story particularly rich was the explanatory shadow cast by the second law of thermodynamics, one of science's deepest principles. The second law suggests that, far from getting more complex, the universe ought to be getting simpler as "entropy" or disorder increase. There is clearly a deep puzzle here (for a brief summary, see Christian, 2011).

In books such as *Cosmic Evolution* (Chaisson, 2001), Chaisson told the story of increasing complexity. The early universe was quite simple. It contained hydrogen and helium atoms; large and homogenous flows of energy; dark energy and dark matter (which we do not understand); and not much else. No stars, no life, no planets or living organisms. Then more complex entities began to appear. Stars seeded the universe with hot spots, creating new energy gradients. Within dying large stars fusion created new chemical elements, making the universe more complex chemically. New forms of matter accreted to form chemically complex objects such as rocky planets. On some of these planets (certainly on our own, but probably on many others, too), living organisms evolved. On our own planet, life multiplied, diversified, and complexified. A similar story seems to be repeated, in compressed and accelerated forms, in the history of our own species. Early human societies were small and relatively homogenous; today's societies contain an astonishing variety of different types of communities and lifeways linked into global networks of staggering complexity.

Chaisson proposed a rough way of measuring complexity. You could measure complexity, he argued, by an object's "energy rate density": the amount of energy flowing through a given mass in a given amount of time. These energy flows explain why complex things can temporarily resist the flow of entropy; the energy holds them together. But of course at larger scales the same flows of energy that maintain complexity in one region are also doing the work of the second law in other regions by turning more and more energy into unusable forms. Curiously, complexity turns out to be an obedient servant of the second law.

Chaisson's argument suggested that it should be possible to roughly measure the "energy rate densities" of different objects and compare the results. The results of such calculations are striking. According to Chaisson's estimates, the energy rate densities of rocky planets such as the earth are almost 40 times greater than those of the Sun, while the energy rate densities of plants are 400–500 times greater and those of modern society perhaps 250,000 times higher than those of the Sun. These are spectacular differences, and, while no one would claim much precision for them, they suggest that there is an objective basis to our sense that modern human society represents a phenomenon of extraordinary complexity. This is enough to justify the claim that human history is remarkable even on cosmological scales.

Fred Spier, a Dutch biochemist and anthropologist who began teaching big history in Amsterdam in the mid 1990s, took the story further. He and his colleague, Johann Goudsblom (who had launched the teaching of big history in the University of Amsterdam), had been influenced by the German sociologist, Norbert Elias. Using Elias' ideas, Spier wrote a book arguing that in big history we could identify and study a number of different "regimes." These were similar to the complex objects described by Chaisson. They were objects or structures or processes that might exist at many different scales, such as stars or planets or living organisms or societies. "Regimes" were dynamic, complex phenomena that had interesting emergent properties, that used flows of energy to stabilize themselves for a while, but would eventually break down (Spier, 1996). In a later book, Spier added the crucial insight that stable "regimes" could only appear where the appropriate "Goldilocks" conditions existed (Spier, 2010). For example, on the early earth, gentle energy flows, diverse chemical elements, and water in liquid form provided the perfect "Goldilocks" conditions for life. Complexity is rare, even in today's universe. To find it you have to look in just the right places.

The idea of increasing complexity offers a unifying theme that links the history of the universe to the history of the earth, of life, and of human societies. It provides exactly the sort of framework for historical thinking that I had looked for throughout my career. It also invites us to explore the nature and meaning of complexity, to ask why some phenomena become more complex than others, to ask why certain "Goldilocks" environments, such as the surface of a rocky planet orbiting a star, seem to encourage increasing complexity, while most environments do not, and to ask about the conditions under which complex phenomena may break down, because increasing complexity is not a simple linear process.

Big History as Increasing Complexity: The idea of increasing complexity frames how I teach big history today. How did the first stars form in a universe with little more than vast, homogenous clouds of hydrogen and helium? How did dying stars forge most of the elements in the periodic table? How did those elements combine chemically to form the materials from which our earth would form? And how did the rich chemistry of the earth's first oceans generate the first single-celled organisms? Seen in this context, natural selection appears as a new and peculiarly powerful method of generating diversity and complexity.

Human history looks like a speeded up version of the same story, as human societies, which were small and relatively homogenous for most of human history, began to get larger and more diverse after the appearance of agriculture. What drives the increasing complexity evident in human history? Though products of natural selection, humans are clearly distinctive. What links biology and human history? Why, to put the question slightly differently, were humans so much better than all other organisms at increasing their control over the biosphere? The answer I have found most fruitful is the idea of "collective learning." Humans alone can share the information they learn with such precision that new information can accumulate within the collective memory. Unlike the languages of other species, human language is so flexible and so precise that information can travel from brain to brain with little distortion, so that, generation by generation, human societies can store more and more information about how to exploit their environments. Collective learning explains our astonishing creativity as a species. Eventually, collective learning generated the knowledge that underpins the huge, powerful and complex societies of today's world. Collective learning explains why we have become the first single species in almost 4 billion years to dominate the biosphere. That is why the appearance of our species counts as a significant threshold in the big history narrative.

The idea of collective learning demonstrates how big history can illuminate familiar phenomena, by viewing them through different scholarly lenses. Studying human history from the perspective of biologists and paleontologists as well as archeologists and historians helps us see our species in new ways. No longer does human history seem self-contained and self-sufficient. We see it, instead, as part of the history of the biosphere. Doing this can help us understand how and why our species has set out on entirely new trajectories, following pathways that have not been explored by any other species in the 3.5 billion year history of life on earth. Big history offers an extraordinarily powerful way of understanding the distinctiveness of our own species.

These ideas shaped my own attempt to write a big history: *Maps of Time* (Christian, 2004). That book arose from a powerful synergy between teaching and researching big history. As I came to grips with more of the big history course, and as the overall shape of the big history argument became clearer to me, I began writing draft chapters as the basis for lectures, and then as possible chapters in a book. That forced me to discuss each part of the course more rigorously and to read more widely, until, by 2002 I had a manuscript ready to submit. In area after area I set myself the goal of trying to make sure I had reached first base, even in areas that were new to me. Could I describe a phenomenon such as the big bang precisely enough that a cosmologist might at least say: "Not a bad account for a historian!" But I also knew that if I tried to go too deeply into each topic I'd never finish the book. As I wrote, ideas generated or tried out in the classroom shaped my writing. At the same time, ideas developed while writing began to shape my lectures. The to-and-fro continued until the moment of publication, as I was lucky enough to have copy editors who asked their own questions about the text and sometimes forced me to rewrite and clarify passages I had thought were done.

The ideas that evolved as I taught and wrote on big history also shaped a later attempt to write a short history of humanity, *This Fleeting World* (Christian, 2008a). That book began as a series of articles for the *Berkshire Encyclopedia of World History* (2004). When Karen Christensen, the founder of Berkshire Publishing, first proposed publishing an encyclopedia of world history, I remember saying to her: "You can't do an encyclopedia of World History. Encyclopedias are bitsy. World History is looking for a larger narrative." She quite rightly challenged me, saying: "OK, help me think of a way of producing an encyclopedia that is not just bitsy." And we soon realized we could do that if we agreed to include articles at different scales, some on detailed events or topics, some on larger periods or themes.

And finally, she said to me: "OK, now you need to write some short articles covering the whole of human history." How could I resist? I had been wanting to do that all my life! So I wrote three articles on the three great periods of human history, the Paleolithic Era, the Agrarian Era, and the Modern Era. Those essays, with a wonderful preface by Bob Bain and Lauren McArthur Harris, turned into a book. I called it *This Fleeting World*, using a quote from a Buddhist sutra reminding us that, from some perspectives, even the 200,000-year story of human history is a mere eye-blink in time.

With that book, I finally managed to write the history of humanity I had thought of writing as a young lecturer in Russian history. But the detour through big history had taught me that I could only understand human history if I could place it within the much larger history of the universe.

Big History and the Evolution of Historical Thought: The Return of Universal History

It might seem that big history is an utterly new phenomenon. But seen in a larger historiographical context, big history represents, rather, a return to old and once commonplace forms of historical thinking.

Fred Spier has shown that there were many attempts to write big history throughout the twentieth century (Spier, 2012; and see Hughes-Warrington, 2002; Benjamin, 2004). H.G. Wells" *The Outline of History* (Wells, 1920), first published just after World War I, was an attempt to write a history of the universe in order to transcend the narrow tribalisms that had generated the Great War. But when Wells wrote, he could provide no absolute dates for events earlier than the first written documents, which had appeared just a few thousand years earlier. Inevitably, his story lacked chronological shape.

In the second half of the twentieth century, the emergence of Big Bang Cosmology, and new techniques for dating past events, including radiometric dating, made it possible to construct richer and more precise histories of the universe (Christian, 2009a, 2009b and McNeill, 1998). Carl Sagan's 13-part television series, *Cosmos*, offered an influential history of the Universe, while Erich Jantsch's unjustly neglected book, *The Self-Organizing Universe*, published in 1980 (Jantsch, 1980), represents the first modern attempt to offer a unifying theory for big history.

Fred Spier and others have also shown that big history belongs to an ancient genre of history writing. In the nineteenth century, philosophers such as George William Friedrich Hegel, Karl Marx, and Auguste Comte attempted to write universal histories, as did the German scientist, Alexander von Humboldt and the Scottish publisher, Robert Chambers (Spier, 2012). Even Leopold von Ranke, so often thought of as the archetypical archive rat, committed to the task of documenting "history as it really happened," assumed that historians should never lose sight of the ultimate goal of constructing a universal history (Stern, 1956, pp. 61–62). But his own attempt at such a history, shaped as it was by the Social Darwinist ideologies fashionable when he wrote, helped give such projects a bad name by showing how easily universal histories could morph into national or racial mythologies.

Further back in time, "big histories" become more common. The idea of writing universal histories seemed normal in the Enlightenment. Similar projects were also common within many other historiographical traditions, including that of China, where the Han historian, Sima Qian, wrote what looks in retrospect, like an attempt at big history. Finally, something like big history is present in all major religious traditions, and indeed wherever we find "origin stories," which means in almost every human community we know.

Far from being a new form of history, big history represents a return to ancient historical traditions. What is strange today is not the presence of big history but its absence for much of the past century (Christian, 2010).

Big History Today

Why did historians and scholars in general turn against universal history in the late nineteenth century? The answer is not yet clear. It may be that, as modern science evolved, scholars felt inundated by a tsunami of new information. Hyperspecialization offered a way of coping. In field after field, scholars turned to smaller and more manageable questions, questions you could draw lines around. Such intellectual modesty came to be seen as the mark of professional scholarship, and overambitious writers such as H.G. Wells or Arnold Toynbee (author of a popular 10-volume *Study of History*, published between 1934 and 1954, that compared the rise and fall of civilizations) were lampooned as naïve amateurs.

Specialization worked. In discipline after discipline, it yielded a rich harvest of carefully tested information and ideas. However, as an educational strategy, specialization had a serious disadvantage: it deprived students of the large cosmological maps that had helped earlier generations find meaning within traditional origin stories. For framework learners like myself, extreme specialization seemed to empty education itself of meaning.

Eventually, the very success of specialist research has made it possible to turn back toward more universal questions. New paradigms emerged in cosmology (big bang cosmology) and geology (plate tectonics), showing that the piecemeal accumulation of data could yield grand generalizations and high theory. New dating techniques transformed our very sense of the past. The modern "chronometric revolution" began in the 1950s when Willard Libby developed Carbon 14 dating techniques. Radiometric dating techniques depended on the regular breakdown of radioactive materials. These and other related techniques built the skeleton of absolute dates around which we can now construct a detailed, chronologically rigorous history of the universe over 13 billion years (Christian, 2008b).

Today, though still marginal within historical scholarship, big history is evolving fast and attracting increasing interest among scholars and educators. If it is to flourish, big history will have to overcome the deep commitment of modern educational and research institutions to specialized disciplines with well-policed borders. Educators distrust syllabi that seem too broad; they may also distrust big historians because, like world historians, they have slipped their disciplinary leash and strayed beyond their formal areas of expertise. Meanwhile, graduate students can pay a high price if they fail to stay with a sharply focused research project. These powerful conventions create many unexpected difficulties for big history, barely visible trip wires that are present in all educational and research institutions and affect all stages of a scholarly career.

Nevertheless, sustained by a growing feeling that we need more transdisciplinary education and research, big history is making headway. By 2010, there existed some 50 college-level courses in big history (Rodrigue and Stasko, 2009). Most were in the United States, but big history was also being taught at colleges and universities in Australia, the Netherlands, Russia, and Korea. Course materials are beginning to appear for such courses, in addition to the scholarly literature listed later. David Christian has recorded a series of lectures on big history that are available through the "Teaching Company" (Christian, 2008c). In 2009, Craig Benjamin edited a forum on big history teaching in the online journal *World History Connected* (Benjamin, 2009). In August 2013, David Christian, Cynthia Brown, and Craig Benjamin published the first textbook for college courses in big history (Christian, Brown, and Benjamin, 2013).

Big history is also making an appearance in high schools. This is tremendously important because the large cosmological maps of big history can help students see the connective tissues between disciplines and find rich meanings in what they learn. Since 2010, with the support of Bill Gates, the "Big History Project" has started building free online courses in big history for high school students (Big History Project, 2013). The Big History Project will provide a rich body of material for the teaching of big history both in schools and for independent learners. Such courses will offer students of the next generation the broad, transdisciplinary perspective they will need to tackle the global challenges of the next 50 years. Of course, big history courses will not replace existing courses. But by providing a unifying perspective that links different disciplines, they may help students approach traditional courses in new ways and help them link what they learn into a more coherent understanding of their world.

New organizational structures are also evolving to support the development of big history. Walter Alvarez is the geologist who demonstrated that an asteroid strike drove the dinosaurs to extinction some

67 million years (Alvarez, 2008). Fascinated by history, Alvarez discovered big history and began teaching big history courses in the geology department of UC Berkeley. In 2010, he organized a symposium for big historians at the Geological Observatory in Coldigioco in Italy, and it was at this symposium that a group of big historians formally constituted the International Big History Association (IBHA, 2010). The IBHA held its first conference at the Grand Valley State University in Michigan in August 2012. That conference brought together scientists, historians, artists, and teachers, and demonstrated the richness and variety of ideas, approaches and expertise available within what is still an embryonic field of scholarship. A second conference will be held in 2014 at the Dominican University outside San Francisco. Dominican University has created an entire freshman program organized around the idea of big history (Dominican University, 2013).

Big history is also evolving as a research field. There is now a small cohort of graduate students pursuing big history themes at the Macquarie University in Sydney, in Amsterdam, and elsewhere. Macquarie University's recently established Big History Institute intends to start the complex process of creating research environments that encourage research across multiple disciplines on transdisciplinary themes. These themes may include increasing complexity, collective learning, the role of information in big history, and the idea of the "Anthropocene epoch" of earth history. Eventually, it will be necessary to create institutional structures, career structures, and publication structures that cut across the disciplinary silos that inhibit transdisciplinary research in modern universities and research institutes.

My personal hope is that as more and more students and scholars become familiar with the unifying story of big history, they will start weaving together the questions, themes, and insights of many disparate disciplines. A generation of students and researchers familiar with the big history story will find it easier to see new links and synergies between disciplines. We will need this sort of transdisciplinary thinking and research as societies face global challenges such as climate change or declining biodiversity, whose solution will require ideas and insights from many different fields of expertise.

References

Alvarez, Walter. 2008. *"T. Rex" and the Crater of Doom*. Princeton, NJ: Princeton University Press.

Benjamin, Craig. 2004. "Beginnings and Endings," in M. Hughes-Warrington, ed. *Palgrave Advances: World History*. London/New York: Palgrave Macmillan, pp. 90–111.

Benjamin, Craig. 2009. "Forum on Big History." *World History Connected* 6/3. http://worldhistoryconnected.press.illinois.edu/index.html. Accessed January 22, 2013.

Big History Project. 2013. https://course.bighistoryproject.com/bhplive. Accessed August 16, 2013.

Braudel, Fernand. 1972. *The Mediterranean and the Mediterranean World in the Age of Philip II*, trans. S. Reynolds. London: Collins.

Chaisson, Eric. 2001. *Cosmic Evolution: The Rise of Complexity in Nature*. Cambridge, MA: Harvard University Press.

Christian, David. 1990. *"Living Water": Vodka and Russian Society on the Eve of Emancipation*. Oxford: Oxford University Press.

Christian, David. 1991a. "The Black and Gold Seals: Popular Protests Against the Liquor Trade on the Eve of Emancipation," in Esther Kingston-Mann and Timothy Mixter, eds. *Peasant Economy, Culture and Politics of European Russia, 1800–1917*. Princeton, NJ: Princeton University Press, pp. 261–293.

Christian, David. 1991b. "The Case for "Big History'," *The Journal of World History* 2/2: 223–238.

Christian, David. 1997. *Imperial and Soviet Russia: Power, Privilege and the Challenge of Modernity*. Basingstoke: Macmillan.

Christian, David. 2004. *Maps of Time: An Introduction to Big History*. Berkeley, CA: University of California Press.

Christian, David. 2008a. *This Fleeting World: A Short History of Humanity*. Great Barrington, MA: Berkshire Publishing.

Christian, David. 2008b. "Historia, complejidad y revolución cronomé-trica," *Revista de Occidente* 323: 27–57.

Christian, David. 2008c. "Big History: The Big Bang, Life on Earth, and the Rise of Humanity," 48 lectures on big history published by the Teaching Company. http://www.thegreatcourses.com/tgc/courses/course_detail.aspx?cid=8050. Accessed October 28, 2013.

Christian, David. 2009a. "History and Science after the Chronometric Revolution," in Steven J. Dick and Mark L. Lupisella, eds. *Cosmos & Culture: Cultural Evolution in a Cosmic Context*. Washington, DC: National Aeronautics and Space Administration, pp. 441–462.

Christian, David. 2009b "The Evolutionary Epic and the Chronometric Revolution," in Cheryl Genet, Brian Swimme, Russell Genet, and Linda Palmer, eds. *The Evolutionary Epic: Science's Story and Humanity's Response*. Santa Margarita, CA: Collins Foundation Press, pp. 441–462.

Christian, David. 2010. "The Return of Universal History," *History and Theory* 49/December, Theme issue: 5–26.

Christian, David. 2011. "13.7 billion years in 18 minutes." *TED Conference*, Long Beach, CA, April 11, 2011. http://www.ted.com/talks/david_christian_big_history.html. Accessed January 21, 2013.

Christian, David, Cynthia Brown, and Craig Benjamin. 2013. *Big History: Between Nothing and Everything*. Boston, MA: McGraw-Hill.

Collingwood, R.G. 1994. *The Idea of History*, Revised edition, Jan Van der Dussen, ed. Oxford/New York: Oxford University Press.

Dominican University. 2013. "First Year Experience: Big History." http://www.dominican.edu/academics/big-history. Accessed January 25, 2013.

Freedom House. 2012. http://www.freedomhouse.org/regions/central-and-eastern-europeeurasia. Accessed January 21, 2013.

Gribbin, John. 1981. *Genesis: The Origins of Man and the Universe*. New York: Delta.

Hughes-Warrington, Marnie. 2002. "Big History," *Historically Speaking* 4/2: 16–17, 20.

Jantsch, Erich. 1980. *The Self-Organizing Universe: Scientific and Human Implications of the Emerging Paradigm of Evolution*. Oxford: Pergamon Press.

Kuhn, Thomas S. 1970. *The Structure of Scientific Revolutions*, 2nd edition. Chicago, IL: Chicago University Press.

McNeill, William H. 1986. "Mythistory, or Truth, Myth, History and Historians," *American Historical Review* 91/1: 1–10.

McNeill, William H. 1998. "History and the Scientific Worldview," *History and Theory* 37/1: 1–13

McNeill, William H. Senior Editor. 2004. *Berkshire Encyclopedia of World History*, 5 vols. Great Barrington, MA: Berkshire Publishing Group.

Rodrigue, Barry and Daniel Stasko. 2009. "A Big History Directory: 2009." *World History Connected* 6/3. http://worldhistoryconnected.press.illinois.edu/6.3/rodrigue.html. Accessed January 22, 2013.

Smith, R.E.F. and David Christian. 1984. *Bread and Salt: A Social and Economic History of Food and Drink in Russia*. Cambridge: Cambridge University Press [re-issued in paperback, 2008].

Snow, C.P. 1971. "The Two Cultures and the Scientific Revolution," in C.P. Snow, ed. *Public Affairs*. London/Basingstoke: Macmillan, pp. 13–46 [1st published 1959].

Spier, Fred. 1996. *The Structure of Big History: From the Big Bang until Today*. Amsterdam: Amsterdam University Press.

Spier, Fred. 2010. *Big History and the Future of Humanity*. Chichester/Malden, MA: Wiley-Blackwell.

Spier, Fred. 2012. "Big History," in Douglas Northrop, ed. *A Companion to World History*. Malden, MA: Wiley-Blackwell, pp. 171–184.

Stern, Fritz. 1956. *The Varieties of History: From Voltaire to the Present*. Cleveland/New York: World Publishing Company.

Swain, Tony. 1993. *A Place for Strangers: Toward a History of Australian Aboriginal Being*. Cambridge: Cambridge University Press.

The International Big History Association (IBHA). 2010. http://ibhanet.org/. Accessed January 22, 2013.

Wells, H.G. 1920. *Outline of History*, 3rd edition. London: Macmillan.

Wilson, E.O. 1998. *Consilience: The Unity of Knowledge*. London: Abacus.

Further Reading

Brown, Cynthia Stokes. 2007. *Big History: From the Big Bang to the Present*. New York: The New Press.

Chaisson, Eric. 2001. *Cosmic Evolution: The Rise of Complexity in Nature*. Cambridge, MA: Harvard University Press.

Chaisson, Eric. 2006. *Epic of Evolution: Seven Ages of the Cosmos*. New York: Columbia University Press.

Christian, David. 2004. *Maps of Time: An Introduction to Big History*. Berkeley, CA: University of California Press.

Christian, David. 2008a. *This Fleeting World: A Short History of Humanity*. Great Barrington, MA: Berkshire Publishing.

Christian, David. 2008b. "Big History: The Big Bang, Life on Earth, and the Rise of Humanity," 48 lectures on big history published by the Teaching Company. http://www.thegreatcourses.com/tgc/courses/course_detail.aspx?cid=8050. Accessed October 28, 2013.

Christian, David. 2010. "The Return of Universal History," *History and Theory* 49/December, Theme issue: 5–26.

Spier, Fred. 2010. *Big History and the Future of Humanity*. Chichester/Malden, MA: Wiley-Blackwell.

9

In Search of a Global Cultural History

Jerry H. Bentley and Karen Louise Jolly, foreword by Alan Karras

Foreword

Jerry Bentley died on July 15, 2012, 7 months after receiving the news that he had pancreatic cancer. The following essay is the last essay that he authored; his wife, Carol Mon Lee, has reported that Jerry would type away on his laptop computer on most days, even as his health continued to deteriorate. Jerry passed away before he could finish this essay. Even so, the piece is extremely polished. Not a word of Jerry's original has been changed, though Jerry's colleague, Karen Jolly, has provided a postscript that brings the project to a conclusion.

After Jerry died, Carol found the essay on his computer. She read it, believed it to be publishable, but recognized that it was unfinished. She sent the essay to me and asked for my help in locating a suitable place for publication. A day or two later, I received an e-mail from this volume's editor, Ken Curtis, telling me about the volume,

Architects of World History: Researching the Global Past, First Edition.
Edited by Kenneth R. Curtis and Jerry H. Bentley.

the nature of the essays to be included – and letting me know that Jerry was supposed to be included in the volume. Ken had a variety of ideas about how to proceed with the volume absent Jerry's essay and wanted to discuss them with me. I quickly wrote back to Ken saying that Jerry had been working before he died on a piece that matched Ken's description of this book. I attached the essay to my e-mail, and Ken responded that he too thought this piece was intended for *Architects of World History*. We asked Carol if this seemed right to her; she believed that it did. She even found a folder on Jerry's desktop with the book's name on it. In such a fashion, we put two and two together.

The essay's appearance in this volume is a testament to the type of detective work historians often undertake. It is also directly related to the ways that Jerry built and fostered networks among world historians. The essay appears with Carol's permission, as do this foreword and Karen Jolly's sequel, which frame Jerry's last work for readers. Though glad to have found the essay's intended home, we are all deeply saddened by the premature loss of one of world history's most iconic figures; he was a true pioneer in the field.

Alan Karras

Over the years, people have frequently asked me how I am able to remember so much information, so many details about the past. After all, my historian colleagues and I write books with thousands upon thousands of factual details. We of course record most of the precise information that we use on note cards, computers, or other storage devices so that our limited brain capacities can focus on larger issues.

A better explanation of historians' vaunted memory skills has to do with the nature of historical thinking. Consider the difference between an encyclopedia and a work of historical analysis. The purpose of the encyclopedia is to compile more or less information on discrete topics. Historical analysis, on the other hand, seeks to probe and understand the relationships between historical developments. This calls for a high order of thinking. It requires historians to consider all of the various sources of information – textual, artistic, archeological, literary, and others – that are relevant to their topics. It calls also for historians to subject these sources to careful and highly critical inspection in order to obtain the most useful information from them. It requires further that historians think creatively about the information they glean from their sources and seek to identify patterns that help explain the course of historical development.

History is not a chest of miscellaneous details or a box of data from which historians simply pluck pieces of information and try to fashion them into some kind of story. Rather, history represents a creative effort by historians to gain insights into the dynamics of historical development. In order to achieve this goal, historians focus their attention on questions and issues that allow them to comment usefully on the course of historical development.

Finding Focus

How do historians identify the questions and issues that they explore? They obviously choose topics that hold particular meaning or significance, such as the experiences of national, racial, religious, or ethnic communities. Thinking about their topics in light of all the relevant sources, they seek to contribute to the understanding of their larger topics through analysis of some dimension that opens windows into the larger patterns of historical development. This is a highly creative effort that involves the construction of new ideas, fresh interpretations, and sometimes even new theories about the dynamics of historical development. Historians become, in effect, architects of the past.

For most of the time since about the 1840s and the development of professional historical scholarship – the approach to the past based on rigorous, critical analysis of documents and other source materials – professional historians focused their attention almost exclusively on the political, diplomatic, and military experiences of national communities. One reason for this focus was the fact that the middle and late decades of the nineteenth century witnessed the brutal and often terrifying but always fascinating processes by which zealous, single-minded leaders in Europe and North forged their territories and peoples into powerful nation-states based on bonds of common language, religion, and cultural inheritance. Another reason for the focus on political history was the fact that the men – almost no women – who studied history in universities mostly expected to assume careers in the government as political leaders, diplomats, or military officers.

No one has ever doubted that political experiences provide crucial contexts for the analysis of historical development. As times changed, however, historians recognized that fresh perspectives could help them understand powerful influences that, alongside political affairs, profoundly shaped the course of historical development. This realization prompted them to expand the horizons of their discipline – to construct new architectures of the past.

During the later nineteenth and twentieth centuries, for example, the process of industrialization brought enormous change to European and North American societies. Particularly in the United States, waves of migrants arrived to work in labor-hungry factories. By the 1920s and 1930s, their children – including women as well as men – were attending newly founded city colleges and universities in large numbers. In their history texts, they found abundant discussion of political leaders and their work. But they found almost no mention of everyday working people – even though they had contributed as much as any other group to the emergence of the United States as a powerful industrial society. Their response was the construction of labor history and social history as fresh approaches that profoundly enriched the understanding of historical development.

As the twentieth century marched along, historians recognized many additional approaches that have led to deeper understanding of the past. The Suffragette and Women's Movements, for example, prompted historians to explore the roles played by women in the past, as well as the nature of sexual and gender groups and the relations between them. Similarly, awareness of environmental problems in the contemporary world prompted other historians to investigate environmental issues in the past, focusing particularly on the relationship between human beings and the natural environment. The histories of science and technology, as well as the relationships between the two, represent additional approaches suggested to historians by the experiences of the past two centuries. Alongside political history, these approaches add layers of fresh perspectives that have profoundly enriched historians' understanding of the past.

One additional new approach merits special mention here – world history. In one way, world history is an old and hoary project because philosophers and theologians had speculated since ancient times about the causes of historical development and the meaning of history itself. Only in the twentieth century, and particularly since the 1960s, have historians applied the methods and tools of professional historical scholarship to the analysis of the global past (for two genealogies of contemporary world history, see Bentley, 2002, pp. 393–416; Bentley, 2011, pp. 343–360). From about the 1870s, European and American imperial ventures alerted national leaders and policymakers to their need for reliable information about the larger world – its peoples, lands, resources, and cultural traditions. At the same time, from the 1870s all the way up to the Great Depression of the 1930s – including even the era of the Great War (1914–1918) – massive volumes of global trade and enormous flows of international migration made it clear that the world's peoples and societies had become interdependent to a degree never imaginable before.

Professional historians were slow to take up the challenge posed by this round of globalization: most remained content to work within the friendly confines of the nation-state. Gradually, however, some historians recognized the value of focusing their analyses not on national experiences but on the encounters, interactions, and exchanges that linked the world's peoples and societies. They began to explore these issues in the 1950s and 1960s, and during the 1970s and 1980s, the world history approach had become an influential movement within the larger discipline of history. In shifting the focus of their analysis, the world historians constructed a new framework – a new architecture – for historical scholarship.

Finding Focus: Cultural History

My own particular interest in historical scholarship has always been cultural issues – the distinctive clusters of beliefs, values, and ideas that informed the intellectual and spiritual lives of their communities. My concern has not been to clarify doctrine or explain the ideas of the major intellectual figures who wrote mainly for each other – even though that is an interesting and worthy project itself. Rather, I have sought to explore the connecting points between the realm of beliefs, values, and ideas, on the one hand, and the practical, everyday lives of peoples living under the influence of these cultural traditions, on the other hand. This is quite a tricky project since the vast majority of the evidence is unavailable to us today. How can we know what went through the minds of peasants, townsmen, and merchants before recent times? Yet this approach to the past is endlessly fascinating and enlightening since it deepens understanding of the cultural traditions that are prime elements in the glue that holds societies together.

Are there personal reasons that help to explain my interest in cultural traditions and cultural history? Yes, undoubtedly so. Growing up, I attended public schools from Grade 1 through completion of my Ph.D. degree. Although I did not have a religious education per se, many of my family members were conservative, fundamentalist Christians, so they regularly took my two brothers and myself to Sunday school and church. There I gained a basic familiarity with the Bible and its teachings – not by any means a deep understanding, but an acquaintance that served me well in later years when I began to study Christianity from much more rigorous, critical, and scholarly perspectives.

At one point during my last year or so in high school, while working through a bout of adolescent feelings of alienation, I became a devout believer myself. Indeed, I toyed briefly with the idea of pursuing a career in the ministry. (This was a very bad idea: I would have made a terrible minister, for lack of patience.) This phase of my life came to an abrupt end when I entered the university. Before Christmas break of the fall term, I had decisively rejected Christianity and indeed all organized religion. This development was partly a result of the fact that, in light of fresh critical perspectives that I encountered at the university, I realized that I simply could not accept the teachings of organized religion. It also reflected my profound disillusionment and even disgust with the sometimes hideous behavior that church leaders organized and actively encouraged. Political and military leaders of course carried out more than their own fair share of atrocities, but it has always seemed to me that there is a particular hypocrisy in the promotion of violence in the name of Jesus of Nazareth.

Nevertheless, I always harbored a profound respect and admiration for those rare and sensitive individuals, the seekers, who made their lives a quest for wisdom, enlightenment, justice, and opportunities to improve the lives of their fellow human beings. My problem with religion was not with the seekers but with the epigone theologians who hardened the seekers' reflections into rigid and formulaic doctrines, some of which actually perverted the seekers' ideas, and with the ambitious leaders who sought to turn their churches into power bases to advance their political agenda – issues that my Sunday school teachers neglected to discuss. (Indeed, as lay volunteers with little if any education in history, they knew very little about these issues themselves.) The first of the seekers I became acquainted with was of course Jesus of Nazareth, but in later years I also came to appreciate others, including Laozi, the Buddha, Muhammad, St. Francis of Assisi, and Mother Teresa, among others.

In this frame of mind, I completed my undergraduate degree with a major in history and entered graduate school. At both levels, my principal interest was the European Renaissance, a period of remarkable cultural ferment, and particularly on the Renaissance humanists, a fascinating cluster of literary figures, scholars, and educators who were the prime instigators of cultural ferment. For my Ph.D. dissertation, I chose a topic that combined my interests in religious issues and the humanists. In due course, I revised my dissertation and published it as my first book, entitled *Humanists and Holy Writ: New Testament Scholarship in the Renaissance* (Bentley, 1983).

In retrospect, it seems clear enough that this project was a way of working my way through my earlier commitment to Christianity by exploring the New Testament through critical and scholarly perspectives. In any case, *Humanists and Holy Writ* analyzed the work of Renaissance humanists who laid the foundations of modern biblical scholarship. The principal figures were Lorenzo Valla (1407–1457) and Erasmus of Rotterdam (1486–1536), although the book also considered the work of several other humanists who contributed to the effort.

How did these humanists transform biblical scholarship? First, they based their study on the Greek text instead of the Latin translation known as the Vulgate, which had served throughout the middle ages as the supposedly definitive text of the New Testament in western Christendom (the region dominated by the Roman Catholic church). Greek was of course the original language of the New Testament, and the humanists performed a profoundly important service by establishing a reliable text of the Greek New Testament. Second, the humanists carefully and critically evaluated the Vulgate against the Greek text. Not surprisingly they discovered thousands upon thousands of passages in the Vulgate that were awkward or misleading or even outright misrepresentations of the Greek text. Third, on the basis of these discoveries, they were able to demonstrate that the New Testament was the product of human hands. This point then enabled them to liberate study and interpretation of the New Testament from the theologians and establish a place for rigorous, critical analysis of the text and its meaning(s) by scholars. Fourth, they profoundly influenced education by showing that any sophisticated study of the New Testament called for deep knowledge of language and literature, and the universities were quick to establish courses to serve this need. Finally, more broadly, the humanists contributed to the larger effort throughout Europe to reconsider inherited ideas and build a fresh understanding of the world on the basis of rational, critical inquiry.

Humanist scholarship did not immediately displace theologically based study of the New Testament. Conservative theologians continued to champion the Vulgate. By the early sixteenth century, however, the world of scholarship had largely passed the conservatives by. The humanists were by no means anti-Christian activists seeking to undermine the basic message of the New Testament. To the contrary, they spent years of effort seeking fresher, deeper, richer understanding of the fundamental text of Christianity. In realizing this goal, they contributed to a remarkable round of cultural ferment throughout Europe.

Alongside religion, issues of politics, morality, and their entanglements have always intrigued me. In my second book, *Politics and Culture in Renaissance Naples*, I sought to bring these issues into clear focus by studying the work of a fascinating group of humanists who were active at the royalcourt of Naples from the 1440s until the Spanish conquest of the kingdom in 1501 (Bentley, 1987). The most important of these humanists were Lorenzo Valla (1407–1457), Antonio Beccadelli, known informally as Panormita (1394–1471), and Giovanni Gioviano Pontano (1426–1503). The kings of Naples attracted many other humanists to their court – mostly poets and literary figures whom they hoped would add luster to their court – but Valla,

Panormita, and Pontano made the principal contributions to political thought and practice in the kingdom.

Like the leaders of all the Italian states – and indeed all European states beyond Italy – the kings of Naples had constantly tense relations with the papacy. Valla helped to undermine the political influence of the popes by exposing document called the Donation of Constantine as a forgery. The Donation purported to record a gift from the fourth-century Roman Emperor Constantine transferring political authority over all Western Europe to Pope Sylvester I and his successors. This very idea is of course absurd on the face of things, but medieval popes had often invoked the Donation as justification for intrusion into political affairs of European states. Using the methods that he and others later applied to analysis of the New Testament, Valla was able to demonstrate definitively that the Donation was a forgery. It included words and terms that had not even been invented in the fourth century, and it referred to events that took place long after Constantine's time. Since the time of Valla's exposé (1440), no one has taken the document seriously. Later scholarship has dated the Donation to the eighth or ninth century. Once again, it became clear that rigorous, careful, critical inquiry had the power to clarify the status of an important document.

Panormita and Pontano played quite different roles at the Neapolitan court. Both enjoyed sterling reputations as humanist literary figures who composed poetry, essays, orations, histories, formal treatises, and widely circulated letters in vast quantities. Both also served as secretaries, ambassadors, and top advisors to the kings of Naples. Thus, both men acquired a range of practical political experience rare, although by no means completely unknown, among the humanists. Accordingly, more than most of their fellow humanists, Panormita and Pontano became well aware of the tensions between the ideals of political theory, on the one hand, and the demands of political practice, on the other hand.

Like most sensible people of their own time and others, Panormita and Pontano shared the ideal of building a powerful, prosperous, just, fair, peaceful, harmonious, and stable state that could sustain itself through time, and they urged this ideal on their patrons, the kings of Naples. The kings did not always agree with their views on things. Their limited influence frustrated the humanists, who lodged frequent complaints that the kings were ignoring excellent advice – and also that the kings were not rewarding them properly for their sage advice. Nevertheless, Panormita and Pontano represented royal positions more or less faithfully when dealing with states beyond Naples. As a result, they negotiated alliances with the other states and advocated policies that led to several peninsular wars. Within the kingdom of Naples itself, they helped the kings overcome two major rebellions by the haughty and entrenched local barons, especially those in the far south of the peninsula where it was difficult to impose effective royal authority.

Yet Panormita and Pontano were not mere recipients of political influence. Rather, they and the other humanist active in Naples deeply influenced cultural life in the kingdom by establishing literary academies, promoting humanist education, and introducing humanist historical writing that reflected the influence of their favorite historians of classical Greece and Rome. These influences spread well beyond the royal court to the cities in the far south of the kingdom and also, although infrequently, to the occasional enlightened baron in the countryside.

Especially intriguing was the way Panormita and especially Pontano drew upon their political experience to develop fresh insights into the nature of political life. Like humanist colleagues in Florence and Venice, they openly discussed the need to adopt hard-nosed policies in the interests of state security – a theme developed most spectacularly in the writings of the Florentine commentator Niccolò Machiavelli (1469–1527). Pont-de obedienta-1499-perspicacity, flexibility, vigilance, industry, judgment, etc.-but also cunning, sham, lies, dissimulation, hypocrisy as needed …

After writing this rumination on the complexities of Machiavelli, Jerry Bentley was unable to continue with the essay. He had, however, already provided the heading of "Finding Focus: Global Cultural History," and here Dr. Karen Jolly completes the essay with a first-person narrative of Bentley's subsequent work:

The same moral concerns Bentley expressed about Renaissance Europe, he carried forward into his study of cultures in world history. One key shift in the previous pages is from a consideration of "architects" of the past to "seekers." Bentley would consider himself more the latter, although clearly he can be counted as one of the architects of global cultural history.

Finding Focus: Global Cultural History

The inaugural issue of *The Journal of World History* (*JWH*) appeared in 1990, shortly after I arrived at the University of Hawai'i as a new assistant professor in medieval European history. Jerry Bentley was the one who interviewed me for the position at the American Historical Association (AHA) meeting, and I distinctly remember him asking if I was willing to teach *world* history, despite having been trained only in Western civilizations. I was daunted by the prospect but willing, and found the faculty and upper division course materials in Asian and Pacific histories at UH under Jerry's mentorship incredibly helpful. As a consequence, my career teaching world history from 1989 to the present is closely tied to Bentley's expanding scholarship in world history. Bentley's transition from the Renaissance humanist scholarship he outlined earlier to world historian is evident in his publication record in the years 1988–1990, precisely when I met him. His enthusiasm for world historiography as a way of thinking about the human condition was palpable and remained a guiding force in my own research and teaching.

In that first issue of *JWH*, Bentley set the agenda for the journal in a few brief pages. The list of comparative and cross-cultural themes he listed as potential article topics foreshadows his own writing in the coming decades:

> comparative studies of historical developments that work their influences in more than one civilization or cultural region;
> analyses of encounters between peoples of different civilizations or cultural regions;

> studies in the historiography of world history;
> reflections on conceptualization and periodization in world history;
> articles dealing with methodology in world history; and
> review articles dealing with recent literature on especially themes of world history
>
> (Bentley, 1990, p. iv).

In addition, the journal promised to review books, including textbooks, and address world history as both a research and teaching field. Bentley did both, in spades. One of the hallmarks of his scholarship was the way he put theory into practice: in scholarly articles and books he developed and defended a framework for world history that he also carried out in his textbooks and teaching.

In the following survey, I trace the trajectory of world historiography through Bentley's diverse publications using the categories he defined in 1990 for the *Journal of World History*. The thread running throughout, however, is what he named as the focus of this essay, cultural history, arguably his most important contribution to world historiography. In a personal interview (June 29, 2012) shortly before his death, Bentley described cultural history as "the study of the place where beliefs, values, and customs intersect with daily lives," undoubtedly echoing the definition he had just composed earlier. This definition of cultural history resonates for me because I arrived in Hawai'i as a cultural historian influenced by anthropology, but without the world comparative dimensions Bentley cultivated and from which I subsequently benefited.

Bentley's conversion from European to comparative history may have been stimulated by his seemingly chance encounter with a group of historians seeking to form the World History Association (WHA), but it also owes much to his location and the cosmopolitan setting of the University of Hawai'i at Mānoa in Honolulu. Bentley was in the right place at the right time with like-minded historians when William H. McNeill gave the keynote address at a 1982 Air Force Academy meeting cosponsored by the AHA that led to the founding of the WHA. But Bentley's development of cross-cultural interactions as a model for world history reflects even more the multicultural environment in which he conducted his research and teaching. In particular, his interdisciplinary conversations with scholars of Asia and the Pacific included philosophy east and west, comparative religions, various centers under the umbrella of the then School of Hawaiian, Asian, and Pacific Studies (SHAPS), and Hawaiian Studies (now in the Hawai'inuiākea School of Hawaiian Knowledge). Engaging actively with these diverse traditions, Bentley explored "comparative studies of historical developments" and began to note transcultural phenomena from a uniquely Oceanic viewpoint.

This comparative framework inevitably led to "analyses of encounters," applied first to his own field of training in Renaissance Europe. His third book, *Old World Encounters* (1993), in many ways signaled Bentley's permanent transformation into a world historian. The book appeared the year after, but pointedly in dialogue with, the Columbian quincentennial, during which a spate of popular and scholarly books celebrated and critiqued what everyone took to be a turning point in world history (Bentley, 1993, pp. vii–viii). But *Old World Encounters* challenged that assumption by getting behind the Columbian moment of "discovery" to chronicle a rich history of premodern encounters between Asian, African, and European peoples.

By the mid-1990s, then, Bentley was becoming a leading spokesperson for world historiography, most obviously in a path-breaking 1996 forum article, "Cross-Cultural Interaction and Periodization in World History," in the *American Historical Review* (*AHR*), but also in an AHA pamphlet of the same year defining world history (Bentley, 1996a, 1996b; see also Bentley, 2001). Bentley added to world history's emphases on migration, commerce, and empires a consideration of cultural exchange. This focus on interactions between cultures led him to propose a new global periodization of six major eras for study and teaching. Patrick Manning notes in his response to the *AHR* article how Bentley's model of cross-cultural contacts "sidesteps a linear interpretation of world history," but he also points out that this focus on cultural interactions could become the "main subject matter of world history" (Manning, 1996, p. 771). In effect, Manning portrays Bentley as blazing a new path in world historiography for others to follow, which they have.

Cross-cultural encounters became a new way to think about global history, moving beyond the exchange of material culture to focus on the *people* involved in these exchanges, with all of their beliefs, values, ideals, and aspirations. This cultural shift in world history intersects with the rise of two trends in scholarship associated with postmodernism in the 1980s and 1990s: postcolonial cultural studies and interdisciplinary globalization studies. Postmodernism questions the confidence in human reason espoused by the humanist thinkers Bentley studied; it is often associated with the deconstruction of Enlightenment concepts and values on which modern western scholarship rests. In particular, postcolonial scholars challenge the dominance of western ways of thinking and seek alternative perspectives among people groups breaking free of that western cultural imperialism. At the same time, many disciplines in the social sciences began to work together to study the effects of globalization on the economy, society, and the environment.

Bentley anticipated and spoke to this conjunction of cultural and global forces and their implications for world history. Early on in the *JWH*, in "Hemispheric Integration, 500–1500 C.E.," Bentley responded to some postmodern readings of medieval European travel literature that characterized it as contributing to later European imperialism and "orientalism" (exoticizing and commodifying "the east"). Bentley rejected this anachronistic reading as, ironically, too Eurocentric. Based on his research in *Old World Encounters*, he put medieval European encounters into a world historical view: "when the focus broadens from a narcissistic, Eurocentric study of European travelers to the analysis of cross-cultural interactions as historical processes, a range of alternative patterns come into view" (Bentley, 1998, p. 251; see also Bentley, 2006, 2007). Within the larger pattern of cross-cultural interactions historically, Europeans abroad were not exceptional; rather, their behaviors are comparable to other societies.

Patterns of historical processes are a key world history concept, but Bentley defines in the "Hemispheric Integration" article two major cultural strands of inquiry to pursue. One is the effect of encounters on shifting ethnic identities, echoing ongoing work in studies of European ethnogenesis, or how people groups come to identify and tell the story of their origins (Gillett, 2006). The second strand examined the spread of and encounters between cultural and religious traditions (Bentley, 1998, p. 253). The article focused initially on the role of individual travelers in transmitting religious ideas and artifacts, but at the end also suggested a broader, more difficult field of inquiry: investigating the intertwining religious, economic, and political forces working on these individuals in their cultural encounters.

As for interdisciplinary globalization studies, in 2004 Bentley pointed to the "unfinished intellectual projects" of globalizing history *and* historicizing globalization (Bentley, 2004, p. 69). The latter process had been missed by many present-minded social scientists who failed to recognize the larger patterns of global exchange in the premodern eras of human history. In particular, Bentley challenged the nineteenth-century concept of the nation-state, assumed as generic by political scientists but actually an anachronistic model for studying other cultures historically, and potentially dangerous in its application in global politics. The ethnic nation state model played a divisive role in the partitioning of Eastern Europe after World War I and in the twentieth-century postcolonial invention of "new" countries. Ostensibly these nations were created out of some historic ethnic identity predating colonialism, but in reality these entities and their boundaries were more imagined by western notions of ethnic nationalism than by the indigenous people groups they reorganized (Geary, 2002; Davis, 2008).

Several challenges face world historians seeking to take a global and comparative approach that avoids Eurocentrism. One is that the interdisciplinary nature of cultural and globalization studies would seemingly make scholarly research in world history increasingly difficult: How can world historians not only keep up with all of the regional fields of study for comparative analysis, but also keep current with the work of scholars in literary studies and the social sciences? Second, the historical profession places a high value on studying sources in their original languages, with many fields, such as my own, requiring three or four languages. To multiply original research for world historians by two or three fields presents a daunting number of languages. Part of the difficulty, though, lies with the solitary nature of historical scholarship found in the image of the lonely scholar in the archives with a stack of books or manuscripts. In contrast, collaboration in world history is an essential component of its methodology and part of the ongoing cross-cultural dialogue that should characterize historical research of all kinds.

One instructive example of such collaboration is an article Bentley coauthored with Pacific voyaging historian Ben Finney in *Acta Astronautica*. Together, they expose a false premise (or an abuse of history) among nonhistorians: those speculating about communication with extraterrestrials often point to terrestrial history of ideas translated between Greek, Arabic, and Latin, but a better analogy lies in the encounters between Europeans and the Maya and the ensuing communication difficulties between two unrelated language groups (Finney and Bentley, 1998). Influenced by an Oceanic perspective from his home in the middle of the Pacific, Bentley likewise challenged geographers as well as historians to consider water, rather than land-based divisions, as a way of understanding human interactions around the globe (Bentley, 1999; see also Finney, 1994; Hau'ofa, 2008; Gulliver, 2011). Rich cultural studies of the Indian Ocean basin, the Atlantic world, and Oceania point to the fruitfulness of this approach (Buschmann, 2006; Matsuda, 2006).

One way to keep up with interdisciplinary global history scholarship lies in book reviews and review articles, as the *Journal of World History* set out to do. Reviews provide the mechanism by which scholars in one field learn about developments in others. In this way, globally minded scholars like Jerry Bentley take what they learned in another field of inquiry back to their colleagues. In a review article for the *Sixteenth Century Journal* covering eight Variorum edited volumes, he gently chastised the series for retaining a Eurocentric approach to European expansion, while nonetheless highlighting the potential it contained for future comparative research (Bentley,

1997). In a more recent example of interdisciplinary dialogue, for the journal *Religions*, Bentley reviewed John Miles Headley's *The Europeanization of the World: On the Origins of Human Rights and Democracy* (2008), arguing that the Europeanization Headley described was based on a prior globalization of Europe, visible only if we adopt a global view of history (Bentley, 2012).

The other way world historians make connections with larger trends is in education, creating access to research materials for teachers of world history at the secondary, collegiate, and graduate level. As a member of the WHA, Bentley was in the front lines of developing the AP World History curriculum, helping establish state standards in world history, and working directly with teachers in local schools. Bentley firmly believed that the best way to get good historical scholarship into secondary education was not to wait for it to trickle down but to be directly involved with developing standards and curriculum. In the process, teachers and students raised questions and issues for scholars of world history to address. This synergy between research and teaching was a hallmark of Bentley's work and set an example for the historical profession as a whole.

But perhaps the most useful and enduring pedagogical contribution is *Traditions and Encounters*, coauthored with colleague Herbert F. Ziegler, first published in 2000 and now in its fifth edition (2011). *Traditions and Encounters* was not the first truly world history textbook to depart from the Eurocentric "west plus the rest" approach, but it established a new model for instruction in at least three ways. First, it abandoned the civilization model by putting "complex urban societies" in relation to other forms of social organization. This switch brought greater attention to interactions on frontiers with nomadic or pastoralist societies, as the authors paid attention to the response of local ethnic groups to the expanding sweep of empire builders. Second, the textbook established categories of time and place not rooted in western history or political territories, such as "The Acceleration of Cross-Cultural Interactions 1000–1500" and "The Origins of Global Interdependence 1500–1800"; or Southwest Asia (instead of the Middle East) and the Atlantic world for trans-oceanic encounters. In a break from most world history textbooks covering pre-1500, volume 1 of *Traditions and Encounters* includes two chapters on the Americas and Oceania before "contact." Last but not least, its title and structure proposed a thematic way to do comparative history that ties the chapters on different regions together: traditions, paying attention to each culture and granting them some space to articulate their emerging worldviews; and encounters, the constant movement and interaction of people groups around the globe throughout history, from migration, empire building, and spread of religions to trade networks, imperialism, and world wars. In short, *Traditions and Encounters* puts into practice what Bentley preached: a truly world comparative history not skewed by the Eurocentric nation-state model.

This new pedagogical model also needed to grow at the graduate level in order to train future historians and teachers, regardless of their regional field specialization, how to think cross-culturally and comparatively. Bentley led the way at the University of Hawai'i in 1985, collaborating with Professor Daniel W. Y. Kwok, then department chair, and the history faculty to create a Ph.D. field in world history, one of the earliest programs to do so. While a few US history graduate programs followed suit (such as Northeastern University and Washington State University), Bentley took the concept abroad and engaged with other historical and academic traditions. In particular, one of his crowning achievements was assisting Capital Normal University in Beijing with establishing a world history program, serving as Distinguished Visiting Professor (2006–2011) and then encouraging them to host the WHA in 2011, at which meeting both Bentley and historian Liu Xincheng, Vice President of CNU, were named "pioneers in world history."

Looking back on the *JWH* in 2008, Bentley reviewed the early issues in light of the aims of the WHA to promote world history as a research field (Bentley, 2008). The key question was whether or even how world history could meet the rigorous standards of historical research on which the discipline has stood since the nineteenth century, with its emphasis on language study and archival work dedicated to a narrowly defined time and place. His answer pointed to the success of the *JWH* in emphasizing encounters over traditions, interconnections, and comparisons, rather than just being a collection of essays about various, seemingly isolated, regions of the world. At the same time, Bentley also called for further work in two areas: engagement with postmodern and postcolonial scholarship, and bringing in multiple perspectives from outside the dominant strands of North American, western European, and Australasian scholarship. Four years later, these remain goals not only for the *JWH*, but also for graduate training and research.

Following this line of thought, world history should move beyond a transnational and comparative framework to develop an entirely new, multicultural historiography that includes diverse perspectives on the past: we need to hear other voices telling their story their way and, maybe, learn to tell our stories their way (Symes, 2011). In the last item published before his death, Bentley ended his review essay of Headley's *The Europeanization of the World* with a plea "to take the larger world seriously, to scour global archives just as assiduously as historians have examined the European record over the past two centuries, and to follow as clearly as Headley has done for the Europeans the contributions that peoples beyond Europe have made to the development of democracy and human rights" (Bentley, 2012, p. 453).

What this would look like remains to be seen, but one starting place might be the emerging field of indigenous studies. Studies of and by indigenous people groups around the globe working together seek to escape the way their histories have been written from a western colonial perspective, often without due attention paid to indigenous language sources – ironic since the western method of history developed in the nineteenth century placed such great emphasis on original language study (Smith, 1999; Nogelmeier, 2010). One example of an alternative perspective on the past that can enrich global cultural histories is found in Hawaiian historiography. As in many languages, the key word for history is rooted in story, *mo'olelo*. But in a fascinating reversal of modern forward-looking conceptions, the Hawaiian phrase for the past is *ka wā ma mua*, the time *in front*, while the future is *ka wā ma hope*, the time *behind* (Kame'eleihiwa, 1992, p. 22; Osorio, 2002, p. 7). A global cultural history could do well to start from this premise.

Ultimately, Bentley's cultural approach to world history rests on a moral framework evident in his own biography, as he moved from a monocultural upbringing through the critical reasoning of renaissance humanism and then along many paths of cultural understanding. In his last essay in the *JWH* in 2005 ("Myths, Wagers, and Some Moral Implications of World History"), Bentley challenged the politicization of history by both members of the right (advocating the triumph of democracy and capitalism) and those on the left (Marxist and postcolonial critiques of modernity). He argued for an "ecumenical world history" that "leaves the end of history open" (Bentley, 2005, p. 78). More importantly, he asks, might we wager on a history that "takes the world seriously, treats its various peoples with respect, sheds light on the dynamics that explain the world's development through time, and might even conceivably contribute to such worthy goals as cross-cultural understanding and global peace?" (Bentley, 2005, pp. 81–82).

References

Bentley, Jerry H. 1983. *Humanists and Holy Writ: New Testament Scholarship in the Renaissance*. Princeton, NJ: Princeton University Press.

Bentley, Jerry H. 1987. *Politics and Culture in Renaissance Naples*. Princeton, NJ: Princeton University Press.

Bentley, Jerry H. 1990. "A New Forum for Global History," *Journal of World History* 1/1: iii–v.

Bentley, Jerry H. 1993. *Old World Encounters: Cross-Cultural Contacts and Exchanges in Pre-Modern Europe*. New York: Oxford University Press.

Bentley, Jerry H. 1996a. "Cross-Cultural Interaction and Periodization in World History," *American Historical Review* 101: 749–770.

Bentley, Jerry H. 1996b. *Shapes of World History in Twentieth-Century Scholarship*. Washington, DC: American Historical Association.

Bentley, Jerry H. 1997. "Revisiting the Expansion of Europe: A Review Article," *Sixteenth Century Journal* 28: 503–510.

Bentley, Jerry H. 1998. "Hemispheric Integration, 500–1500 C.E.," *Journal of World History* 9: 237–254.

Bentley, Jerry H. 1999."Sea and Ocean Basins as Frameworks of Historical Analysis," *The Geographical Review* 89: 215–224.

Bentley, Jerry H. and Herbert F. Ziegler. 2000. *Traditions and Encounters: A Global Perspective on the Past*, 2nd edition 2003, 3rd edition 2006, 4th edition 2008, 5th edition 2011. Boston, MA: McGraw-Hill.

Bentley, Jerry H. 2001. "Shapes of World History in Twentieth-Century Scholarship," in Michael P. Adas, ed. *Agricultural and Pastoral Societies in Ancient and Classical History*. Philadelphia, PA: Temple University Press, pp. 3–35.

Bentley, Jerry H. 2002. "The New World History," in Lloyd Kramer and Sara Maza, eds *A Companion to Western Historical Thought*. Oxford: Blackwell, pp. 393–416.

Bentley, Jerry H. 2004. "Globalizing History and Historicizing Globalization," *Globalizations* 1/1: 69–81.

Bentley, Jerry H. 2005."Myths, Wagers, and Some Moral Implications of World History," *Journal of World History* 16: 51–82.

Bentley, Jerry H. 2006. "Beyond Modernocentrism: Toward Fresh Visions of the Global Past," in Victor H. Mair, ed. *Contact and Exchange in the Ancient World*. Honolulu, HI: University of Hawaii Press, pp. 17–29.

Bentley, Jerry H. 2007. "Early Modern Europe and the Early Modern World," in Charles H. Parker and Jerry H. Bentley, eds *Between the Middle Ages and Modernity: Individual and Community in the Early Modern World*. Lanham, MD: Rowman and Littlefield, pp. 13–31.

Bentley, Jerry H. 2008. "The Journal of World History," in Patrick Manning, ed. *Global Practice in World History: Advances Worldwide*. Princeton, NJ: Markus Wiener, pp. 129–140.

Bentley, Jerry H. 2011. "The Task of World History," in Jerry H. Bentley, ed. *The Oxford Handbook of World History*. Oxford: Oxford University Press, 343–360.

Bentley, Jerry H. 2012. "Europeanization of the World or Globalization of Europe?," *Religions* 3: 441–454.

Buschmann, Rainer F. 2006. *Oceans in World History*. New York: McGraw-Hill.

Davis, Kathleen. 2008. *Periodization and Sovereignty: How Ideas of Feudalism and Secularization Govern the Politics of Time*. Philadelphia, PA: University of Pennsylvania Press.

Finney, Ben. 1994. "The Other One-Third of the Globe," *Journal of World History* 5: 273–297.

Finney, Ben and Jerry H. Bentley. 1998. "A Tale of Two Analogues: Learning at a Distance from the Ancient Greeks and Mayans and the Problem of

Deciphering Extraterrestrial Radio Transmissions," *Acta Astronautica* 42: 691–696.

Geary, Patrick. 2002. *The Myth of Nations: The Medieval Origins of Europe*. Princeton, NJ: Princeton University Press.

Gillett, Andrew. 2006. "Ethnogenesis: A Contested Model of Early Medieval Europe," *History Compass* 4/2: 241–260.

Gulliver, Katrina. 2011. "Finding the Pacific World," *Journal of World History* 22: 83–100.

Hau'ofa, Epeli. 2008. *We Are the Ocean: Selected Works*. Honolulu, HI: University of Hawaii Press.

Holsinger, Bruce. 2005. *The Premodern Condition: Medievalism and the Making of Theory*. Chicago, IL: University of Chicago Press.

Kame'eleihiwa, Lilikalā. 1992. *Native Land and Foreign Desires: Pehea Lā E Pono Ai?*. Honolulu, HI: Bishop Museum.

Manning, Patrick. 1996. "The Problem of Interactions in World History," *American Historical Review* 101: 771–782.

Marr K. Matsuda 2006. "AHR Forum: Oceans of History," *American Historical Review* 111: 717–780.

Nogelmeier, M. Puakea. 2010. *Mai Pa'a I Ka Leo: Historical Voice in Hawaiian Primary Materials, Looking Forward and Listening Back*. Honolulu, HI: Bishop Museum Press.

Osorio, Jonathan Kay Kamakawiwo`ole. 2002. *Dismemebering Lāhui: A History of the Hawaiian Nation to 1877*. Honolulu, HI: University of Hawaii Press.

Smith, LindaTuhiwai. 1999. *Decolonizing Methodologies: Research and Indigenous Peoples*. New York: St. Martin's Press.

Symes, Carol. 2011. "What new historical paradigms could we develop?," *American Historical Review* 116: 715–726.

Index

Architects of World History: Researching the Global Past, First Edition.
Edited by Kenneth R. Curtis and Jerry H. Bentley.